THE HIS~~TORY~~
OF

# INDIAN TRIBES
## of
# HUDSON'S RIVER

# 1700 - 1850

BY
E.M. RUTTENBER

## HOPE FARM PRESS
## &
## BOOKSHOP

**1992**

*This publication is a
facsimile reprint of the original*

Second Edition
1999
ISBN # 0-910746-09-5

Hope Farm Press & Bookshop
252 Main Street
Saugerties NY 12477
www.hopefarm.com

Picture waking up one morning to the arrival of a fascinating people unlike any you had ever seen, who could do things you never thought possible and had riches beyond your imagining. They seemed a friendly people, and although you didn't understand what they said, they led you to believe that they wanted to live with you in peace. Then imagine how you would feel when you realized that the strangers had weapons that could kill from afar, that through lies and trickery they were stealing your land and all you owned and that they squandered the wealth of the nature you revered while poisoning you with rum and disease.

Imagine all that and you begin to feel what the Indians must have felt in 1609 when Henry Hudson first sailed into New York harbor ... wonder, awe and horror ... as the end of their way of life arrived on the incoming tide.

# Introduction

The History of **THE INDIAN TRIBES OF HUD-
SON'S RIVER** begins with Hudson's arrival, as
the author carefully reconstructs the history of the
dozens of tribes in the Northeast included in
the great nations of the Lenni Lenape, the Mahicans
and the Iroquois. Every sachem (or King) is identi-
fied, and the location, customs and traditions of each
tribe are documented. Significant attention is paid to
the various tribal interactions with the colonists and
how these affected each nationality's struggle for
controlling interest in the New World. Volume I
brought us up to the year 1700 when a short-lived
peace prevailed in the Northeast.

Volume II, Indian Tribes of Hudson's River 1700-
1850, begins with France's dispute with England
over the succession to her throne (known here as
Queen Ann's War) and how it affected both nationali-
ties in the struggle for dominance in the New World.
Here, the English gained dominion of the lower
reaches of the Hudson from the Dutch and allied
with the Iroquois to push their control to the North
and East, while the French solidified their positions

in Canada and New England by allying with the Hurons and the Abenaquis.

During this period New York readied defenses but was mostly unaffected, while other areas fared badly. The Abenaqui Indians, goaded by the French, wrecked havoc throughout New England. Casco, Wells, Deerfield and Haverhill were ravaged as the "sad narrative of rural dangers and sorrows" told of death in the heart of Massachusetts, as well as along the coast, and on the southern and western frontiers. Meanwhile, in North Carolina, authorities decimated the Tuscarora Indians to make room for the German Palatines settling there. The remaining Tuscaroras migrated North and became the Sixth Nation of the Iroquois Confederacy, swelling the ranks of the English allies as the stage was set for the bloody French and Indian Wars.

Throughout this narrative, arcane bits of history keep appearing. For instance: the Moravians said that "Kingston (the first capitol of New York) had earned the title of 'the Sodom of New York'"; that on July 4th, 1754 George Washington, leading a force of 150 Virginians, was defeated by the French at Fort Necessity in the Ohio River valley; that Tamany was the name of the revered and legendary chief of the Lenapes and May 1st, celebrations in his name in Philadelphia were the beginnings of the Tamany Society (infamous in New York City politics); and that Sir William Johnson had no less than 100 children by Indian squaws.

Above all else, the most compelling truth was that... "The Indians were the principle contestants and the principle sufferers in these wars (and) if they rapidly became a 'contemptible people', it was in consequence of the influences by which they were surrounded". And so it would be throughout their history. The French and Indian Wars were followed by the Revolutionary War and the War of 1812, just as injustice was followed by "disintegration and dispersion" for the Indian Tribes of Hudson's River.

In addition to this "most complete and well-documented" Native American history, there is a 100 page appendix consisting of additional biographical data and extensive examination of the similarities and differences between the two primary Indian languages, the Algonquin and Iroquois, and among their many various dialects. Also included is an analysis and interpretation of the Indian names, giving their geographic or historic origins. Lastly, the complete index for both volumes has been included to make referencing easier.

On the whole, this is as good a history of the Native Americans of the Northeast as is available and, with its extensive documentation and footnotes, will prove to be an invaluable and readable reference. However, as in any work of this scope, especially one written over 100 years ago, some inconsistencies and/or inaccuracies may occur. Inevitably also, events are recorded here as they were discerned at the time, not as they might be presented today. With that understanding, this work is offered intact, in two volumes, with no corrections or additions, with hopes that the reader will use it as part of an on-going instruction in Native Amercian history.

R.F. Saugerties NY 1992

# HISTORY

OF THE

# Indian Tribes of Hudson's River;

THEIR

ORIGIN, MANNERS AND CUSTOMS; TRIBAL
AND SUB-TRIBAL ORGANIZATIONS;
WARS, TREATIES, ETC., ETC.

BY

## E. M. RUTTENBER,

*Author of the History of Newburgh.*

" 'TIS GOOD TO MUSE ON NATIONS PASSED AWAY
FOREVER FROM THE LAND WE CALL OUR OWN;
NATIONS AS PROUD AND MIGHTY IN THEIR DAY,
WHO DEEMED THAT EVERLASTING WAS THEIR THRONE."
*Sands.*

ALBANY, N. Y. :
J. MUNSELL, 82 STATE STREET.
1872.

# PREFACE.

THE pioneer in new fields of historic inquiry encounters many obstacles from which those who follow the more beaten paths of investigation are exempt, and especially so if the inquiry involves conclusions differing materially from those which have been generally accepted. The experience of the author in prosecuting the investigations, the results of which have been embodied in the work which is now submitted to the public, have been no exception to this rule. Not only had the history of the Indians who occupied the valley of Hudson's river never been written, but the incidental references to them, in the histories of nations more prominent at a later period — treating them as mere fragmentary bands without organization or political position among the aboriginal nations — being regarded as erroneous, the inquiry involved the rejection, to a very great extent, of the conclusions of others, and the investigation and analyzation of original sources of information. To extract the truth and embody it in consistent narrative, has involved no little labor and research, and the careful weighing of words; and, although the results

1

may not be stated in the clearest terms or the most flowing rhetoric, nor entirely without error, they are nevertheless believed to fully sustain the conclusion that the tribes in question have a history which entitles them to a high rank in the annals of aboriginal nations, and which assigns to them native abilities as distinguished, eloquence as pure, bravery and prowess as unquestionable, as was possessed by those who, preserved for a greater time in their national integrity by their remoteness from civilization, became of more esteem in their relations to the government but less noble in their purposes.

It has been the object of the author to trace the history of the Indians from the earliest period; to show their original position in the family of nations, and that which they subsequently maintained ; the wrongs which they suffered, and the triumphs which they won ; their greatness and their decay.   In the narrative, liberal use has been made of current histories, so far as their statements were found to be in accordance with the facts. Acknowledgment, it is believed, has been fully made, and even to an extent which is not customary.   Very full notes have been introduced for the purpose of explaining the text and enabling the reader to judge of the correctness of the conclusions drawn therefrom. As far as possible the narrative has been divested of the recitation of events which do not pertain to it, and though necessarily running beyond the limits of the territory regarded as the valley of the Hudson, has been as closely confined to it as possible, too closely perhaps, as it is believed that the eastern

Indians have the same claim to consideration as a confederacy as the western.

The work is submitted to the judgment of the public, with a desire that the author may be lost in the theme which he has presented, and the truth of history vindicated in behalf of a people that have left behind no monuments to their memory save those erected by their destroyers.

NEWBURGH, N. Y.

## CHAPTER VIII.

THE MAHICANS IN COUNCIL — QUEEN ANNE'S WAR — MI-
GRATIONS — MISSIONARY LABORS — THE WAR OF 1746.

PEACE, such as had not fallen upon the wildernesses of the New World since the Europeans added their conflicting interests to the field of savage contests, prevailed at the opening of the eighteenth century. The contending tribes had buried the hatchet at Montreal, and *Senecas* and *Hurons*, *Onondagas* and *Ottawas*, *Mohawks* and *Abenaquis*,[1] through their representatives smoked together the pipe of peace. Beside their ancient river the *Mahican* warriors hunted the deer, and their hand-maidens cultivated the fields, wove wampum in the woods, and chanted their maternal songs. Large numbers of them gathered around the " tree of welfare" which had been planted for them, and their dispersed New England relatives, at Schaticook, and in the councils with the tribes lifted up the voice of thanksgiving and proclaimed signifi- cant history. " We are glad to see you and your lady," said So- quans, the *Mahican* speaker, to Governor Bellomont at a confer- ence at Albany, August 31st, 1700; " 'Tis now about two years ago since we first saw you. The sun of peace shined then and so it does still. In the times of old there were not any Christians on this river, and the first Christians that came settled upon Rensselaer's land, whom we loved as soon as we saw them, and with whom we made a strict alliance and a covenant chain which has been-kept inviolable ever since. This chain we are now come to renew. We are resolved to live and die here in this government, and do pray that our father will support and protect us." " I thank you for your kind expressions," replied Bellomont ; " and you may be sure I will do every thing to maintain the covenant chain firm and steadfast. I should be

---

[1] Peace was established between the Abenaquis and the Five Nations, Oct. 7, 1700.—*Colonial History,* IV, 758.

very glad if you would invite your friends the *Pennacokes* and eastern Indians to come and settle with you. Since the Five Nations and you are linked together in interest, it would be an advantage to engage those other Indians in the same interest."[1] At a conference held July 18, 1701, Soquans again appeared with joyful heart. "We are now two hundred fighting men belonging to this county of Albany[2] from Katskill to Skachkook," said he, "and hope to increase in a year's time to three hundred. Our neighbors, the *Maquas*, have not been so fortunate, for their tree was burnt. We have been so happy and fortunate that our number is increased to that degree that we cannot all be shaded by one tree, and therefore desire that another tree, besides that at Skachkook, may be planted for us, for we are in hopes that our number will daily increase from other parts. It is now ninety years ago since the Christians first came here, when there was a covenant chain made between them and the *Mahikanders*, the first inhabitants of this river, and the chain has been kept inviolable ever since. We have been so happy as never to have had the least flaw or crack in the chain. There have been breaches round about us, and great differences, but that chain, wherein the *Maquas* and we are linked, has been kept inviolate, and we pray that our father will keep the same so forever." "We will plant you another tree," responded Lieutenant Governor Nanfan, "which shall be so large and flourishing that the branches will shade and cherish as many of your friends as will be persuaded to come and live with you. You know now by the experience of ninety years that we have the best laws and government in the world. You may depend upon it that I will do every thing to maintain the covenant chain firm and inviolate."[3]

Similar were the addresses delivered at a conference held by Governor Cornbury, on his first visit to Albany after his appointment: "You desired," said Soquans, "to know the number and strength of our people, which we now acquaint you with, viz: one hundred and ten Indians at Skachkook, and eighty-seven

[1] *Colonial History*, IV, 744.
[2] The county of Albany then embraced the entire country west of the Connecticut river, and north of Roelof's Jansen's kill on the east, and north of the Katskill mountains on the west.
[3] *Colonial History*, IX, 902, etc.

below the town (i. e., below Albany), in all one hundred and ninety-seven fighting men. You renewed the covenant chain two days ago (July 18, 1702), and we come now and ratify the same and make the chain stronger, which has been kept inviolable, between us and the Christians of this province, these ninety years. About twenty-six years ago, Sir Edmund Andros, then governor of this province, planted a tree of welfare at Skachkook, and invited us to come and live there, which we very luckily complied with, and we have had the good fortune ever since, that we have increased that tree, and the very leaves thereof have grown hard and strong ; the tree is grown so thick of leaves and boughs that the sun can scarce shine through it, yea the fire itself cannot consume it ; and we now desire, that our father may strengthen that tree and cause the leaves to grow so thick that no sun at all may shine through it."

The *Pennacooks* who had found refuge in Canada,[1] sent repeated invitations to their kindred at Schaticook to join them, promising them " houses, land and provisions," in the name of the French governor. These invitations were rejected, and Paasquin and Ackkonepak, two young *Pennacook* sachems, accompanied Soquans to Albany to acquaint the governor of their action. They were kindly received and their determination commended. " Tell your kindred," said Governor Cornbury, " to come and live with you. They shall not only have land assigned them gratis, but a fort shall be built of stockadoes to secure you and them from any sudden attempts of the enemy ; your land is tough and hard, I will order next spring a plow to break up the ground for them to plant in, and they shall be protected and secured as well as any other Indians under the queen of England's protection. If they are inclined to be instructed in the Christian religion, the minister here shall teach them." And the Pennacooks accepted the mission, and went out after their brethren.

The relations existing between the government and the *Mahicans* under the treaty of 1664, had further illustration at this time. In August, 1702, Minichque, one of their sachems, while visiting Albany, was mortally wounded by a party of four

[1] *Ante,* p. 63.

negroes.   The authorities took immediate charge of him, nursed him tenderly, and arrested the offenders and brought them to trial.   Minichque and his brethren were satisfied, and the former, although lamenting that his death should have been caused by those who had " no courage nor heart," charged Soquans to make intercession for his murderers.   " Upon his death-bed," said Soquans, in performing this mission, " our great sachem desired that no revenge should be taken, saying that he forgave the offenders, and prayed that they might be reprieved."   " Since blood was shed, blood must be shed again," replied Cornbury, and on the 19th of August the principal offender was executed in atonement for the wrong which he had  committed.

Through all these conferences[1] and proceedings, two principal facts are conspicuous : the equality of the *Mahicans* in all treaties with the authorities, from the earliest Dutch adventurers at Fort Orange to the more powerful occupation by the English, and the duality of the organization called the *Schaticooks*, in which the principals appear as *Mahicans* and the New England fugitives as *Pennacooks*.   Had equal fullness in record been made at earlier periods, the first point would not have so long been in obscurity.   That it finally appears is due to the wisdom of Governor Bellomont and to the selection of Colonel Peter Schuyler — than whom the *Mahicans* had no more sincere friend — as secretary to  the commissioners of Indian affairs, under instructions, " upon any message from any or all of the Five Nations of Indians, or from the nation of Schakook or river Indians," to immediately call the commissioners together, and " to keep a record of all proceedings in reference thereto."   The faithfulness of this record preserves the truth of history, and places the *Mahicans* in the position which they justly occupied, but which had perhaps been clouded by the destructive wars through which they had passed, and the demoralization which had fallen upon them incident to their proximity to the marts of European

---

[1] Conferences with the Indians were not the most pleasant affairs. They were almost invariably held in the old Albany Court House.   Gov. Bellomont writes of one which he held with the Five Nations in October, 1700 : " My conference lasted seven days and was the greatest fatigue I ever endured in my whole life.   I was shut up in a close chamber with fifty sachems, who besides the stink of bear's grease, with which they plentifully daub'd themselves, were continually either smoking or drinking."— *Colonial History*, IV, 714.

traffic. Yet judged by this standard, their ancient rivals, the *Mohawks*, were not their peers. Zinzendorf writes of the latter that •their passion for strong drink, by making them hopelessly indolent, had rendered them unworthy of their position as head of the Six Nations ; that though chiefest in dignity, they were "despised because of their levity and paid off with the title," while the *Onondagas* were the actual "Judahs among their brethren." Years of intimate association with the Europeans had made the one "prophets without honor in their own country," while the absence of such association had magnified the dignity and prowess of the others.

The peace of 1698 was of short duration. James II, the dethroned king of England, died in exile in France in September, 1701, and Louis acknowledged the son of James as the successor to the throne. The death of King William followed in March, 1702, and Anne was declared his successor. The war which followed, and which was known in Europe as the war of the Spanish succession, was called in America, Queen Anne's war. It continued until the peace at Utrecht, April 11, 1713. New York scarce knew of its existence, although the province was put in condition for defense. The Indians, who had hitherto been the principal contestants and principal sufferers in these wars, were at peace. The Five Nations refused to break their treaties by attacking the *Abenaquis* who had espoused the cause of France, while the *Abenaquis* in turn refused to make war upon the Five Nations. But while New York escaped, New England was ravaged with ruthless hand. Casco, Wells, Deerfield, and Haverhill, were given to flame and sword ; the aged and those of tender years shared the fate of the vigorous and manly ; death hung on the frontiers ; the prowling Indian seemed near every farm house. "There is," says Bancroft, "no tale to tell of battles like those of Blenheim, or Ramillies, but only one sad narrative of rural dangers and sorrows. The Indians stealthily approached towns in the heart of Massachusetts, as well as along the coast, and on the southern and western frontiers. Children, as they gamboled on the beach ; reapers, as they gathered the harvest ;

24

mowers, as they rested from using the scythe ; mothers, as they
busied themselves about the household, were victims to an
enemy who disappeared the moment a blow was struck.    Such
were the sorrows of that generation." [1]

Special efforts were made, early in 1710, to induce the Five
Nations and the *Mahicans* to violate their neutrality and embark
in the conflict.    The success of the French, in establishing
themselves among the northern and western Indians, annoyed
the English of New York, who saw in embroiling the peaceful
tribes in war the only mode of arresting more formidable alliances.    Nicholson, who had been appointed governor in 1688,
and who had fled to England during the Leisler revolution, had
met with some successes on the northern coast, and was anxious
to have the Indians in the field as part of an expedition for the
reduction of Quebec, which he had planned and in which he
hoped to win unfading laurels.    To promote the ends of both,
and at the same time contribute to the relief of New England,
he sailed for Europe, taking with him Colonel Peter Schuyler and
representative chiefs of the *Mohawks* and *Mahicans*.    On their
arrival in England this delegation was received with marked
distinction.[2]    "Clothed like tragedy kings, by tailors of the
theatre, taken in the coaches of state, they were waited upon
by Sir Charles Cottrell, and, on the 19th of April, introduced
to her majesty by the Duke of Shrewsbury.    They were entertained by many noble persons, particularly the Duke of
Ormond, who favored them with a review of the life-guards.
Their portraits were taken and are now preserved in the British
Museum, together with their names." [3]    So much attention, so

---

[1] *Bancroft*, III, 216.

[2] *Bancroft*, III, 209.

[3] The best and most methodical account
of the visit of these chiefs was published
in the great annual history by Mr. Bo-
yer, entitled " *The Annals of Queen
Anne's Reign, for* 1710," from which the
following is an extract :    " On the 19th
of April, *Te-Gee-Neen-Ho-Ga-Prow* and
*Sa-Ga-Yeau-Qua-Prah-Ton* (King Hendrik, *Colonial History*, v, 358), of the
Maquas ; *Elow-Oh-Kaom* and *Oh-Yeath-
Ton-No-Prow*, of the river sachems, and
the *Ganajohhore* sachem, five kings or

chiefs of the six nations, which lie between
New England and New France or Canada,
who lately came over with the West In-
dia fleet, and were clothed and entertained
at the Queen's expense, had a public au-
dience of Her Majesty at the palace of
St James.    They made a speech by their
interpreter, which Major Pidgeon, who
was one of the officers came with them,
read in English to Her Majesty."    Sir
Richard Steele, in the *Tatler* of May
13, 1710, gives an account of the visit.
Miner, in his *History of Wyoming*,
endeavors to locate one of the visiting

great a display of the power and glory of England, had its effect ; the chiefs readily promised to return and rally their clans to the field; were hurried home with this promise fresh on their lips, and started on their mission of war.

Events moved slowly in the wilderness at that time, and a full year elapsed before the response came. On the 17th of August, 1711, the chiefs met Governor Hunter, with their warriors. The sachem of *Schaticook* brought thirty-eight men ; the *Mahicans*, fifty-eight under Wampasa, whom they had chosen as their captain ; the *Shawanoes*, twenty-six ; the *Mohawks* one hundred and forty, and the remaining tribes of the Five Nations, about five hundred. Each delegation was separately received, that of the Five Nations, on account of · its numbers, being especially honored by a salute of five guns as they passed in review before Fort Albany. The conference opened on the 24th when, " each nation seated on the ground by themselves," Governor Hunter thanked them for their response to the queen's commands, and informed them that they would be expected to join General Nicholson in the expedition against Canada, which had been organized.[1] This expedition had already sailed from Boston, with seven veteran regiments, and was to be met by the colonial forces of New York, New Jersey and Connecticut, with their Indian allies, under the walls of Quebec.[2] Roasted oxen, barrels of beer, the firing of cannon, and some " private presents" to the proper chiefs, completed the work, and all professed their readiness to march at the queen's command.

The French were not idle spectators of these preparations, and in their efforts to defeat them brought out in strong colors the power and influence which they had established over their Indian allies through their priests. A great war festival was held at Montreal, and the war song chanted by seven or eight hundred warriors, many of whom were the flower of the *Iroquois* and *Mahican* nations, whom the priests had drawn thither.

chiefs among the Delawares, but is not sustained by the record. The Canajoharie chief, whose name is not given, died in England soon after his arrival. The first conference after their return was held at Albany, Aug. 10, 1711, of which the record says : " Some of ye sa-chems of ye Five Nations and river Indians, particularly those lately come from Great Britain, waited upon His Excellency, Gov. Hunter," &c. — *Colonial History*, v, 217.

[1] *Colonial History*, v, 267, etc.

[2] *Bancroft*, III, 221, etc.

From the far west the response was even more enthusiastic. Tribe after tribe, even the *Osages* and *Missouris*, sprang to the relief of the French. " Father," said they to Vaudreuil, " behold thy children compass thee round. We will, if need be, gladly die for our father — only take care of our wives and our children, and spread a little grass over our dead bodies to protect them against the flies."

Circumstances prevented actual collision. The fleet sailed from Boston, after many delays, only to be invested by heavy fogs, and to meet with the wreck of eight of the vessels of which it was composed and the loss of eight hundred and eighty-four men drowned.[1] The land forces were moved to the support of the fleet. " On the 29th of August," says Governor Hunter, " I left them all upon their march beyond Albany towards the lakes, completely armed, clothed, accoutred and victualled, to be followed next day by eight hundred Indians of the Five Nations and their allies from Albany." How far the march extended does not appear ; it was arrested by the disaster to the fleet, and became a successful and unmolested retreat.

The *Tuscaroras*, of North Carolina, one of the southern tribes of *Iroquois*, did not escape from the war so fortunately. Resisting the encroachments of the proprietaries of Carolina, who had assigned their lands to the German Palatines, they were almost destroyed in their fort on the river Taw, on the 26th of March, 1713, having lost eight hundred in prisoners, who were sold as slaves to the allies of the English. The largest portion of the survivors of this disaster, " unwilling to submit and unable to contend," removed to the north, joined the confederated tribes of New York, and were accepted and established as the sixth nation, or " children," of the *Iroquois*.[2] They were located immediately west of, and in juxtaposition to,

[1] *Colonial History*, v, 277.

[2] At a conference at Albany, Sept. 25, 1714, the Five Nations, in their address to Governor Hunter, said : "We acquaint you that the Tuscarore Indians are come to shelter themselves among the Five Nations. They were of us and went from us long ago and are now returned, and promise to live peaceably among us, and since there is peace every where, we have received them. We desire you to look upon the Tuscarores that are come to live among us as our children who shall obey our commands and live peaceably and orderly."—*Colonial History*, v, 387.

the *Oneidas*,[1] and as they increased in strength became useful to their associates.[2]

Peace and intimate association with their European neighbors, which had proved so disastrous to the *Mahicans* in former times, did not improve their condition. They came regularly to the conferences, but in smaller numbers and in a condition betokening great indulgence in intoxicating liquors. At the conference of 1720, the commissioners specially commended their faithfulness to their covenant, as distinguished from the Five Nations, who had " suffered themselves to be deluded by the French and their emissaries," but did not hesitate to ascribe the poverty of which they complained to " drinking and laziness," and to advise them to " be sober and active in hunting and planting" in the future.[3] In 1722, Governor Burnet, in renewing the ancient covenant with them, remarked : " I need not tell you how destructive your intemperance has proved, and how much your people are diminished by your excessive drinking of rum, the women as well as the men being guilty of being often drunk. Let me advise you to be more sober in the future, and not to spend what you get by hunting in strong drink, and above all not squander your Indian corn for rum." But was it the fault of the Indians that the assertions of the governor were but too well founded? Said the *Mahicans* in their answer, through Ampamit [4] their speaker : " We are sensible that you are much in the right, that rum does a great deal of harm. We approve of all that you said on that point, but the matter is this, when our people come from hunting to the town or plantations and acquaint the traders and people that we want powder and shot and clothing, they first give us a large cup of rum, and after we get the taste of it we crave for more, so that in fine all the beaver and peltry we have hunted goes for drink, and we are left destitute either of clothing or ammunition. Therefore, we desire our father to order the tap or crane to be shut, and to prohibit the selling of rum, for as long as the Christians will sell rum

---

[1] " The *Oneidas*, the proprietors of that country, gave you a settlement then out of kindness."—*Johnson to Seth, chief of the Tuscaroras at Oghkwaga.*

[2] *Schoolcraft's Notes on the Iroquois,* 104, etc. *Gallatin,* 82, 83.

[3] *Colonial History,* v, 563.

[4] Said to have been chief of an island in the Hudson.

our people will drink it. We acknowledge that our father
is very much in the right to tell us that we squander away
our Indian corn, but one great cause of it is that many of
our people are obliged to hire land of the Christians at a very
dear rate, and to give half the corn for rent, and the other half
they are tempted by rum to sell, and so the corn goes, and the
poor women and children are left to shift as well as they can."
And he might have added, that the land which they called their
own was not unfrequently mortgaged to those who had furnished
them corn, after defrauding them of that which they had
produced, and the mortgages very promptly foreclosed.    Without this addition, however, Governor Burnet felt the force of
the argument of this aboriginal prohibitionist, and took the
point from his rebuke by remarking, in reply, that they " looked
better " and were " better clothed " " than the other Indians,
who do not live among the Christians," and that therefore they
would do well " to stay among them."    No promise did he give,
however, that he appreciated and would enforce the divine
command, " Lead us not into temptation," by preventing the
sale of rum and the consequent plunder by which the Christian
name was reproached.    Commanding them to distribute their
presents equally between those living above Albany and those
living below Albany, he dismissed them.

The New England provinces maintained war with the eastern Indians for some years after peace had been established with
France.    The doctrine that the Indians had no rights which
Christians were bound to respect, was firmly held by the successors of Underhill and Church, who hesitated not to provoke
and continue hostilities when peace was within their reach.    But
the war grew tedious as well as disastrous, and the authorities
there appealed to the *Iroquois* to take up the hatchet in their
behalf.[1]    The latter made loud protestations of what they would
do, but contented themselves with hiding the hatchet in their
bosoms and sending messengers to the *Abenaquis*.    A year later
(1724), the New England commissioners remonstrated with them,

[1] This overture was not to the Five Nations alone, but embraced the *Mahi-cans* and *Schaticooks*. Delegates from the tribes named were invited to Boston, and were there entertained with a feast and presents, as was customary in such nego-tiations. — *Niles' History, Massachusetts Historical Collections*, v, 347.

and charged that they had not only laid the hatchet by their side, but had accomplished nothing by negotiation. The reply was pointed : " The matter of peace rests with you," said their speaker ; " whenever you will give up the lands which you have wrongfully taken, and restore the hostages which you have retained without cause," peace can be secured. They had made full inquiry and were satisfied that the eastern Indians were not the aggressors, and they knew that should they attempt to force them to peace, a general war would ensue. " Though the hatchet lies by our side," continued their speaker, " yet the way is open between this place and Canada, and trade is free both going and coming, and so the way is open between this place and Albany and the Six Nations, and if a war should break out and we should use the hatchet that lays by our side, those paths which are now open would be stopped ; and if we should make war it would not end in a few days as yours doth, but it must last till one nation or the other is destroyed. We have been three times with the eastward Indians and could not prevail, and we know what whipping and scourging is from the governor of Canada. The eastern Indians seem to be inclined to peace, and inasmuch as we have tried three times and could not effect it, we would have you try them yourselves." [1] The *Iroquois* were in no humor to attack so formidable a foe as the *Abenaquis*. Their last conflict had been at least a drawn battle, and having formed a peace with them as well as with the governor of Canada, whose allies they were, they declined, as they did in 1704, to reopen a conflict which might involve their own existence. The name of *Mohawk !* if it once had terror [2] for the fugitive *Pequot*, upon whose head a price was set, had none for those who boasted that they received the first kiss of the morning sun— the tribute which they paid was not to the *Iroquois*.

The record of the years immediately subsequent is but a disconnected detail of migrations and reorganizations among the Indian tribes. In 1726, two of the sachems of the *Pennacooks*, at Schaticook, being dead, Governor Burnet appointed Wawiachech in their place. Instead of increasing in numbers as they had

[1] *Colonial History*, v, 723, 725.

[2] This is one of the fables of history, which is quoted by almost every writer.

anticipated, they steadily decreased by desertions to Canada.
These desertions were explained, by those who remained, as
being caused by debts which they had incurred and were unable
to pay, or the payment of which they wished to escape.[1]  While
this explanation was not without some truth, the overtures made
by the French, and the entreaties of their relatives, were probably the predominant impelling motives.   Houses, lands, protection, and a more complete recognition by the government,
were temptations that these wanderers, who, like Esau, had
parted with their birthright for a mess of pottage, could not
resist.

   Nor were their *Mahican* neighbors fully satisfied with their
condition.   A considerable number of the better classes among
them felt keenly the devouring curses to which they were
exposed by their proximity to the established centre of trade,
and fled from their devouring touch to the friendly embrace
of their "grandfathers," the *Lenapes*, and settled beside the
*Minsis* and *Shawanoes* in the valley of Wyoming at the forks
of the Susquehanna.[2]  Among the first of these emigrants was
Keeperdo, or Mohekin Abraham, who, in 1730, left his lands
at the mouth of Wood creek unoccupied.   Whether he was the
founder of the Pennsylvania organization or not does not appear ;
but the organization itself maintained a separate and recognized
existence in all the changes of the *Lenapes* and their confederates.   In those changes Keeperdo shared — accepted, with his
associates, the reproach of "women," joined in the ceremonies
of its removal, and, in 1771, was found in the Ohio country.[3]

[1] *Colonial History*, v, 798, 799.

[2] "We reached Skehandowa (April 23,
1737), where a number of Indians live,—
Shawanos and Mahicanders."—*Memorials
Moravian Church*, 1, 69.

[3] In the Manuscripts of Sir William
Johnson, in the State Library (vol. 21,
p. 40), is a letter endorsed : "Letter from
Ohio concerning land —rec'd it Oct. 16th,
1771." This letter was from Mohekin
Abraham, who writes : "I understand
the Mohikans at Stockbridge are wanting
to sell a certain tract of land lying above
Albany, from the mouth of Wood creek
upwards." This sale he requested to have
stopped as he was the owner, that he was
well known by many old people about
Albany, and in conclusion says : "It may
be reported that I am dead, as it is forty
years since I left that country." Signed,
"Mohekin Abraham, or Keeperdo."
The tract was covered by a patent to
Philip Skene, and embraced what was
known as Skenesborough, now White-
hall, in the present county of Washington.
Skene located thirty families on it in 1761.
The Mahicans at Stockbridge claimed
the ownership, but it does not appear that
the tract was ever paid for. The letter
of Keeperdo is important as defining more
clearly the extent of the Mahican country.

As this band retreated towards the west, another appeared from the east in the territory of the *Mahicans.* Gideon [1] Mauwehu, a *Pequot* chief, originally of some prominence in that unfortunate nation, and whose natural abilities were of no ordinary stamp, with a few of his followers found a home in the present town of Dover, on Ten Mile river, in the county of Dutchess. Here he had lived but a short time, when, on one of his hunting excursions, he came to the summit of a mountain in the present county of Kent, Connecticut. Looking down from this eminence he saw the Housatonic winding through a narrow but fertile valley, shut in by wooded hills. Delighted with the scene, he returned to his wigwam, packed up his property, and journeyed with his family and followers to this new found land of quiet and plenty. From here he issued invitations to his old friends and to the *Mahicans* of the Hudson. Immigrants flocked in, and in ten years from the time of settlement, it was thought a hundred warriors had collected around him.[2] To his village he gave the name of Pishgachtigok, which had already been applied to that of the fugitive *Pennacooks* on the Hudson, and which there as well as on the Hudson,[3] was corrupted into Schaticook, by which it was known to the authorities of Connecticut, who subsequently established there a reservation on which the name of Mauwehu was represented for five generations.[4] What relation this organization sustained to the *Mahicans* does not appear, although the authority of the latter was no doubt recognized, so far as recognition was customary under tribal laws. With the authorities of New York, Mauwehu had no direct connection.

Almost simultaneously with the appearance of Mauwehu in the valley of the Housatonic, the axe of the pioneer was heard in its ancient forests. In 1722, Joseph Parsons and others purchased from the *Mahicans* there a tract of land embracing territory sufficient for two townships, and prepared to locate a

[1] A name given to him by the Moravian missionary, Mack, by whom he was baptized in 1743.—*Latrobe's Missions,* II, 43, 44, etc.

[2] *De Forest's History Indians of Connecticut,* 407, etc.

[3] The situations were similar and the name, Pisgachtigok, or the confluence of two streams, was applied to both.

[4] Eunice, the last of royal line, died on the reservation in 1860.

settlement. That which the people of New England then regarded as an absolute essential in such enterprises — a reservation for the use and support of a minister — was included in their charter. Subsequent investigation having proved that the location of a minister among them could be greatly promoted by availing themselves of the aid of the Society for the Propagation of the Gospel in Foreign Parts, and that the prospect of improving the condition of the *Mahicans* by direct association was better than through the intercourse had with them at the forts, where missionaries had been stationed, it was determined to make application to that society for a missionary. The application was granted, but on condition that the consent of the *Mahicans* should be first obtained. A committee accordingly visited them at Westenhuck in July, 1734. The relations existing between the *Mahicans* and the Massachusetts government being intimate and friendly — Konapot, the *Mahican* chief, having been commissioned captain, by Governor Belcher, and Umpachenee, his subordinate, made a lieutenant, in the colonial service — this consent was readily obtained. In September following, the Rev. John Sergeant was appointed to the mission and entered upon its duties in October. In 1735, the mission was definitely located on the W-nahk-ta-kook, or the Great Meadow, the great council chamber of the nation, where a township six miles square was laid out by the legislature as a reservation under the name of Stockbridge, by which name the *Mahicans* who were then located there, as well as those who subsequently removed thither, were known to the authorities of Massachusetts and New York.[1]

Following closely upon the establishment of the Stockbridge mission, the Moravians began their labors in the *Mahican* country. With a zeal remarkable for its voluntarily assumed sacrifices, and more pure than that which characterized the labors of other organizations, because without political interests to serve, they had pushed their way into the territory of the *Creeks* and

[1] *Stockbridge, Past and Present.* Twenty miles distant, at a village called *Kaunaumeek*, David Brainerd, a licentiate acting under similar authority, established a mission in 1743. He was aided in his labors, by a young Mahican, John Wauwaumpequnnaunt, and met with so much success that he was enabled to induce his people to remove to Stockbridge.

*Cherokees* of Georgia, in 1735. Driven thence by the political troubles with the Spaniards, they established a colony at Bethlehem, on the Delaware, and, in 1740, founded a mission in the present county of Dutchess. The pioneer in the latter field was Christian Henry Rauch, who arrived in New York, in July of that year, seeking missionary labor, and where he soon after met a company of *Mahicans* who were there to renew their covenant with the government. Ascertaining that he could converse with them in the Dutch language, he visited them repeatedly at their encampment, but found them almost invariably in a state of beastly intoxication on the liquor which the government had given them, ferocious in appearance and but little disposed to extend the encouragement which he sought. Finding them sober at last, he addressed two of their chiefs, Tschoop and Shabash, and obtained their consent to accompany them to their village as a teacher. Led by them he reached Shekomeko, in the district now known as Pine plains, on the 16th of August, and immediately commenced a work which was not without encouraging reward. Tschoop,[1] known as " the greatest drunkard among his followers," was converted ; Schabash joined him soon after. At the end of two years thirty-one baptized Indians attended his ministrations, " all of the *Mahikander* tribe," and in 1743, the number had reached sixty-three.

Rauch's labors were not confined to Shekomeko alone. At Pisgachtigok, Mauwehu and his brother were among his converts, while at Wechquadnach,[2] or Pachquadnach, Totatik,[3] Westenhuck, and Wehtak,[4] he was not without sincere followers. At Shekomeko, Wechquadnach and Pisgachtigok, mission

---

[1] Schweinitz, in his *Life and Times of David Zeisberger*, says the name of this chief was Wasarnapah ; his English name prior to his baptism, Job ; and the name he received in baptism, John ; that he never bore the name of Tschoop among his people, but that it originated among the Moravians in consequence of their German mode of pronouncing Job. Wasarnapah was the ruling chief at Shekomeko. He was a man of remarkable powers of mind, and in whose mien " was the majesty of a Luther." He died of small pox at Bethlehem, Aug. 27, 1746.

*Loskiel*, II, 93, 94. Schabash received in baptism the name of Abraham. He was subsequently elected chief or king of the Mahicans on the Delaware, and died at Wyoming in December, 1762.—*Memorials Moravian Church*, I, 147.

[2] Now North-east Centre, Connecticut. The name is preserved in Wachquadnach lake or Indian pond.

[3] On the east side of the Housatonic opposite the mouth of Poughtatuck creek.

[4] Or Wyatiack, near Salisbury, Litchfield Co., Conn.

houses were established, the success at the latter being greater than that at Shekomeko. In this field Rauch, Gotleib, Buttner and Samuel Mack labored for twenty years, and until driven out by persecutions which their success provoked. In the war of 1755, they were accused of being emissaries of the French ; subsequently they were arrested under the law of 1700, forbidding the presence of priests in the province without a license from the government ; the traders, whose traffic in rum was materially abridged by their teachings, lost no opportunity to misrepresent them and accuse them falsely ; finally, they were ejected from the lands at Shekomeko under a claim that they belonged to the white people and not to the Indians. After a temporary rest at Wechquadnach and Pisgachtigok, they removed, with many of their followers, to Pennsylvania, where they formed a colony to which they gave the name of Freidenshutten, (tents of peace). Their stay here was short. Gnadenhutten (tents of grace) received them for a time, and from thence they shared the roving fortunes of the Moravians, followed in all their wanderings by their faithful *Mahican* converts.[1]

Meanwhile the commissioners of the society in Scotland for Propagating the Gospel had entered upon the work of diffusing Christian knowledge among the Indians, and had commissioned the Rev. David Brainerd to labor among the Delawares. Having transferred his mission among the *Mahicans* to the Rev. Mr. ·Sergeant, Brainerd visited the Delaware country in the spring of 1744. At Minnisink he encountered the opposition of the Indians,[2] but established himself at the Forks of the Dela-

[1] *Heckewelder's Narrative; Life and Times of David Zeisberger ; Loskiel's History of the Mission of the United Brethren ; Memorials of the Moravian Church ; The Moravians in New York and Connecticut ; Documentary History of New York; Stone's Life of Brant, etc.*

[2] "I then set out on my journey toward Delaware; and on May 10th, (1744), met with a number of Indians in a place called Minnissinks, about a hundred and forty miles from Kaunaumeek (the place where I spent the last year), and directly in my way to Delaware river. With these Indians I spent some time, and first addressed their king in a friendly manner, and after some discourse, and attempts to contract a friendship with him, I told him I had a desire (for his benefit and happiness) to instruct them in *Christianity*. At which he laughed and turned his back upon me and went away. I then addressed another *principal* man in the same manner, who said he was willing to hear me. After some time, I followed the *king* into his house, and renewed my discourse to him : but he declined talking, and left the affair to another, who appeared to be a rational man. He began and talked very warmly near a quarter of an hour together ; he enquired why I desired the Indians to become

ware, at which place, and at Crossweeksung, "in New Jersey, towards the sea," he met with considerable success.[1] His brother, John Brainerd, about the same time, established a mission at Bethel, New Jersey, where he drew together a permanent congregation.

But the changes of this period were not confined to the *Mahicans* and *Lenapes*. It is said that in 1748, a band of fugitive *Nanticokes*, under their chief sachem, White, put themselves under the protection of the Six Nations at Conestoga on the Delaware.[2] If the Moravian missionaries were correctly informed, their presence was a source of weakness rather than of strength to their allies. Loskiel states that they "instructed the Delawares and Iroquois in preparing a peculiar kind of poison," which was capable of infecting whole townships and tribes with "disorders as pernicious as the plague," and that they "nearly destroyed their own nation by it." Their history, until their final disappearance in the west, was not particularly distinguished, perhaps for the reason stated by Loskiel.

A more important acquisition — at least temporarily — by the *Iroquois* at this time, was that of the *Mississagies* as the seventh nation of the confederacy. The *Mississagies* were a northern *Alqonquin* nation whose place of residence was on the waters of

*Christians,* seeing the Christians were so much worse than the Indians. It was they first taught the Indians to be drunk, and *they* stole from one another, to that degree, that their rulers were obliged to hang them for it, and that was not sufficient to deter others from the like practice. But the Indians, he added, were none or them ever hanged for stealing, and yet they did not steal half so much; and he supposed that if the Indians should become Christians, they would then be as bad as those, and hereupon he said, they would live as their *fathers* lived, and go where their *fathers* were when they died. I then freely owned, lamented, and joined with him in condemning the ill conduct of some who are called Christians; told him these were not Christians at heart, that I hated such wicked practices, and did not desire the Indians to become such as these, and when he appeared calmer, I asked him if he was willing that I should

come and see them again. He replied, he should be willing to see me again, as a *friend*, if I would not desire them to become *Christians*. I then bid them farewell, and prosecuted my journey towards Delaware."— *Brainerd's Mission.*

[1] He died in 1747, of consumption, a martyr to the work which he had undertaken.

[2] The Nanticokes, or tide water people, had their seats, when the Europeans first met them, on the eastern shore of Maryland. At the time of the removal referred to in the text they were not considerable in numbers. Gallatin says they were the allies of the Six Nations. Their lands in Maryland were sold, through the agency of Sir William Johnson, in 1760, and the money paid to the chiefs.— *Colonial History*, VIII, 117. They were repeatedly represented in the conferences with the Delawares and the Shawanoes.

a river which enters the north shores of Lake Huron, between Point Tessalon and La Cloche. In pushing the policy which the government of New York had established, of promoting trade by securing the alliance of Indian tribes with the Six Nations, the latter had been induced to open negotiations with many of their former enemies.[1]   As one of the fruits of this policy, the *Necariages*, a remnant of the once powerful *Hurons*, or *Wyandots*, had been induced to visit Albany, in 1723, and to ask to be received as the seventh nation. The commissioners of Indian affairs accepted them as such,[2] but the confederates never acknowledged them. When the *Mississagies* tendered a similar alliance, however, they were received by the confederates, and at a conference, held at Albany on the 23d of August, 1746, were publicly acknowledged by them as the seventh nation.[3]   The alliance did not long continue. When the war of 1755 broke out, it was found that the Six Nations were at War with their new allies.

A more permanent acquisition was that of the *Ochtayhquanawicroons*,[4] a *Tuscarora* clan,[5] who appeared on the Susquehanna river, in the present county of Broome, in 1722, and around whom subsequently gathered several *Mahican* families who had previously found homes with the *Mohawks*, but who had become " dissatisfied with the ruling politics [6] of that tribe; " *Skaniadaradigh-*

---

[1] In 1740, George Clark, then acting as governor, secured the assent of the Six Nations to the proposition to "take into the covenant chain all the nations of Indians lying to the westward and southward as far as the Mississippi," as the "most likely way to establish an universal peace among all the Indians and to make it lasting."

[2] *Colonial History*, v, 695. Schoolcraft classes the Necariages as the seventh nation, but admits that they were never so received. The fact appears to be that no nation was ever received into the confederate compact; even the Tuscaroras had no such relation. In all their national action but five tribes were represented.

[3] " We, the Six Nations, are now assembled together as one man, and we take in the Mississagies as the Seventh Nation ; and what is now spoken by one mouth, are the joint and sincere thoughts of

every heart."—*Colonial History*, vi, 321. The Mississagies numbered at that time eight hundred warriors. They were at treaty conference for the last time in 1755.—*Colonial History*, vii, 259.

[4] *Colonial History*, v, 675. They were subsequently called the Onoghquageys, Oghquagas, Aughquages, Ochquaquas, Onenhoghkwages, Auquaguas, Onehohquages, etc. — *Index Colonial History ; Proceedings of the Provincial Convention of New York*, ii, 340, 419, 423, etc.

[5] Dr. O'Callaghan says they were chiefly Mohawks (note, *Colonial History*, v, 675), but a different conclusion is clearly deducible from the conference minutes of Feb. 2, 1756, in which the name " Aughquages, as distinguishing the original organization, is immediately followed by that of Tuscaroras in brackets.—*Colonial History*, vii, 51. It is quite probable there were Mohawks residing among them.

[6] *Colonial History*, vii, 278. " A party

*roonas,* from Maryland,[1] a portion of the *Chugnuts,*[2] a Susquehanna family, and several clans of the *Minsis* or Esopus Indians
living upon the east branch of the Delaware river ; [3] They were
not without favorable record· in the wars of 1745 and 1755,[4]
but derive their historic interest mainly from the distinguished
services of their chief, Thomas King,[5] and from the fact that
through them the history of the Esopus clans is linked with the
war of the Revolution.[6]

At a later period, and apparently about 1746, the *Oneidas*
sent off a colony from their principal castle, to a point about
twelve miles from Oneida lake, where they established a settlement which they called Canowaroghere or Onawaraghharee,[7] and
which was subsequently recognized as " the second Oneida
castle." Several families of the Long island clans, dispossessed
of their lands and surrounded by European settlers, were subsequently added to the colony,[8] giving to it influence in point of
numbers.

Meanwhile the Esopus clans who had not followed the fortunes of their kindred, the *Minsis,* maintained their succession of
sachems and held annual conferences with the justices at Kingston.[9] Thither came Ankerop, chief sachem, in 1722, and
complained that a " white man had offered violence to an Indian

of Aughquages and Mahicanders under
Thomas, an Aughquage chief.— *Ibid,*
187. The Mahicans here spoken of were
entirely distinct from those who settled at
an early period among the .Lenapes, or
those who were subsequently located at
Otsiningo.— *Ibid.,* 104.

[1] *Colonial History,* vi, 983. Supposed
to be a remnant of the Powhattan confederacy, who were removed under the
treaty with Virginia in 1722, and called
by Gallatin Sachdagughroonas. The date
of their settlement at the north corresponds with that of the treaty with .Vir-
ginia.— *Gallatin,* 58, 59.

[2] Their village was on the south bank
of the Susquehanna, opposite Binghamton.

[3] " The Delaware Indians, who live on
the east branch of the Delaware river,
near the head of it, have given us the
strongest assurances that they will live
and die with us."— *Colonial History,* vii,
50.

[4] " I assure your excellency I never saw
a people better inclined to assist us than
they are."— *Colonial History,* vi, 361.

[5] This chief was actively employed as
the principal deputy of the Five Nations
in the treaties with the Lenapes and Shawanoes. He died at Charleston, South
Carolina, after attending the congress of
Indian nations at Scioto, in 1771. Johnson speaks of him as a man of " superior
capacity and fidelity."— *Colonial History,*
viii, 290, 300, etc.

[6] *Proceedings of the Provincial Convention of New York,* i, 339, 808 ; ii, 340,
419, 423, etc.

[7] *Colonial History,* vii, 512, 611, etc.

[8] *Ib.,* viii, 476.

[9] The records of these conferences are
scattered, some being found at Kingston,
others in the Clinton and Johnson papers
in the State Library, and others in the
office of the secretary of state.

whom he had met carrying rum," and the justices promised the punishment of the offender.   The justices, on their part, charged that the Indians " had hired negroes to fight against the Christians," which the sachem denied.   Not a conference passed without a claim for lands taken from the Indians without compensation, many of them entirely unfounded, according to the English interpretation of boundaries, but doubtless well founded in the absolute knowledge of the claimants, who, in their sales, had designated hills and not intervening valleys.   The principal purpose of the conferences, however, appears to have been to dismiss the Indians with assurances of friendship, a few blankets and considerable rum.   If they rapidly became a " contemptible people," it was in consequence of the influences by which they were surrounded.   In their wanderings a few of them came under the teachings of the Moravians, and united with the *Mahican* converts in Pennsylvania, but to them as an organization no missionary work was undertaken.   The people of Kingston cared little for their own improvement, much less for that of the Indians, and preferred rather to earn for themselves the sobriquet of " the Sodom of New York,"[1] than to perform those acts of charity and mercy which spring from a proper appreciation of the Christian character.   Had they followed the exterminating policy of the Puritans it would have been more to their credit.

The *Wappingers*, too, maintained an organization on the Hudson amid all the changes which surrounded and attended them.   Many of them had been drawn off to new homes ; a few appeared among the Moravians and at Stockbridge, but the seat of the tribe remained in the highlands.[2]   Nimham, who was made chief sachem in 1740, gave them prominence by service in the field and by his persistent efforts to recover lands of which they had been defrauded.

The result of these and other changes was, that at the close of the half century the *Lenapes* had an active, vigorous organization of five tribes ; the *Iroquois*,[3] one of seven tribes, and the

[1] *Memorials of the Moravian Church,* I, 58.
[2] *Colonial History,* VII, 869.
[3] Including the original Lenape divisions with the addition of the *Shawanoes* and *Mahicans.*   There were also several detached clans of minor importance associated with them.

*Mahicans*, although divided by provincial lines, one that could still call its followers from Quebec to Manhattan. Although the changes which had produced these new combinations were in a great degree the result alike of the selfish efforts of the European nations who were contesting the supremacy of the continent, and of the pressure of an incoming civilization, they were not less the work of aboriginal diplomats who had purposes of their own to serve. The lessons which Philip had taught his people and his allies were deeply impressed. Fugitives from the fields on which he had met disaster, bore them to congenial soil among the *Lenapes* and *Shawanoes;* to the north, among the *Abenaquis*, sharpening their desire for revenges which were unatoned ; on the prairies of the west and amid the wildernesses of Canada, they were the theme of thought and preparation. The English saw the gathering storm and sought shelter behind their allies, the *Iroquois ;* the French welded its gathering folds, and bade the avengers onward.

The war of 1744, while without positive results to the principal contestants, was the turning point in the supremacy of the *Iroquois*, as well as in the ardor of their attachment to the English. At the opening of the war a conference was held with them at Albany, in which Governor Clinton informed them of the condition of affairs, and asked their cooperation in promoting the mutual safety and defense of the English and themselves, " and the annoyance of the common enemy." The chiefs hesitated. " We cannot answer to every particular concerning the war," said they, " but do promise that we will keep all our people at home and there await orders. We are inclined to peace, till the enemy attack some of his majesty's subjects, and then we will join together to defend ourselves against them.[1]

The conference with them in October of the following year was not more successful. The chiefs thanked the governor for the Information which he had given them concerning the war, but the hatchet which they accepted they would keep in their bosoms. " We are," said they, " in alliance with a great many nations, and if we should suddenly lift the hatchet without acquainting them, they would perhaps take offense at it.

---

[1] *Colonial History*, VI, 265.

We will, therefore, before we make use of the hatchet, send four of our people to Canada, to demand satisfaction for the wrongs they have done, and if they refuse, then we shall be ready."

In a word, they had determined to remain neutral, and to that end had had consultation with their allies as well as with the French. The general character of these consultations may be inferred from that which they held with the *Mahicans* at Stockbridge, in 1744, when, Mr. Sergeant states, the embassadors were met in the most cordial manner. " Uncle," said the *Mahican* chief, " I ask you a question. I hear you have agreed with the French *Mohawks* to sit still, in case of war between their friends and ours. You well know how that matter is. I desire you to tell me what we are to do in that affair. If you say we must sit still, we will sit still. If we are to see those Indians help their friends, we must help ours." " Cousin," replied the *Mohawk*, " the information you have received of our engaging with the French *Mohawks* to stand neuter in case of war between the French and English, is very true. Those Indians have promised us that they would not meddle with the war, but sit still in peace, and let the white people determine the dispute themselves. We have promised them the same, and desire you to join with us in the same peaceable disposition."

Neutrality was maintained until 1746, when the French and their Indians became the aggressors. Meanwhile the New England authorities had erected a chain of stockades and block-houses along the frontier from Maine to the Connecticut river, and from thence across the Hoosic mountains to the territory of New York. Upon the Hoosic river, within the bounds of what is now the town of Adams, one of these blockhouses, known as Fort Massachusetts, was attacked in August, 1746, by a force under Vaudreuil, consisting of French troops and Indians numbering nine hundred and sixty-five men. The fort had but eleven effective defenders, who were compelled to surrender after a few hours' active resistance. The significance of this result was not in the loss of the fort, but in the fact that the enemy had crossed the Westenhuck and invaded neutral territory.

At the time of this occurrence a conference was being held at Albany, with the Six Nations, who as yet had given no evidence of intention to lift the hatchet. Governor Clinton had exhausted persuasive appeal; had told them that the king expected and ordered them to join with their whole force in the' contest, thereby giving them "a glorious opportunity of establishing their fame and renown over all the Indian nations in America,' by the conquest of their "inveterate enemies, the French," who, however much they might "dissemble and profess friendship," would never forget the slaughter which the Five Nations had inflicted upon them in former years, and who, for the purpose of their destruction, were "caressing the nations" who had been their "most inhuman enemies," and who desired "nothing so much as to see the name of the Six Nations become decayed and forgot forever." The issue, as it was understood by the French and the Indians, was fairly stated, but it awoke no response.

When the news came that Hoosic had been attacked, the aspect of affairs was immediately changed. Three days after the governor's last appeal (August 23d), the chiefs replied: "Last year you gave us the hatchet to be made use of against your enemies. We accepted it and promised to make use of it if they should commit further hostilities, which they have now done by destroying Saraghtoga[1] and shedding a great deal of blood. Hitherto we have made no use of the hatchet, but as you now call upon us we are ready, and do declare, from the bottom of our hearts, that we will from this day make use of it against the French and their children." To this determination the *Mahicans* and the *Schaticooks* gave their assent.

But nothing more than a petty warfare followed. In New England the English suffered some disasters, but in New York they escaped, with the exception of an engagement near Schenectady, July 21st, 1748, the account of which is much confused, and the destruction, about the same time, of the residence of Mr. Keith, near Schaticook, and the slaughter of several of the members of his family, by a company of St. Francis In-

---

[1] A settlement on the Hudson in the vicinity of the present village of Schuy- lerville, from which the present name of Saratoga is derived.

dians.[1]  On the part of the English, the *Mohawks* and *Mahicans*
appear to have taken the field in some numbers, and to have
lost warriors by death and captivity.  At the Cedars they made
a successful attack in the summer of 1747, but at the Cascades
they were defeated with loss.

Pending formidable aggressive movements against the French,
the war was closed by the treaty of peace at Aix la Chapelle.
The news of the conclusion of this treaty reached Governor
Clinton on the eve of the assemblage at Albany of a grand conference, with the Six Nations and their allies.  Great effort had
been made for the success of this conference, and in point of
numbers these efforts were rewarded.  If the Six Nations
could do nothing else, they could always rally a host at a distribution of presents ; the flow of rum was an attraction which
they could not resist.  Albany never saw such a gathering of
painted warriors ; a larger number never, perhaps, assembled
in one place, or one in which there were more tribes represented.
The enmities of years seemed to be forgotten ; *Mahicans*
and *Minsis* joined hands with the *Senecas ;* the descendants of
*Miantonimo* smoked the pipe with the *Mississagies.*  Except
in numbers, however, the conference was a failure.  The
" covenant chain " was brightened in ancient form, but instead
of the command, " On to Canada ! " which Clinton had expected
to issue, " Peace ! " was the injunction which fell upon the ears
of the assembled chiefs.

The *Mohawks,* and *Mahicans,* the representative tribes addressed, were disappointed.  While the other tribes in the English
alliance had, with the exception of a few of their warriors, ab-
stained from hostilities, they were seriously compromised.  They
had lost friends whose deaths were unavenged ; the axe of the
French was sticking in the heads of their people ; in Canada
prisons their brethren were rotting in irons ; they had taken up
the hatchet with reluctance, and would not lay it down until
their friends were released and a definite proposal made guaran-
teeing their protection in the future.  " We will still keep the
hatchet in our hands," said the former ; " we will still keep our hands
on the cocks of our guns," said the latter.  With them the question

[1] *Stone's Life and Times of Sir William Johnson,* I, 350, 354.

of peace remained an open one until the exchange of prisoners was completed in June, 1750.[1] For two or three years later the *Mohawks* carried the hatchet in their hands, the English having neglected to call them together and remove it by a distribution of presents, a custom for which they had a most tenacious regard.

In the meantime, five tribes of the confederacy made peace with the French, asserting thereby not only their national independence but subscribing their totems to the declaration "that they had not ceded to any one, their lands;" that they "were not subjects of England."[2] To the French this was an important declaration. If the nations represented claimed independence, then could treaties be made with them and the foundation of territorial lines established; but if already under allegiance to Great Britain, the question of boundaries was still an open one. The *Mohawks* alone took their rank with the English; the practical division of the confederacy, upon a very vital point, was established, and a new element added to the controversy which had so long existed between the Indian nations and the English.

[1] *Colonial History*, x, 211.          [2] *Colonial History*, x, 187.

## CHAPTER IX.

The War of 1755 — Rehabilitation of the Lenapes
and Shawanoes — The Conspiracy of Pontiac.

HE treaty of Aix la Chapelle was a very imperfect paper. By its stipulations "all Nova Scotia, or Acadia, with its dependencies," was ceded to Great Britain; the "subjects of France, inhabitants of Canada," were not to "disturb or molest in any manner whatever," the Five Indian Nations which were "subject to Great Britain," nor the "other American allies" of that government; the boundaries between the English and French possessions, along the rivers St. Lawrence and Mississippi, and the limits even of Nova Scotia, one of the original causes of the war, were left entirely undetermined, and no provision was made for the removal of the forts which the French had erected at Crown point, or Lake Champlain, and at Niagara. The key to its interpretation, if such it had, was the status of the "Five Indian Nations" claimed as "subjects to Great Britain." If the nations referred to were not "subjects to Great Britain," then were the prohibitions of the treaty void, so far as they circumscribed the operations of the French or defined the boundaries of their possessions. Availing themselves of this interpretation, the French forstalled the English by securing from the *Onondagas, Senecas, Cayugas,* and *Oneidas,* the declaration already quoted that they were independent tribes, and resumed the prosecution of the policy, which they had inaugurated as early as 1731, of connecting the St. Lawrence with the gulf of Mexico by a chain of forts along that river to Detroit and down the Ohio to the Mississippi. While the English were disputing with them in regard to the Nova Scotia peninsula, La Galissoniére was sent out, in 1749, with three hundred men to trace and occupy the Ohio valley, and faithfully did he perform his work. At the mouth of every principal river plates of lead were deposited in the soil bearing the inscription, that, from the farthest ridge whence water trickled towards the Ohio, the country belonged to France, and the lilies of the Bourbons were nailed to forest trees in token of possession.[1]

The determination of the French reopened the original controversy. The establishment of the contemplated forts was fraught with danger to the English colonies. Not only would they cut off the western Indian trade, but would build up a power behind the English settlements which would be to them a perpetual menace, even if it did not involve their very existence as subjects of Great Britain. Self-interest as well as self-defense demanded that their construction should be anticipated if possible — if not, that their occupation by the French should be resisted. The colonies were themselves divided in regard to the jurisdiction to which they were respectively entitled by their charters; but, without waiting for the determination of the dispute, Virginia organized what was known as the Ohio company, for the ostensible purpose of securing the Ohio valley for the English world. Obtaining a patent in March, 1749, for five hundred thousand acres, this company sent out, in October, 1750, Christopher Gist to make treaties with the Indians and select locations for colonies, while Pennsylvania, for a similar purpose, dispatched George Croghan. At Logstown, these agents met and together prosecuted surveys, and consummated treaties, covering a broad expanse of territory, resting from their labors finally in the heart of the territory of the *Miamis.*

The *Senecas,* the *Lenapes,* and the *Shawanoes,* whose territory was thus invaded by the rival civilizations of Europe, at first received their visitors approvingly; but at length comprehending that they were to be the ultimate sufferers, remonstrated. "Where," said Tanadiarisson, the Half-King, as the ruling *Seneca* chief was called; "where lie the lands of the Indians? The French claim all on one side of the river, and the English all on the other;" and, repairing to the French commandant at Erie, he declared that it was the wish of his people that both parties should withdraw. Met with open refusal, he returned

[1] *Bancroft,* IV, 43 etc.; *Life and Times of Sir Wm. Johnson,* I, 386, etc.

to his council, and added to the pending conflict a third party in interest — the aboriginal proprietors who were resolved to defeat the purposes of their European neighbors in such manner as opportunity should develop.

Strong in all the resources of civil and military centralization, the government of Canada moved with a resolution and celerity that for a time set at defiance the efforts of their slow-footed and divided adversaries. By the end of 1753, they had a connected line of forts, extending from Montreal to what is now called French creek, in Pennsylvania, but to which they gave the name of the Riviere aux Boeufs.[1] To this latter fort, Virginia sent, in December, Major George Washington, to demand the reason " for invading the British possessions in time of peace," and to warn the trespassers to retire. Civilly was he treated ; the answer which he received was not unexpected. The French commandant knew no law but the orders of his general ; to those orders he should " conform with exactness and resolution." The *casus belli* which Virginia sought was supplied.

Promptly voting £10,000, Virginia dispatched, in May, a force of one hundred and fifty men, under Washington, to the invaded territory, instructed " to make prisoners, kill or destroy all who interrupted the English settlements." Not a moment too soon did he reach the field. The French, sweeping down from Venango, had compelled the English to evacuate the trading post which they had established at the Fork,[2] and had occupied the place with fortifications. Warned by the Half-King, Washington hurried to the Great Meadows, where he held a conference with the friendly *Lenape* and *Seneca* chiefs. Before the rising sun of another day the French were attacked in ambush. An action of about a quarter of an hour ensued ; ten of the French force were killed, including Jumonville, their commander, and twenty-one wounded.[3] Bearing tidings of the

[1] On account of the number of Buffalo found in its vicinity.— *Sparks's Washington*, II, 436.
[2] Now the city of Pittsburg, Pa. It was here that the Indian path separated, one leading to the Seneca country and the other to the west. Hence the name, the *Fork*.
[3] Washington was severely criticised for this attack, and was charged with the murder of Jumonville.— *Memoirs Hist. Soc. Penn.*, v, 45, etc.

disaster, a soldier reached the headquarters of the French commandant ; a council of war was instantly assembled ; its deliberations almost as instantly resulted in sending out an overwhelming force to meet and crush the advancing English. Washington fell back to the Great Meadows, where he threw up the breastworks of Fort Necessity and manned its feeble ramparts. But resistance was hopeless. Without supplies of ammunition or of food, capitulation was a necessity. Accepting permission to retire with his forces, Washington turned his face homeward. On the morning of the fourth of July, 1754, the French flag waved in triumph in the valley of the Ohio.

Not alone in the celerity of their movements had the French anticipated the English. With a zeal as remarkable as it was contagious among the Indians, they had pushed the alliances and strengthened the tribes immediately dependent upon them to an extent which had transferred to them the active power which had formerly been exercised by the Five Nations, when, armed by the English, they had first been commissioned a roving police over their contemporary tribes. In this respect the change had been wonderful indeed since the confederates rallied in the war of 1688. The liberality of the French had removed much of the ancient prejudice against them ; the labors of the priests had won converts until in Canada the *Iroquois* were represented by as many organizations as they were in New York, who completely neutralized the action of the parent stocks ; the *Mississagies*, the seventh tribe of the confederacy, had dropped from their ranks ; the *Senecas* were estranged, and at Onondaga the council fire of the nation was constantly attended by the emissaries of France. As early as 1720, they began to appear in the character of mediators, rather than that of aggressive allies, and in 1745, they had with great difficulty indeed been brought out in even inconsiderable force in behalf of the English.

Perhaps this result was due in a great measure to the policy of the English in seeking through their alliances the promotion of trade ; in neglecting to supply them with priests as self-sacrificing as were those sent out by France ; in supplying the more immediate tribes with intoxicating liquors to their destruction, and in failing to cultivate the intimate relations with them

27

which formed so conspicuous a feature of the policy of the French. Whatever the cause, the French experienced little difficulty in transferring to themselves the moral support of the *Senecas*, and in securing the active alliance of the *Lenapes* and *Shawanoes*, as well as of the more western tribes, and to direct their blows for the possession of the Ohio valley against the English as their worst enemies.

For their negative rather than their positive power, continued alliance with the confederates was desirable to the English. As enemies, they would be dangerous from their familiarity with the English settlements; as allies, they would still interpose a barrier to the incursions of their relatives in the Canada alliance. Their threats[1] intimidated Clinton; the rapidity with which events were culminating in hostilities, aroused the reluctant assembly; the funds necessary to provide presents for a renewal of the ancient alliance with them was voted, and Colonel Johnson dispatched to their castles to invite their attendance at a conference at Albany. The *Mohawks* responded sullenly: "Had any other person been sent, we would not move a foot;" at Onondaga, the king declared he did not understand what the French and English intended to do in reference to the Ohio country, but for his people he could say, that they were already "so hemmed in by both, that hardly a hunting place was left, so that even if they should find a bear in a tree, there would immediately appear an owner of the land to challenge the property."

The conference at Albany was appointed for the fourteenth of June, 1754, and was to be held in conjunction with a convention of delegates from the several colonies, called to consider a plan for a general union for mutual protection. The attendance was not large; the colonies were not fully represented; the confederates were still halting between two opinions. The proceedings were opened with an address by acting governor De Lancey, in which the tribes were invited to "renew and strengthen their ancient covenant" with the English, and to call back the clans who had removed to the territory of the French. "The French," said he, "profess to be in perfect friendship with us

[1] *The Life and Times of Sir William Johnson*, I, 422.

as well as with you. Notwithstanding this they are making continual encroachments upon us both. They have lately done so in the most insulting manner, both to the northward and westward. They are endeavoring to possess themselves of the whole country, although they have made express treaties with the English to the contrary. It appears to us that their measures must necessarily soon interrupt and destroy all trade and intercourse between the English and the several Indian nations on the continent, and will block up and obstruct the great roads, which have hitherto been kept open, between you and your allies and friends who live at a distance. We want, therefore, to know whether these things appear to you in the same light as they do to us, or whether the French, taking possession of the lands in your country, and building forts between the lake Erie and the Ohio, be done with your consent or approbation."

Hendrik accepted the belt, and replied that it should be taken to Onondaga for consultation. The confederates had been shamefully treated by their allies, while the French had used their utmost endeavors to bring them over in their favor. "This," said he, "is the ancient place of treaty, where the fire of friendship always used to burn; and 'tis now three years since we have been called to any public treaty here. 'Tis true there are commissioners here, but they have never invited us to smoke with them. But the Indians of Canada come frequently and smoke here, which is for the sake of their beaver. But we hate them. We have not yet confirmed the peace with them. 'Tis your fault, brethren, that we are not strengthened by conquest; for we would have gone and taken Crown point, but you hindered us. We had concluded to go and take it, but we were told that it was too late and that the ice would not bear us. Instead of this, you burnt your own fort at Saratoga, and run away from it, which was a shame and a scandal to you. Look about your country, and see, you have no fortifications about you; no, not even to this city. Look at the French; they are men; they are fortifying everywhere. But, we are ashamed to say it, you are all like women, bare and open without any fortifications." [1]

[1] *Colonial History,* vi, 870; *Life and Times of Sir Wm. Johnson,* i, 456, etc.

The *Mahicans* who acknowledged the jurisdiction of the authorities of New York, as well as those living under the government of Massachusetts, were present, and also the *Schaticooks*. The latter, replying to the governor, said : " Your honor may see that we are young and inexperienced, our ancient people being almost all dead, so that we have nobody to give us advice, but we will do as our fathers have done before us." The reception of the *Mahicans* from Stockbridge was delayed, the governor regarding them as belonging to Massachusetts. The records of the Indian commissioners were examined, and the fact made apparent that while under the territorial jurisdiction of Massachusetts, they were not the less the representatives of the *Mahican* nation ; that they had always been present at the treaties with the Five Nations, and had been included therein.[1] Their address was historical and forcible. Their fathers had first welcomed the Europeans and given them lands ; had formed with them a covenant chain which had never been broken. That chain they would now renew, rub bright and defend its links.[2]

The conference closed on the eighth of July. Every effort had been made to conciliate the chiefs, and presents and promises were lavished upon them. The heart of Hendrik grew happy. " We are highly pleased that all things have been so amicably settled," said he, " and hope that all that has passed between us may be strictly observed on both sides. If we do not hold fast by this chain of friendship, our enemies will laugh us to scorn." Thirty wagons conveyed to Schenectady the rum and other presents which he had received for his people ; in full faith that his lands would be protected, and a church built at Canajoharie, in which should be taught the principles of peace and good will, he departed.

While the conference with the Six Nations was as satisfactory as could have been expected, proceedings not directly connected therewith were had which ultimately destroyed not only the good which was anticipated, but plunged the confederates themselves into greater discord,[3] and aroused the *Lenapes* to war.

---

[1] *Colonial History*, vi, 865.
[2] *Colonial History*, vi, 881.
[3] *Colonial History*, vii, 956.

Sundry individuals of Connecticut had, after exploring the Susquehanna valley, determined to locate a settlement at Wyoming. The territory being regarded as the property of the Six Nations, although in the occupation of the *Lenapes* and their confederated clans, a deputation was sent to Albany to confer with them and effect its purchase. The governor of Pennsylvania promptly interposed objections to the procedure, and the delegates from that province were instructed to prevent its consummation if possible. The motive was entirely selfish. The proprietaries of Pennsylvania were also in attendance seeking the purchase of the same lands. The Connecticut agents succeeded, through the aid of Colonel Lydius. The tract purchased extended about seventy miles north and south, and from a parallel line ten miles east of the Susquehanna, westward two degrees of longitude, and included the whole valley of Wyoming and the country westward to the sources of the Alleghany. Failing to secure this tract for themselves, the proprietaries of Pennsylvania added to their purchase of 1737, " a tract of land between the Blue mountain and the forks of the Susquehanna river." These purchases were not made in open council with the representatives of the tribes, but from a few of the chiefs, several of whom were in a state of intoxication when they signed the deed of conveyance; but the purchasers, and especially the Connecticut company,[1] insisted upon their validity.[2]

The convention of deputies from the several colonies was continued in session until July 11th. A plan of union was agreed to and referred to the several colonial assemblies, and a declaration adopted recommending that the Indians in alliance with the English should be placed under a competent superintendency; that forts should be built for the security of each nation; that vessels of war should be placed on the lakes, and that any further advances of the French should be prevented. The latter only was approved; the union of the colonies failed. Regarding the transfer of powers to a confederate organization as too much of an encroachment upon the liberties of the people, the colonial assemblies refused their assent, while the parent

[1] Known as the Susquehanna company. It was organized in 1753.  [2] *Life and Times of Sir Wm. Johnson,* I, 468, etc.

government rejected the plan on the ground that it favored the democratic at the expense of the aristocratic element.

The echo of Washington's guns on the Ohio meadows was speedily wafted to Canada, and scarcely had the last commissioner departed from Albany before the forests became alive with savage hordes let loose by the French upon the settlements. On the 28th of August, the St. Francis Indians fell upon Schaticook and Hoosic ; killed several persons, destroyed houses, barns and cattle, and swept off, either as prisoners or willing attendants, the remnant of *Pennacooks* residing there.[1]   Bakerstown, in New Hampshire, was next visited, and there, as well at other points, men and women fell under the blows of their assailants, or were carried away captive.

Even more disastrous results were inaugurated in Pennsylvania and the Ohio country when the Albany purchases became known.   The *Senecas* openly repudiated the contract.   The lands which had been sold were theirs ; were occupied by their children and their allies, and they would not listen to its sale. Their principal chief, who had been one of the intoxicated grantors, was driven out from their cantons ;[2] the *Lenapes* and *Shawanoes* were urged to hostilities.   The latter required but little encouragement.   To them the famous " walking treaty," had been a sore grievance, a shameless fraud.   That treaty was drawn by Penn in 1686, and conveyed an immense tract on the Delaware, the boundaries of which were described as beginning at a certain tree above the mouth of Neshamony creek ; thence by a course west-north-west to the Neshamony ; thence back into the woods " as far as a man could walk in a day and a

---

[1] On the 28th of August a party of French Indians, said to be of Bekancourt, a place between Quebeck and Montreal, made an incursion into this province and burnt the houses and barns full of grain at Hoosic, a place lying about eighteen or twenty miles east from that part of Hudson's river which is ten miles above Albany. They carried off with them the few remaining Indians at Schaticook, being between fifty and sixty in number, men, women and children. They had a little while before, when I was in Albany, assured me of their fidelity.— *Report of Gov. DeLancy, Colonial History*, VI, 909.

[2] Johnson says that this chief fled to the French for protection against his incensed people, but immediately adds : " A powerful party who followed his fortunes, took up arms shortly after, attacked a body of provincials at Lake George, whom he totally defeated, and killed forty-five. Since which he was concerned in the most important services against us, cut off some of our settlements, and occasioned the deaths of more than four hundred of our people."— *Colonial History*, VII, 956

half ; " thence to the Delaware again, and so down to the place
of beginning.    Sixty years later, Penn's successors were the
surveyors of this tract, and, in order to secure as good a bargain
as possible, prepared a road for the " walk," provided expedi-
tious means of crossing the intersecting streams, and selected
the swiftest pedestrians in the province, that thereby might be
accomplished as great a distance as possible within the time
limited.    The line on the Delaware was not fixed by the treaty,
and advantage was taken of the omission to run the course not
parallel with the river, but by one which extended north-east
for a hundred miles and more, till it struck the Delaware near
the mouth of Laxawaxen creek, far above Easton.    A million
acres of land were thus embraced, when, by a fairer computa-
tion, three hundred and fifty thousand would have confined
their claim.[1]

This was the largest, but not the least of the frauds which
the *Lenapes* had suffered.    In the Minnisink country they had
also been defrauded.    The famous Minnisink patent covered
lands which had been purchased from them but never paid for,
the purchasers having made the grantors drunk pending the
execution of the deed, obtained their signatures when they knew
not what they were doing, and then refused the promised compensation on the plea that it had already been given.[2]    The
Esopus chiefs, and the *Hackinsacks* and *Tappans*, joined in the
complaint ; the borders of New Jersey and New York, as well

[1] *Memoirs Historical Society of Pennsylvania*, v, 68.

[2] " An elderly man who lived in the
Highlands, and at whose house I dined
on my way from New York some years
ago, told me that he lived with or in the
neighborhood of one Depuy, and was
present when the said Depuy purchased
the Minnisink lands from the Indians ;
that when they were to sign the deed of
sale he made them drunk and never paid
them the purchase money agreed upon.
He heard the Indians frequently com-
plain of the fraud, and declare that they
would never be easy until they had satisfaction for their lands."—*Manuscripts of
Sir Wm. Johnson*, XXIV, 14.    Depuy was
probably the agent employed to make the
purchase.    He was well known to the
Moravians, his residence being on the
old Mine Road, which they traveled.—
*Memorials of Moravian Church*, 1, 46.
" The examinant (John Morris) says he
often heard the Delawares say that the
reason of their quarrelling with and killing the English in that part of the country was on account of their lands which
the Pennsylvania government cheated
them out of, and drove them from their
settlement at Shamokin by crowding upon
them, and by that means spoiled their
hunting, and that the people of Minnisink
used to make the Indians always drunk
whenever they traded with them, and
then cheated them out of their furs and
skins, also wronged them with regard to
their lands."—*Colonial History*, VII, 332.

as the wilderness of Pennsylvania, were filled with the threatening protestations of disfranchised proprietors animated by a common determination to hold possession of their ancient homes.

Hitherto their protestations had been without favorable result. The authorities of Pennsylvania, to provide against evil consequences, had appealed to the Five Nations to send delegates to a council at Philadelphia, when they had complained of the " walking " boundaries in 1742. The *Iroquois* delegates heard the complaint, as well as received private presents from the proprietaries. Subsidized by rum and trinkets, they commanded the *Lenapes* to yield possession of the lands. " We conquered you; we made women of you ; we charge you to remove instantly ; we don't give you liberty to think about it; we assign you two places to go to, either to Wyoming or Shamoking," was their answer, and the debate was closed.

The *Lenapes* had removed as they were bidden, and settled in the valley of Wyoming, but with that removal and settlement the " undisciplined feeling of natural equity " was fully developed in them. Whatever of doubt hung over their right of possession to the lands from which they had been ejected, there was none in regard to those to which they had been assigned. The Five Nations had given them the latter, and they were theirs. In the sale to the Connecticut company these lands were included ; in that to the agents of the Pennsylvania proprietaries, their more western hunting grounds were cut off without their consent. Remembering that by precisely similar means they had been despoiled of their former homes, they resolved to fight to the last in defense of their rights ; to revenge this last and crowning outrage, and to wipe away with blood the well remembered wrongs which had rankled in their bosoms for years. The chiefs of the east met those of the west in council at Alleghany, rehearsed the wrongs which they had suffered, and declared that wherever the white man had settled within the territory which they claimed, there they would strike him as best they could with such weapons as they could command ; and, that the blow might be effectually dealt, each warrior-chief was charged to scalp, kill and burn within the precincts of his birthright, and all simultaneously, from the frontiers, down into the heart of the settlements, until the English should sue for peace and promise redress.[1]

The summer was spent in hostile preparations and in establishing alliances. The *Senecas* gave them arms, removed from them the petticoat, and bade them take the hatchet; the " six different nations of French Indians "[2] plead their cause with the *Mohawks,* and " advised and entreated them " to break the Albany sales, and to " have some consideration for those they called brothers; "[3] the council at Onondaga repudiated the offensive contracts. October came, and no sooner had the biting frost reddened the maple and hardened the yellow corn in the husk, than, with their allies, painted black for war, in bands of two or four abreast, they moved eastward with murderous intent, and the line of the Blue mountain, from the Delaware to the Susquehanna, became the scene of the carnival which they held with torch and tomahawk during many coming months. The defenseless settlers were harassed by an unseen foe by day and by night. Some were shot down at the plow, some were killed at the fireside ; men, women and children were promiscuously tomahawked or scalped, or hurried away into distant captivity, for torture or for coveted ransom. There was literally a pillar of fire by night and a pillar and cloud by day going up along the horizon, marking the progress of the relentless Indians, as they dealt out death, and pillage, and conflagration, and drove before them, in midwinter's flight, hundreds of homeless wanderers, who scarce knew where to turn for safety or for succor in the swift destruction that was come upon them.[4]

The attacking force appeared in two distinct yet united organizations — that of the eastern *Lenapes,* under the lead of Teedyuscung; that of the western under Shingas.[5] Both

[1] *Thompson's Alienation.*

[2] These were representatives of the Six Nations who had removed to Canada at the instigation of the French priests.

[3] *Colonial History,* vi, 938.

[4] *Memorials Meravian Church,* i, 193.

[5] " *Shingask* was his proper name, which interpreted is a *bog meadow.* This man was the greatest Delaware warrior of that time ; were his war exploits on record they would form an interesting document, though a shocking one. His person was small, but in point of courage and activity, he was said never to have been exceeded by any one." (*Heckewelder's Narrative,* 64). Pennsylvania offered £200 for his scalp. His brother, Tamaque, or King Beaver, was also a distinguished warrior and chief.— *Ib.,* 61, 64.

were equal in determination, though perhaps unequal in strength, the western being the most formidable in numbers, in position, and in the direct aid which they could obtain from the French. The defeat of Braddock in July, was the signal for the aggressive action already outlined in general terms. The western organization was first to strike. On the 16th of October they fell upon the whites of John Penn's creek, four miles south of Shamokin. Here they killed or took captive twenty-five persons; and it was only the twenty-third of the month when all the settlements along the Susquehanna, between Shamokin and Hunter's mill, for a distance of fifty miles, were hopelessly deserted. Early in November the Great and Little Cove were attacked and the inhabitants either put to death or taken prisoners, and the settlements totally destroyed.

These blows were promptly seconded by the eastern organization under Teedyuscung. Assembling his allied *Lenape*, *Shawanoe* and *Mahican* warriors at Nescopec, he marked out the plan of the campaign for the coming autumn and winter. Its operations were to be restricted to the " walking purchase," within which it was resolved to chastise the English first, by waging against them a war of extermination. From their lurking places in the fastnesses of the Great Swamp, the wronged warriors, led by Teedyuscung in person, sallied forth on their marauds, striking consternation into the hearts of the settlers. Falling upon the farms along the Susquehanna and Delaware, they fired the harvested grain and fodder in barns and in barracks, destroyed large numbers of cattle and horses, and killed thirteen persons. On the 24th of November the Moravian mission at Gnadenhutten was surprised and ten of its converts scalped, or shot, or tomahawked, or burned to death in their dwellings. This was but the prelude to the tragedy which was to be performed. Along the northern line of the tract which had been so fraudulently surveyed, the tide of devastation rolled its blackening current. Within a month, fifty farm houses were plundered and burned, and upwards of one hundred persons killed on the frontiers on both sides ·of the Kittatinny, or endless hills. " All our border country," writes a chronicler of the day, "extending from the Potomac to the Delaware, not less than one hundred and fifty miles in length and between twenty and thirty in breadth, has been entirely deserted, its houses reduced to ashes, and the cattle, horses, grain and other possessions of the inhabitants either destroyed, burned or carried off by the Indians ; while such of the poor planters who, with their wives, children and servants, escaped from the enemy, have been obliged, in this inclement season of the year, to abandon their habitations almost naked, and to throw themselves upon the charity of those who dwell in the interior of the province."

The *Minsis*, unleashed, performed their part — for each tribal clan, it will be borne in mind, was, by the terms of the compact, required to strike within the territory which they claimed as their

birthright — and on the borders of Ulster and Orange counties in New York, and in the western settlements of New Jersey, were repeated the fearful ravages of the more remote districts of Pennsylvania. Except in the town of Goshen, the settlements here were at considerable distance from each other and much exposed to the surprises of the Indian enemy. The incursions of the Indians were frequent; the people, especially in the northern part of Orange and southern part of Ulster, were kept in almost perpetual alarm and under such " continued military duty as to be rendered incapable of taking care of their private affairs for the support of their families." An extent of country, on the west side of the Wallkill, of fifteen miles in length and seven or eight in breadth, which was "well and thickly settled, was abandoned by the inhabitants, who, for their safety, removed their families to the east side of the river, and became a charge on the charity of their neighbors," while others " removed to distant parts, and some out of the province.[1]

" Fatigues of body, in continually guarding and ranging the woods, and anxiety of mind which the inhabitants could not

[1] *New York Manuscripts*, LXXXII, 107, etc.

avoid by their being exposed to a cruel and savage enemy," increased by the perpetual lamentations and cries of the women and children," were not the only evils which the inhabitants suffered.   Three men were killed at Cochecton ; five men at Philip Swartwout's ; Benjamin Sutton and one Rude, two of the Goshen militia, were killed at Minnisink ; Morgan Owen was killed and scalped about four miles from Goshen ; a woman, taken prisoner at Minnisink, was killed and her body cut in halves and left by the highway ; Silas Hulet's house was robbed and he himself narrowly escaped.   " From about the drowned lands for fifteen miles down the Wallkill, where fifty families dwelt, all save four abandoned their fields and crops." [1]

Meanwhile General Edward Braddock, whose defeat has been incidentally noticed, had arrived in Virginia with two regiments of English troops, and at a conference with the royal governors, on the 14th of April, had planned four expeditions against the French ; the first was to effect the complete reduction of Nova Scotia, the second was to recover the Ohio valley, the third was to expel the French from Fort Niagara and form a junction with the expedition to the Ohio, and the fourth, under the command of Colonel Johnson, was to have for its object the capture of Crown point, for which purpose he was to have the militia of New York, Massachusetts and Connecticut, and the warriors of the Six Nations under his command.   To aid in securing the services of the latter, as well as to effect a more complete organization of the Indian alliances, he was appointed superintendent of Indian affairs, with full power to make treaties in the interest of the crown.[2]

Returning from Alexandria, where the conference had been held, Johnson entered upon the work which had been assigned to him.   From Mount Johnson, to which he removed the council-fire which had for so many years been kept burning at Albany, he sent a belt to each of the confederate tribes,

[1] " All the families between the deponent's house and Minnisink, to the amount of one hundred and fifty persons, have deserted those settlements and come into four frontier houses, one of which is the deponent's : that deponent's house, which is now a frontier house on that side, and which was, last year, fifteen or sixteen miles within the settlements at Minnisink, is about sixteen miles from Hudson's river."—*Affidavit of James Howell, New York Manuscripts*, LXXXII, 107, etc.

[2] *Colonial History*, VI, 961.

acquainting them of his appointment and asking them to
come and meet him.   Over a thousand sons of the forest
accepted the invitation, and, on the 21st of June, seated themselves before him in council.   While ready to do him personal
service and honor, they had many complaints to make — were
deeply entangled by their pledges to the French as well as ·to
their tribal blood in Canada.   Johnson listened to them with
patience, and, after answering all their inquiries, delivered to
them a ringing appeal to join him.   The chiefs listened and
applauded; drank the rum which had been provided, accepted
the presents, and danced the war dance, but that was all.   To
march with him to the frontiers they were not prepared, and
plead the shortness of the warning, the want of time to call in
their scattered people, the disgraceful termination of the contest of 1745, their relations with their Canada brethren; indeed,
there was apparently no end to the reasons which they could not
assign to conceal their indifference to the English cause and the
divisions which existed among themselves.

From this boasted "bulwark" against the French, turn for
a moment to the conduct of the nations in the French alliance,
led by the flower of the Hudson river tribes.   At the call of
Vaudreuil three and thirty nations rallied to his ranks.   From
the rivers of Maine and Acadia, and the wildernesses of Lake
Huron and Lake Superior, the martial airs of France were
shouted in the many tongues of the allied nations as they pressed
with swift destruction upon the border settlements and returned
laden with the trophies of the fray.

Hendrik and his *Mohawks*, bound by personal ties to Johnson, with here and there a warrior from the other tribes, to the
number of fifty, left Albany with Johnson on the 8th of August.   At the "carrying place" some two hundred warriors
joined him,[1] giving to him, with the militia, a force of about
thirty-five hundred men.   The French, marching in about
equal force to attack Oswego, were called back and sent, under
Baron Dieskau, to the defense of Crown point.   Leaving the
largest portion of his forces at that Fort, Dieskau pushed on

[1] The French report says: "All the Mohawks were there, some Oneidas, some Tharhkarorin, some Mahicans, and one Onondaga."— *Colonial History*, x, 322.

intending to attack Fort Edward, cut off Johnson's retreat, and annihilate his army. Misled by his guides, he found himself on the road to Lake George and only four miles distant from Johnson's encampment at Ticonderoga. Leaving his position, Johnson detached one thousand men and two hundred Indians to bring on an engagement. The opposing forces met on the 8th of September. Finding the French too powerful, the English fell back to Ticonderoga; the French pursued and resumed the battle under the walls of Johnson's position. After a severe engagement, from twelve until four o'clock, the French retreated. The losses on both sides were heavy, that of the English being one hundred and fifty-eight killed, including King Hendrik and thirty-eight of his warriors, ninety-two wounded and sixty-two missing, while that of the French was between three and four hundred.[1] Johnson was wounded slightly, and Dieskau mortally. The French retreat was unmolested; Crown point was not reduced. Such was the victory which gave to Johnson a baronetcy, and to American history Fort Ticonderoga.

Johnson returned to his residence in November, and was met at Schenectady by a message from the governor of Pennsylvania asking his aid in arresting the depredations of the *Lenapes* in that province. Summoning the chiefs of the Six Nations (Jan. 7th), he informed them that " the *Shawanoes* and *Delawares* and river Indians[2] were committing hostilities in the southern part of New York, as well as in New Jersey and Pennsylvania;" that they had " burned several out settlements and killed many people who had never offended them ;" that as the offenders were " looked upon as allies and dependents of the Six Nations," and living within the limits of their country, it was expected that they would reprimand them " for what they had already done, prevent their doing any more mischief, and insist on their turning their arms against the French."[3]

The mission was promptly undertaken by the *Mohawk, Oneida* and *Tuscarora* chiefs.[4] They had already sent a belt to the *Lenapes* and their allies desiring that they would not

[1] *Life and Times of Sir Wm. Johnson.*
[2] The reference is to Mahican and other clans residing on the Delaware.

[3] *Colonial History*, VII, 44.
[4] These were the only nations represented at the conference.

join with any but the Five Nations ;[1] now they would "appoint with them a conference at Tiyoga and endeavor to put a stop to any more bloodshed." The loyal *Seneca* villages[2] exercised their influence in the same direction. Visited by a party of *Lenapes* on their way to Niagara, they tried to persuade them to stop, and called to their aid their most venerable chief; but neither belts nor personal appeals had any effect upon the followers of Shingas. Replying to the loyal *Senecas* they exclaimed : " We have once been women and ashamed to look down at our petticoats, but as you have taken off our petticoats, and encouraged us to begin a quarrel with the English, we are determined never to submit again to that ignominious state while there is one of us alive. It seems to us that you now want to throw all the blame on us, and make peace, which we will not hearken to, but will go to our father the French, who will assist and protect us."[3] Thither they went, and to the commandant at Niagara declared : " Father — We are now at war with the English. When we first began, being very poor, we struck them with billets of wood." In reply, the commandant gave them a hatchet, and arms and ammunition, and lighted afresh the torch of war which they had waved along the borders.

Not more successful were the direct appeals of Johnson's embassadors to Shingas. " Get sober," said they to him, in the metaphorical language of Indian speech ; " Get sober—your actions are those of a drunken man." But the days of yore were gone, when the trembling *Lenape* stood cowering in the presence of the *Mengwe.* Unhesitating submission to the mandates of the tribes that had so long oppressed and insulted his nation, was no longer written on his heart. Of the old confederacy the most powerful part were now his friends, while around him had gathered his grandchildren in formidable numbers. To the words of the embassadors he returned scoff for scoff, and scorn for scorn. " We are men," said he ; " we are men and warriors. We will acknowledge no superiors upon

---

[1] When speaking of themselves in official transactions Five Nations only were recognized. The Tuscaroras had no territorial rights or authority.

[2] The Onondagas, Cayugas and Senecas preferred neutrality, with the exception of two Seneca villages who remained loyal to the English. As already stated, the great bulk of the Senecas were actively aiding the French.

[3] *Manuscripts of Sir William Johnson,* IV, 131.

earth. We are men, and are determined to be no longer ruled over by you as women. We are warriors, and are determined to cut off all the English save those that make their escape from us in ships. So say no more to us on that head, lest we make women of you as you have done of us." [1]

At Otseningo the embassadors were more successful, the *Lenapes* and their allies there being more immediately under the influence of the *Oneidas*. From thence they returned, on the 27th of December, bearing with them the message that the offending chiefs there had promised to " stop and repent," but as a condition thereto the English must return the captives which they had taken; that they " must see every one of them returned again " or it " would not be well ;" for this they would wait two months, and if the captives were then returned, they would " contrive to make up the matter and settle affairs, and not till then ;" meanwhile they promised that their young men who were on the war path should be called back." [2]

In February, 1756, Johnson again called the attention of his allies to the matter, and reminded them that unless they exerted themselves to " maintain their superiority," they would " not only lose that authority " which had been hitherto acknowledged, but would have the *Lenapes* their enemies. Red Head, the *Onondaga* sachem, replied, that when first requested to do so a message had been dispatched to the *Lenapes*, which had subsequently been " backed with a second message;" that both messages having proved abortive, they had " obtained an interview," through the *Oneidas*, at which the *Lenapes* had promised that hostilities should cease. They would cheerfully renew their efforts, and would appoint a meeting at Otseningo, at which, by a full representation of the tribes, they would endeavor to exercise that influence in which they had hitherto failed.

Pending this new mission, a delegation of friendly *Lenapes* met Johnson in conference, on the 29th of February. The *Oneida* and *Tuscarora* embassadors opened the proceedings, and stated that the *Shawanoes* were on their way to Chugnut [3] where

---

[1] *Thompson's Alienation*, 77; *Memoirs Historical Society Pennsylvania*, v, 98.
[2] *Colonial History*, vii, 44, 49.

[3] On the south side of the Susquehanna river, opposite Binghamton. It was a very small portion of the Shawanoes that were represented.

they would live under the protection of the Six Nations; that the *Lenapes* had given the strongest assurances of peace, and that they earnestly desired that a fort might be erected for their protection. Johnson expressed his gratification at the disposition of the chiefs in attendance; promised that a fort should be built for the protection of the *Lenapes* and that they should be cared for and supplied with arms and ammunition. Adam, on the part of the latter, expressed his appreciation of the kindness which they had received, and promised never to forget it. The visit was of no significance touching the action of the *Lenapes* proper, but appears to have been gotten up to indicate that the *Oneidas* and *Tuscaroras* still had the influence which they claimed.

On the 21st of April, the embassadors of the second mission made their report. They had visited the *Lenapes* and *Shawanoes*, and had succeeded, they said, in " convincing them that they had acted very foolishly and very unjustifiably," and that they had "promised and agreed " to unite with them against the " common enemy ; " but at the same time had expressed the desire that they might have a hearing at Onondaga to convince them that harmony and friendship with them was desired, in which request the embassadors united. Johnson accepted the proposition; he would hold a council at Onondaga twenty days hence, and charged the chiefs, then present with the duty of extending the invitation.

About the same time an important change took place in the *Lenape* government. Tadame,[1] their king, was treacherously murdered, but by whom is not stated, and Teedyuscung, that " lusty, raw-boned man," whose voice had already been heard in the wilderness, became his successor. Enjoying the confidence of his people, as well as possessing great native ability, he had already become a power to be both feared and conciliated. For peace with the English he was ready, but it must be a peace which recognized the rights of his nation; to no other would he listen, and spurned alike the threats and the blandishments of those who would influence him to a different policy.

[1] We have not met with a more specific reference to this chief. He appears to have been the successor of Allumpanees who died in 1747, after having long out lived his activity.— *Minor's History Wyoming ; Memorials Moravian Church*, 1, 67.

In the meantime, Pennsylvania declared war against the *Lenapes* and *Shawanoes*, and sent out a force of three hundred men, under the charge of Benjamin Franklin, to build a fort at Gnadenhütten[1] or Shamokin, and restore the fugitive Moravian Indians and their missionaries to their lands.    Johnson doubted the policy of these movements, regarding it as the part of wisdom to have awaited the result of the negotiations which he had inaugurated, and which he believed only awaited the council which he had appointed at Onondaga for their consummation. That council assembled in June, but Teedyuscung did not attend, nor were his subordinate chiefs present in numbers sufficient " to enter upon business and conclude affairs relating to them with proper authority."[2]     To entertain and conciliate them special effort had been made.    Thirty Indians from the Delaware river, who had been taken prisoners by the English, and whose release had been insisted upon, were taken up in full clothing and armament, as a peace offering, and ample presents were provided for distribution.    On the last day of the session Teedyuscung made his appearance, but would do nothing, and the conference was adjourned to Mount Johnson.[3]

The adjourned conference was more successful.    Teedyuscung, having satisfied himself that the English were not only sincere in their desire for peace, but had been convinced that the Six Nations, in their present condition, were wholly unable to control his people, made his appearance, and was urged to explain the reason for the hostilities which had been committed, and to enter upon a covenant of peace.    But he was not prepared to comply.    " I cannot take upon me at this time to give a determinate answer to you," said he, " but I shall punctually deliver your speech to all my nation on my return home, and you shall have our fixed resolutions and positive answers as soon as possible."    Dismissing him, Johnson called the confederate

---

[1] Fort Allen.    It was located at the Moravian town of Gnadenhütten, on the Lehigh river, opposite the mouth of the Mahoning, and adjoined the Lenape town of Shamokin where Teedyuscung had his residence.    It was built in January, 1756, by Benjamin Franklin.— *Pennsylvania Colonial Records*, VII, 15.

[2] There were only two young warriors of the Delaware nation present.— *Colonial History*, VII, 146.

[3] Neither did the deputation from the Delawares come till that meeting was near upon a conclusion.— *Colonial History*, VII, 153.

chiefs to advise with him what further course to pursue, and it was agreed that the latter should visit Teedyuscung in his tent and persuade him to declare his intentions at the session of the following day. To this the king consented, and, at the appointed time, stated that he could only agree for himself and his people at Tiyoga; that his brethren on the Ohio must determine for themselves, but for himself and those whose representative he was, he promised to follow the example of the Six Nations — a promise at that time of very doubtful import. Paxinos, the *Shawanoe* king, made similar pledge, and Abraham, on behalf of the *Mahicans* at Otsiningo, united in the assurance of harmony. A formal declaration or covenant of peace and friendship was then made, and the war dance celebrated.

Still Johnson was not altogether satisfied that his work was well done. He knew that the *Lenapes*, and their allies, aspired to if they did not possess the independence which they claimed, and that so long as this was denied, peace would not be possible. The necessities of the English were great,[1] the determination of the *Lenapes* and their allies undisguised. Selfishness became the ally of justice — the diplomacy of Teedyuscung secured the triumph of his people. In the watches of the night Johnson meditated, and on the morning of the 12th of July, after consultation with the sachems of the Six Nations, declared to the *Lenape* king, and the representatives of the *Shawanoes* and *Mahicans*, that, in consideration of the promise they had made, and in full confidence of their future suitable behavior, they were " hereafter to be considered as men," by all their brethren the English, " and no longer as women," and expressed the hope that the Six Nations would follow his example and remove the " invidious distinction."[2] Decking the chiefs with medals, and the kings with silver gorgets, he covered the embers of the council-fire, and sent from his presence a rehabilitated race.

[1] The good consequences that will attend the accommodating of this unhappy breach are great. It will give a great turn to the affairs of the present war in North America, and I trust may, by a little time and proper management, enable us to withdraw the Delawares and Shawanese that are settled on the Ohio from the French interest. I doubt their present connections are too strong to hope for this success now.— *Hardy to Lords of Trade*, May 10, 1756.

[2] *Colonial History*, VII, 151, 160.

While the attention of Johnson was mainly devoted to the pacification of the more important Indian nations, the domestic clans of *Minsis* and *Mahicans*, who remained in the valley of the Hudson, were not neglected.    To the former, proclamation was made in December, 1755, through  the justices of Ulster, inviting them to remove from the " back settlements, where they might be taken for enemies and destroyed," to the " towns where they would be protected and assisted."    Accepting these assurances, many of them came forward ;  but the promised protection and assistance was not, in all cases, extended.    At Wilemantown, in Ulster county,[1] at the house of Charles Stevenson, where a number of them assembled, they were attacked, on the second of March, by a party of armed men, headed by Samuel Slaughter, and a man and his squaw killed.    Moving from thence to a wigwam about a mile and a half distant, three Indians, two squaws and two  children fell victims to Slaughter's misguided zeal.[2]    Those who reached Kingston, while spared hostile attack, were suffered to remain dependent upon such charity as was usually extended to their race.    Under the circumstances in which they were placed, they readily accepted the offer which was made to them to remove to the *Mohawk* country.    To that end *Mohawk* chiefs were sent to them, with an interpreter, and provision made for their transportation. On  the  22d of May they appeared before Johnson, were addressed and assigned to lands in the Schoharie county.[3]

Many of the *Mahicans* of the upper Hudson and *Wappingers* of Dutchess followed in the same direction.    On the 28th of May, Johnson writes : " The river Indians whose families are at Fishkill, have had a meeting with the *Mohawk* Indians, and it is agreed that they shall remove and live with the *Mohawks*. Two of those Indians are going down to fetch up their women, children, etc., and I send an interpreter with them.    As the removal of these Indians and their incorporation with the *Mohawks* is an affair that will be, I hope, of happy consequence towards the public tranquillity at this juncture, I must desire you

[1] Near Walden, Orange county, in the state of New York.
[2] *New York Manuscripts*, LXXXII, 88 ;    *Documentary History of New York*, II, 763, 764.
[3] *Colonial History*, VII, 94, 96, 100, 113.

will give all assistance in your power to the Indians who are going down, and take care that no just cause of dissatisfaction be given to them."[1] When Johnson returned to his residence on the 9th of July, he found, as the fruit of this order, one hundred and ninety-six " *Mohicander* or river Indians," men, women and children, awaiting his pleasure. In the afternoon he clothed the men " from head to foot, gave them ammunition, paint, etc., in the presence of the Six Nations and the *Shawanoes* and *Delaware* kings."[2] They were warmly greeted by their brethren who had left them many years before, and who were then present, as well as by the *Nanticokes*, in whose immediate vicinity they were assigned lands at Otsiningo.[3] Thither they went, and in the subsequent assemblies of the tribes took their place as the allies of the *Senecas*. After serving Johnson faithfully for a time, and especially in his expedition against Crown point, they joined the fortunes of their brethren in the *Lenape* confederation and lost their identity in their subsequent wars.

The peace which Johnson had made with Teedyuscung was only partial. In consenting to it the latter had defined his authority as limited to the territory which he specially represented. For himself, and those who acknowledged his authority, he had promised—the *Lenapes*, *Shawanoes* and *Mahicans* of the Ohio country—he would influence if he could. To attend any peace conference with Johnson, they had refused, as also had the *Minsis*. Said the latter: " We have murdered the English from Canastota to Esopus. Warraghiyagy (Johnson) may pretend to make peace, but peace is not in his power. The governor of Pennsylvania is master this way, and will not listen to peace," and such was the interpretation which Teedyuscung himself

[1] *Manuscripts of Sir Wm. Johnson*, IV, 54.

[2] *Colonial History*, VII, 153.

[3] " Last spring," said Jonathan, who represented them at the conference of April 23d, 1757, " last spring, with this belt the Nanticokes took us by the hand and bid us sit down by them. They said to us, ' you Mohikanders and we Nanticokes will be one people and take you Mohikanders by the hand as brethren, and fix you here at Otsiningo, where the Six Nations have lighted a council fire and the Senecas appointed lands for you to cultivate. Call all your dispersed brethren together and sit down here with them as their habitation, and we Nanticokes assure you that whoever shall pinch or hurt you, we shall feel it, and the Six Nations shall do the same.' This belt we propose to send among all our dispersed people ; we acquaint you herewith, and whenever you see any of our scattered people passing up the river, you will know they are removing to Otsiningo."—*Colonial History*, VII, 253.

gave to Johnson's jurisdiction.   Monakadook,[1] the *Seneca* Half-King, who had been sent to the Ohio *Lenapes* to invite them to Onondaga, was the bearer of a message from them to the governor.   On his arrival he found that Teedyuscung had preceded him, and had informed him that he had been empowered by ten nations [2] to conclude a peace, and was prepared to negotiate.   Monakadook could give the governor no information on the subject, and was made the bearer to Johnson of the inquiry : " Who is this Teedyuscung who claims to be king of the Delawares ? " coupled with the declaration that his protestations of a desire for peace must be false, "as the Delaware Indians were still murdering" his people.[3]

Johnson professed entire ignorance in regard to the commission which Teedyuscung claimed he had received, and it is not probable that he had any information on the subject.   The inference is that the chiefs who were negotiating in his interest, having failed to control the *Lenapes*, had concealed from him their further action in the matter, hoping to effect the end which he sought by other means, with a view to maintain a reputation which they no longer possessed.[4]   Johnson promised to make inquiry at Onondaga in regard to the matter.   What the result of this inquiry was does not appear; but the governor of Pennsylvania was convinced, and modified his declaration of war, making it applicable only to " implacable and obstinate enemies, and not against any that now are or hereafter may be disposed to hearken to the Six Nations in our favor."   By November he

---

[1] So called by the Iroquois.

[2] Including, as subsequently appeared, his own immediate tribes and the Six Nations.

[3] *Colonial History*, VII, 197.   The governor sent a more formal message by Captain Newcastle, in October, inquiring into the character and credentials of Teedyuscung, and, it is said was informed by one of the Six Nations that the Delaware chief " did not speak the truth when he told the governor that he had authority from the Six Nations to treat with Onas."

[4] This inference is strengthened by the speech of the Mohawk orator at Lancaster.   " In former times our forefathers conquered the Delawares, and put petticoats on them.   A long time after that, they lived among you, and, upon some differences between them and you, we thought proper to remove them, giving them lands to plant and hunt on at Wyoming and Juniatta.   But you, covetous of land, made plantations there and spoiled their hunting.   They complained to us, and we found their complaints true.   You drove them into the arms of the French.   It is our advice that you send for the Senecas and them, treat them kindly, and give them back some part of their lands, rather than differ with them. It is in your power to settle the difference with them if you please."—*Gallatin,* 78

had fully learned who Teedyuscung was, and at Easton held a
formal conference with him.  The *Lenape* king stated his complaint boldly and plainly.  To the governor's inquiry for speci-
fications in regard to alleged wrongs in the sale of lands, he
replied : " I have not far to go for an instance.  This very
ground under me (striking it with his foot), was my land by
inheritance, and is taken from me by fraud.  When I say this
ground, I mean all the land lying between Tohiccon creek and
Wyoming, on the river Susquehanna.  I have not only been
served so in this government, but the same thing has been done
to me as to several tracts in New Jersey, over the river."
When asked what he meant by " fraud," he gave instances of
forged deeds, under which lands were claimed which were never
sold.  " This," said he, " is fraud."  " Also, when one chief has
land beyond the river, and another chief has land on this side,
both bounded by rivers, mountains and springs, which cannot be
moved, and the proprietaries, ready to purchase lands, buy of one
chief what belongs to another, this likewise is fraud."  In regard
to the lands on the Delaware, he said his people had never been
satisfied since the treaty of 1737.  The boundary of the land
then sold was to have gone only "as far as a man could walk
in a day and a half from Nashamony creek," yet the person
who measured the ground did not walk but ran.  He was, moreover, as they supposed, to follow the winding bank of the river,
whereas he went in a straight line.  And because the Indians
had been unwilling to give up the land as far as the " walk "
extended, the governor sent for their cousins, the Six Nations,
to come down and drive them from the land.  When the Six
Nations came down, the *Lenapes* met them for the purpose of
explaining why they did not give up the land ; but the English
made so many presents to the Six Nations that their ears were
stopped.  They would listen to no explanations ; and Canasa-
teego[1] had abused them, and called them women.  The Six
Nations had, however, given to them and the *Shawanoes* the
lands upon the Susquehanna and Juniatta for hunting grounds,
and had so informed the governor ; but notwithstanding this the
white men were allowed to go and settle upon those lands.

[1] A viceroy chieftain who had been set over them by the Six Nations.

Two years ago, moreover, the governor had been to Albany to buy some land of the Six Nations,[1] and had described the boundaries by points of compass, which the Indians did not understand, by which the deeds were made to include lands both upon the Susquehanna and the Juniata which they did not intend to sell.  When all these things were known to the Indians, they had declared that they would no longer be friends to the English, who were trying to get all their country away from them.  He had come now to smoke the pipe of peace with them, and hoped that justice might be done to his people. [2]

The conference continued nine days, and was the occasion for the display of no little tact and good judgment on the part of Governor Denny, as well as on that of Teedyuscung.  The former, as some of the *Iroquois* chiefs expressed it, " put his hand into Teedyuscung's bosom, and was so successful as to draw out the secret, which neither Johnson nor the Six Nations could do ;" while tne latter secured a truce at least involving peace on the basis that himself and his people were to remain on the Wyoming lands, and that houses should be built for them by the Pennsylvania proprietaries.  He was to go to Johnson's council-fire and explain what had been done, obtain his confirmation and take advice as to the future.  Several matters were left unadjusted, Teedyuscung declaring that he was not empowered to consider them, and that the parties interested were not properly represented to make action binding.  He proposed that a meeting should be held at Lancaster in the spring, at which all the matters in dispute should be definitely adjusted, and with that understanding the council closed.

But at the meeting which was then appointed, Teedyuscung was not present,[3] and it was not until the 21st of July that the adjourned council was held.  On its assemblage the *Lenape* king presented his credentials as the representative of the *Lenapes, Minsis, Mahicans, Shawanoes* and *Nanticokes*, east of the Alleghany mountains, fully empowered by them and by the *Senecas, Onondagas, Cayugas, Oneidas* and *Mohawks*, " to set-

[1] At the congress of 1754.
[2] *Life and Times of Sir Wm. Johnson ; Colonial History*, vii, 260, etc.

[3] The attendance of the Indians was prevented by the severity of the winter, the snow being too deep to permit them to travel.

tle all differences subsisting between them and their brethren, the English." George Croghan represented Johnson, as superintendent of Indian affairs. A patient, earnest and honest investigation was had. Surrounded by three hundred of his people ; counselled by Paxinos, chief of the *Shawanoes*, and Abraham, chief of the *Mahicans*, and advised by a delegation of Quakers, one of whom, Charles Thompson, acted as his clerk,[1] Teedyuscung conducted his case. " The land is the cause of our difference," said he, " and if I can now prevail with you, as I hope I shall, honestly to do what may be consistent with justice, then will I with a loud voice speak, and the nations shall hear me. The complaint I made last fall, I yet continue. I think some lands have been bought by the proprietor or his agents from Indians who had not a right to sell, and to whom the lands did not belong. I think also when some lands have been sold to the proprietor by Indians who had a right to sell to a certain place, whether that purchase was made by miles or hours' walk, the proprietors have, contrary to agreement or bargain, taken in more lands than they ought to have done, and lands that belonged to others. I therefore now desire that you will produce the writings and deeds by which you hold the land and let them be read in public and examined, that it may be fully known from what Indians you bought the lands you hold and how far your purchase extends. What is fairly bought and paid for, I make no further demands about, but if any lands have been bought of Indians to whom they did not belong, and who had no right to sell them, I expect satisfaction for those lands ; and if the proprietors have taken in more lands than they bought of true owners, I expect likewise to be paid for that. But as the persons to whom the proprietors may have sold those· lands which of right belong to me, have made some settlements, I

---

[1] " At this council Teedyuscung insisted upon having a secretary of his own selection appointed, to take down the proceedings in behalf of the Indians. The demand was considered extraordinary and was opposed by Governor Denny. Teedyuscung persisted in his demand, and it was finally acceded to. Charles Thompson, master of the free Quaker School in Philadelphia, was appointed. He was afterwards secretary to the Continental congress, and filled that station for many years. He died in 1824, aged 94 years, full of honors. The Delawares adopted him and gave him a name signifying, the man of truth. — *Life and Times of Sir Wm. Johnson*, 11, 14.

don't want to disturb them or force them to leave them, but I expect a full satisfaction shall be made to the true owners for these lands."

The deeds which he questioned, it was proposed should be sent to Johnson to examine; but to this he objected: "We do not know Colonel Johnson; he may be an honest and sincere man. We do understand he treats his Indians very well, but we are sensible that some of the nations are there that have been instrumental to this misunderstanding in selling lands in this province, having in former years usurped that authority and called us women, and threatened to take us by the foretop, and throw us aside as women. But after a long space I believe it is evident, nay there are witnesses present who can prove that it is otherwise. Let the deeds be produced here and put down with the minutes." The governor complied with the request, and the deeds were compared by Thompson, who certified to the correctness of the transcripts which were made. They were five in number.[1] It was agreed that they should be sent to Johnson for transmission to the king, and that awaiting his decision upon the questions which the Indians had raised, there should be peace.

These matters having been made satisfactory, Teedyuscung announced his purpose. "I shall, as I promised," said he, "speak to the different nations with a loud voice. I will faithfully let them know what you have promised, and as we are witnesses that you are wealthy and powerful, and well disposed to assist such as shall come in as brothers, I will let them know it. Those who come to me with hostile intent, I will stop, and if they will not by reasonable terms turn about and join with me, I will then make an end of them or they of me; and if there is a great number, so that I may not be able to withstand them, I will take all prudent steps to let my brethren the English know." "Now," said he, in conclusion, "you

[1] 1. A paper copy of the last Indian purchase, July, 28, 1686 - 2. A release from the Delaware Indians, August 25, 1757. 3. A release from the Five Nations for the lands on the Susquehanna river, October, 11, 1736. 4. A release from the Six Nations of lands eastward to Delaware river, dated October 25, 1736, with another endorsed, "Dated July 9, 1754." 5. A deed of release for Indian purchase, dated August, 22,1749.— *Colonial History*, vii, 313.

may remember I was styled by my uncles, the Six Nations, a woman in former years, and had no hatchet in my hand, but a pestle or hominy pounder. But now, brethren, here are some of my uncles who are present to witness the truth of this. As I had no tomahawk and my uncles were always styled men and had tomahawks in their hands, they gave me a tomahawk ; and as my uncles have given me a tomahawk and appointed and authorized me to make peace with a tomahawk in my hand, I take that tomahawk and turn the edge of it against your enemies the French."

The papers which were transmitted to Johnson were immediately sent by him to the lords of trade, accompanied by the statement that " some of the Six Nations were disgusted with the deed which had been given at Albany, while others were conniving at the hostilities which were being committed, and that he conceived the " most effectual method of producing tranquillity," would be the voluntary and open surrender of that deed, leaving the proprietaries to fix with the Indians, in the best manner they could, " the bounds for their settlements." This opinion he had other reasons for entertaining. The Six Nations, whose consequence he never forgot to magnify, would never be satisfied " unless the deeds of the Albany purchase " were " surrendered up, and the claims founded thereon in a great measure set aside ; " the *Lenapes* were equally determined, testimony having been furnished him that they had been heard to declare " most solemnly" that " they would never leave off killing the English as long as there was one on their lands ; that they were determined to drive them all off their lands, naming Minnisink almost to the North river east (in the provinces of New York and New Jersey) ; also Bethlehem and the lands on a parallel line to it west," which the English had cheated them out of.[1]

In this conclusion he was most amply justified by the results which had been experienced. Peace had been declared, but no exchange of prisoners had taken place, and while Teedyuscung himself maintained the truce which had been agreed to at Easton, on the Ohio, his allies and kindred spurned the overtures made to them and maintained their alliance with the French. Send-

[1] *Colonial History*, VII, 331.

ing their emissaries eastward, the latter propagated prejudices against the good intentions of the English, magnified the prowess, kindness and generosity of the French, and successfully plead the wrongs which had been committed against them in the sale and occupation of their lands.[1]   The *Minsis* were ready listeners to these appeals, and active participants in the hostilities which were continued.[2]   Indeed, hostilities were not suspended in any direction.   In August, 1757, says Niles,[3] "one James Tidd was scalped in the Minnisinks.   About this time, also, one James Watson, with James Mullen, went out on some business and were fired upon by a party of Indians:   Watson was found killed and scalped; Mullen was carried off, as was concluded, not being found or heard of.   About the 19th of September, Patrick Karr was killed and scalped at a place called Minnisink bridge.

"Some time in the first part of October, in Ulster county, the Indians fired into the furthermost house in Rochester, and killed two women, but were repulsed by two men.[4]   Just before the other Indians came up, one of the company that was foremost seized a young woman as she was washing at the door; upon which she screamed out; another woman rescued her, beat off the Indian and shut the door.

"On the 16th of May, 1758, about two clock in the afternoon, about thirteen Indians rushed into the house of one Nicholas Cole, on the frontiers of the Jerseys, if I mistake not.   Cole not being at home, they immediately pinioned his wife, and tomahawked their son-in-law, about eighteen years old, and dragged her out of doors, where her eldest daughter, about thirteen years old, lay murdered, and a boy aged eight, and her youngest daughter, aged about four.   At last, the poor, helpless

---

[1] *Colonial History*, vii, 87.

[2] *History of the French and Indian War, Mass. Hist. Soc. Coll.*, v.

[3] "I am inclined to think the Minnisink Indians who formerly lived on those lands, if not the only are at least the chief perpetrators of those hostilities and ravages which the frontiers of your province and that of New York, have and are daily suffering."— *Johnson to Gov. of New Jersey, July,* 19, 1758.

[4] The official account states that this raid was by a party of Senecas and river (Delaware) Indians.   The attack here spoken of, was on the house of Peter Jan, in the south-western part of Rochester.   Jan's house was burned and one of his daughters, and two men who acted as scouts, were killed.   Jan's wife and two daughters, and himself and two sons who were in the field, escaped.— *Documentary History*, ii, 763, 764.

old woman saw the cruel savages thrust their spears into the body of her gasping infant. They rifled the house, and then carried her and her son off, after they had scalped the slain above mentioned.

" Soon after they were joined by two Indians with two German captives they had taken that day, and killed and scalped another, in one Anthony Westbrook's field, near Minnisink, so called, in Susquehanna county, if I mistake not. Not long after Cole returned home ; where to his great surprise he found his four children murdered, and his wife and other son missing. Upon which he went to Minnisink (Napanoch) fort, and got a few soldiers to assist him in burying his children and the German. The soldiers joined with some of the neighbors that evening to cross Delaware river at day-light, and waylay the road to Wyoming ; and as four of them were going to one Chambers's, about two o'clock at night, they heard the Indians coming down the hill, to cross the Delaware, as was supposed, when one of the four fired on them. They immediately fled, giving a yell after their manner. The woman they led with a string about her neck, and the boy by the hand ; who, finding themselves loose, made their escape along the road, and happily met at James McCarty's house, the boy first, and afterward the woman.

" The daughter of one widow Walling, living near Fort Gardiner, between Goshen and Minnisink, going out to pick up some chips for the fire, was shot at by three Indians. Her shrieks alarmed the people. Her brother, looking out at a garret window, and seeing a fellow dispatching and scalping his sister, fired at them, and was pretty certain he wounded one of them. The old woman, during this, with her other daughter and her son, made off and escaped.

" About this time (beginning of June), a sergeant went from Waasing[1] to Minnisink with a party of men, but returned not at the time they were expected. Upon which a larger party went out in search of them, and, at their arrival at Minnisink, found seven of them killed and scalped, three wounded, and a woman and four children carried off. Near about the same time, in

[1] Wawarsing probably.

the frontiers of the Jerseys, a house was beset by a party of Indians, where were seventeen persons, who were killed, as I remember the account. A man and a boy traveling on the road with their muskets were fired on by some Indians in ambush. The man was killed ; but the boy escaped, having first killed one of the Indians. Not far from this time—whether before or after I am not certain—the Indians killed seven New York soldiers. This slaughter was committed at a place called Westfalls, in the frontiers of New Jersey."[1]

Such is the imperfect record of these hostilities. That they were not more numerous is due to the erection, by Governor Hardy, in the summer of 1757, of a number of blockhouses along the frontiers of Orange and Ulster county, covering a distance of thirty miles,[2] and affording a refuge to the settlers. At these blockhouses garrisons of regular troops or militia were constantly stationed, and moved to the defense of more exposed situations. They were far from being a perfect protection, however, and, as already shown, were themselves the object of hostile attack.

There was some excuse on the part of the Indians for the continuance of hostilities. The proprietaries of Pennsylvania had manifested no willingness to relinquish their claim to the lands which they had so fraudulently acquired, nor had New Jersey made overtures of restitution. To Johnson's letter to the lords of trade, the proprietaries had entered a remonstrance, denying that any cause of complaint existed in reference to the lands which they held, and at home were unsparing in their

[1] A party of Indians lay in ambush to get an opportunity to take the lower fort at Mr. Westfall's. They sent two of their party to espy it, who discovered that there were only two women in the fort. While the two spies returned to inform their party, a small company of soldiers, marching from New Jersey to Esopus, came along and stopped at the fort. They were scarcely seated before the Indians rushed in and fell on the men with their tomahawks. The soldiers fled to the chamber from which they shot at the Indians, and after a desperate fight compelled them to retire, though several of the soldiers were killed.—*History Orange County*, 381.

[2] "From a place called Machakamak to the town of Rochester." (*Gov. Hardy's Message*). Machakamak, is now the village of Port Jervis. The blockhouse at this point was called Col. Jersey fort, and was still standing at the outbreak of the war of the Revolution. The location of the other blockhouses is not marked on Sauthier's map. These blockhouses were joined on the south by those erected by New Jersey of which one was known as Westfall's fort, at the lower neighborhood.

denunciations of the Quakers for having, as they asserted, assisted the Indians against the interests of the province. The papers forwarded by Johnson, however, were too plain a statement of facts to sustain them in their position, and the order was returned directing him to appoint a commission to make an examination of the case. Anticipating the action of this commission, the governor of Pennsylvania appointed a conference with the Indians at Easton, in October, 1758. Teedyuscung attended as the representative of thirteen nations,[1] assumed the position which he had formerly occupied, and sustained himself with eloquence and dignity. Finding that nothing could be done unless the land question was satisfactorily disposed of, the proprietaries came forward and surrendered the confirmatory deed which had been received from the Six Nations at Albany in 1754,[2] and recognized the right of the government to arrange the boundaries of the lands included in the treaty of 1742. A treaty was concluded, after a session of nineteen days. All that Teedyuscung had asked was granted; the boundary lines were agreed to; New Jersey paid the *Minsis* £1,000 for the lands which they claimed in that province, and received a concurrent deed from all the *·Lenape* tribes; an exchange of prisoners was agreed to,[3] and peace folded her wing over the long harassed frontiers.

The divisions which existed among the Six Nations, so apparent in the early stages of the controversy with France, increased as the war progressed. In April, 1757, the *Senecas*,

---

[1] The tribes represented were classified as the Mohawks, Oneidas, Onondagas, Cayugas, Senecas, and Tuscaroras, comprising the Six Nations, the Nanticokes, Conoys, Tuteloes, and Chugnuts, of the Susquehannah; the Lenapes, Minsis, Shawanoes, Mahicans, and Wappingers of the Delaware. In the Wappingers will be recognized the families gathered at Fishkill in 1756, and in the Mahicans the clans of that nation whose removal to the Delaware country had commenced in 1730 (*ante, p.* 194).

[2] Not the deed to the Connecticut company. (*Documentary History,* II, 775); also *Colonial History,* VII, 388, where Johnson says: " Brethren, you have been acquainted that at the late treaty at Easton, in Pennsylvania, the proprietary agents, in behalf of their constituents, gave up their claims to the lands on the Ohio, which were sold to the proprietaries in 1754, at Albany, and here I have in my hands the instrument of release and surrender."

[3] It is said that a portion of the prisoners taken by the Lenapes had been given to the Six Nations, but the confederate title is probably used in this as in many other cases when the designation should have been specific to have properly recorded the fact. These prisoners were returned at Canajoharie, April 13, 1759.

*Onondagas*, and *Cayugas*, threw off the disguise of active friendship which they had professed for the English, and sent a large
belt to Canada to make peace with the French. "Our promise,"
said they, "to remain firm to the English was given with the
understanding that the war should be prosecuted vigorously;"
now that they saw the French victorious on every side, and the
English army retreating as it were, they considered themselves
released from all previous obligations and determined to make
peace for themselves, and thenceforth to remain neutral. With
them the victorious party were desired as friends; besides, so
many of their number were already in the ranks of the French,
that those who remained attached to the English had no security
from destruction but neutrality.

The advantages of this neutrality were in favor of the French.
Although by its terms the English were not deprived of any
numerical force, yet the fact that the confederacy was divided
in its allegiance had its influence at home as well as among the
nations more remote. The *Mohawks* were compromised by it,
and became idle spectators to the numerous incursions of the
French Indians, while to the Indians of the Ohio country it was
an encouragement to continue their revolt. Eventually it
drifted into war in behalf of the French; for the time being it
was turned by Johnson to the best advantage possible. "As you
have declared yourselves neutrals," said he to the three tribes,
"I shall expect you to act as neutrals and not permit either
the French or their Indians to pass through your settlements to
make war upon the English, and that you do not directly or
indirectly give our enemies or their Indians information to our
prejudice. Should you violate these rules of behavior, we shall
look upon the covenant chain as absolutely broken between us."
This promise they gave, and their neutrality was confirmed.

With war rolling its folds of fire on the north and west, and
allies within their bosom who were indifferent if not willing
spectators to its progress, the English had no mean task before
them to retain their supremacy. At one time, indeed, even
this seemed hopeless; [1] but, better counsels prevailing in the pro-

[1] "For God's sake," wrote the officer of Massachusetts, in 1757, "exert yourself
in command at Albany, to the governor to save a province; New York itself may

vinces as well as on the part of the home government, the lost ground was recovered and the banners of England floated in undisputed possession of Canada.

In the Ohio country the conflict was continued long after its close at the north, and developed the strength of the ties which had been formed between the western Indians and the French. Usually the first, they were now the last to yield. The *Senecas* joined them; the *Lenapes* saw all their ancient wrongs repeated and riveted upon them in the success of the English. Already had the advanced couriers of the latter penetrated the Ohio valley; here and there in convenient proximity forts had been erected to overawe them and protect their enemies. Every promise which the English had made having been apparently violated, the war-belt of the *Senecas* invited the nations in the French alliance to take up the hatchet in their behalf.[1]

The plot was discovered in time to arrest immediate hostilities, but not to defeat the formation of a more formidable conspiracy. As the tribes felt the chain of English domination drawing closer and closer around them, one among their number, Pontiac, the king of the *Ottawas*, counseled, in the summer of 1762, the formation of a league to drive the English from the continent. The great interior tribes responded. The *Senecas* gave to the movement one thousand warriors; the *Lenapes* and *Shawanoes*, nine hundred; the *Mahicans* and *Wyandots*, two hundred; the Ottawa confederacy under Pontiac a number equal to their allies.[2] Moving quickly to their work, one after another, LeBœuf, Verrango, Presque Isle, Sandusky, St. Joseph, Miami, and Michillimackinac fell into the hands of the conspirators.

---

fall; save a country; prevent the downfall of the British government upon this continent."—*Bancroft.*

[1] "I understood and was told by them (the Delawares) that the breaking out of this war was occasioned by the Seneca Indians who went about with a bloody belt and tomahawk to all the nations engaged in this trouble "— *Manuscripts of Sir Wm. Johnson*, VIII, 14.

[2] The following is Johnson's estimate:

*Friendly Indians.*—*Mohawks*, two villages, 160 warriors; *Oneidas*, two villages, 250; *Tuscaroras*, one village, 140; *Onondagas*, one large village, 150; *Cayugas*, one large village, 200—total, 900 warriors.

*Hostile Indians*—*Senecas*, two villages, 1050; Delawares, of the Ohio, 600; *Shawanoes*, 300; *Wyandots* and *Mahicans*, near Fort Sandusky, 200—total 2150 warriors.—*Manuscripts*, XXIV, 186.

The *Mohawks, Oneidas, Tuscaroras, Onondagas* and *Cayugas* held to their covenant with the English, but only as neutrals. Teedyuscung followed their example, having, in a treaty at Easton, in May, 1762, fully adjusted his dispute with the proprietaries. It was his last treaty. The *Senecas* and the western *Lenapes* were alike offended by his course,[1] and determined to advance their ends by his destruction. Resorting to a mode of warfare favorite among the Indians and especially calculated to serve a double purpose, a party of *Senecas*,[2] ostensibly on a mission of peace, visited Wyoming in April, 1763, and after lingering about for several days, in the night time treacherously set fire to the house of the unsuspecting king, which, with the veteran himself, was burnt to ashes. Remaining on the ground, they inspired the followers of the murdered king with the belief that the work had been done by the Connecticut settlers. Stimulated by these representations, the infuriated *Lenapes* fell upon the unsuspecting whites, on the 14th, and massacred about thirty, drove off their cattle, rifled their stores, and at night applied the torch to dwellings and barns, and lighted up the valley with their destruction.

The fall of Teedyuscung accomplished the purpose which its perpetrators had designed,— the *Lenapes* were consolidated in interest, and the alliances of the *Senecas* made complete. The governor of Pennsylvania sent troops to the scene of conflict,

[1] The Indians went away much dissatisfied, especially the Six Nations, *i. e.*, the *Senecas*. The *Shawanoes* and *Delawares* left most of their presents on the road to the Ohio.—*Manuscripts*, VI, 144.

[2] Stone and other writers use the term Iroquois, implying the participation of the confederacy in the transaction, and assuming that they were offended at the growing power of Teedyuscung. Such an interpretation does not correspond with the apparent facts. The Indians were Iroquois it is true, but it is also true that they were *Senecas* or those engaged in stirring up hostilities in the west. Heckewelder says: "Fearing that he might not fall into their measures of joining in a new war against the English, they perhaps concerted the plan of destroying him." Nothing was ever positively known. His successor, *Netawatiewes*, held the throne untill 1776, when by his death, it devolved upon *Coquehagechton*, alias White Eyes, who, during the early part of the Revolution, was distinguished for his friendship to the colonists and for his efforts to keep his people neutral. He died at Tuscorawas (Fort Laurens) of small-pox in 1778. "The person on whom, by lineal descent, the station of head-chief of the nation devolved, being yet young in years, the surviving chiefs *Gelellmand*, alias Killbuck, *Machingwe Pushis*, alias *Large Cat*, and *Tetepachksi* officiated in his stead." The young king was killed in the massacre of peaceable Indians by Williamson at Pittsburg, in 1781.—*Heckewelder's Narrative*, 153, 193, 198, etc.

but the immediate participants in the massacre anticipated their arrival and withdrew to Tioga, while the Moravian Indians, who had taken no part in the transaction, removed to Gnadenhütten. Failing to reach the guilty, a band of lawless whites determined to punish the innocent, and with a hatred born of the pernicious teachings of Church, banded together to exterminate the whole Indian race, "that the saints might possess the land." Sixty in number, these maddened zealots fell upon the *Canestogoes,*[1] a small clan of *Oneida* dependents residing upon their reservation in the most inoffensive manner, hacked their chief in pieces in his bed, murdered three men, two women and a boy, and burnt their houses. But few of the Indians were at home, being absent selling their little wares among the people. On their return the magistrates of Lancaster collected them and placed them in one of the public buildings for protection. Thither they were followed by the fanatics, the building broken open and the massacre commenced. "When the poor wretches saw they had no protection, and that they could not escape, and being without the least weapon of defense, they divided their little families, the children clinging to their parents; they fell on their faces, protested their innocence, declared their love for the English, and that in their whole lives they had never done them any harm, and in this posture they received the hatchet. Men, women and children, infants clinging to the breast, were all inhumanly butchered in cold blood."[2]

The Moravian Indians at Gnadenhütten fled to Philadelphia, and were followed thither by their maddened persecutors, whose numbers now swelled to an insurgent army. The governor called the troops for the protection of the fugitives; the Indians begged that they might be sent to England. An attempt was made to send them to the *Mohawk* country, but after proceeding as far as Amboy, they were recalled. Another season of terror

[1] The Conestogoes are presumed to have been the remnant of the old Susquehannocks, whose destruction was accomplished by the English of Maryland aided by the Five Nations. They were removed from Maryland and settled among the Oneidas until they lost their language, when they were sent to Conestoga. Their name would seem to have been derived from that of the chief under whose charge they were placed.—*Gallatin,* 55.

[2] *Proud;* see also *Life and Times of Sir Wm. Johnson.*

ensued, and the governor hid himself away in the house of Dr. Franklin. The Quakers were alone equal to the occasion, and firmly resisted the intended bloodshed. Persuaded to listen to the voice of reason, the insurgents at length abandoned their murderous purposes and returned to their homes, and the besieged Indians again sought rest in the wilderness.[1]

The combination under Pontiac failed, but not from any lack of courage and determination on the part of the confederates. While maintaining the siege of Detroit, belts, which had been sent in all directions by the French, assured the tribes which had been in alliance with them that their power had departed. The courier who took the belt to the north, offered peace to all the tribes wherever he passed ; and to Detroit, where he arrived on the last of October, he bore a letter in the nature of a proclamation, informing the inhabitants of the cession of Canada to England ; another addressed to twenty-five nations by name, and particularly to Pontiac, and a third to the commander, expressing a readiness to surrender to the English all the forts of the Ohio and east of the Mississippi.[2] The next morning Pontiac raised the siege, accepted " the peace which his father the French had sent him," and departed with his followers, disappointed but unrelenting.

The *Lenapes* and their allies had, in the meantime, performed their allotted work. Ruined mills, deserted cabins, fields waving with the harvest but without reapers, attested their ruthless warfare east of the Alleghanies, while at Fort Pitt they held successful siege. The Virginia troops under Boquet, who had been sent out against them, barely escaped destruction. At Edge hill, on the 5th and 6th of August, 1763, stratagem alone saved him. Taking advantage of the intrepidity of his assailants, he feigned a retreat. The allies hurried to charge with the utmost daring, when two companies, that had been purposely concealed, fell upon their flank ; others turned and met them in front ; and the Indians, yielding to the irresistible shock, were routed and put

[1] It is a singular fact, that the actors in this strange and tragic affair were not of the lower orders of the people. They were Presbyterians, comprising in their ranks men of intelligence, and of so much consideration that the press did not disclose their names, nor the government attempt their punishment.—*Stone.*

[2] *Bancroft,* v, 133, 164.

to flight. The loss to the English of one hundred and fifteen men, or about one-fourth of their force, attested the bravery of the assailants.[1]

During the winter of 1764, Johnson succeeded in persuading some of the warriors of the neutral nations to unite with a company of militia under his son, John Johnson, for the invasion of the *Lenape* territory. On the 26th of February, a company of insurgents, under command of Captain Bull,[2] was surprised and made prisoners in their encampment 'near the Susquehanna. The prisoners were removed to Johnson Hall, from whence Bull and thirteen of his warriors were sent to New York and lodged in jail, and the remainder distributed among the confederates. Another *Iroquois* party under Brant, burned the *Lenape* town of Kanestio and six other of their large villages lying on the head waters of the Susquehanna.

Seconding the efforts of Johnson, New Jersey and Connecticut sent out an army of eleven hundred men to attack the *Senecas*, while Pennsylvania and Virginia contributed a greater number to subdue the allies in the Ohio valley. The *Lenapes* fled from their burning villages to the *Senecas*, and the latter, fearing the destruction of their own towns, sent, early in April, a deputation of four hundred of their chief men to Johnson Hall to sue for peace. The overture was taken advantage of by Johnson to gain important concessions. The *Senecas* were required to stop hostilities and engage never again to make war upon the

[1] Johnson pays this tribute to the prowess of the Lenapes and their allies : " The Ohio Indians begun on the frontiers of Pennsylvania, Virginia, and the communications to the posts, three of which, Presque Isle, Verrango and La Bœuf, they took immediately. After laying waste all the frontiers they invested Fort Pitt, and reduced the garrison to much danger. Col. Boquet, with six hundred men and a large convoy, marching to its relief, was attacked by only ninety-five of them (for I have the best authorities of white men then with the Indians and of several different Indians, who all agree that that is the true number), who killed about sixty of his people and greatly obstructed his march. In short, to pursue them through their different successful expeditions and depredations would be entering into a tedious detail of facts well known and still sensibly felt here."—*Colonial History*, VII, 962.

[2] " Made them all prisoners to the number of forty-one, including their chief, Captain Bull, son to Teedyuscung, and one who has discovered great inveteracy against the English, and led several parties against them during the present Indian war." (*Johnson, Colonial History*, VII, 611.) In *Memorials of Moravin Church*, I, 252, it is stated that Teedyuscung had three sons, Amos or Tachgokanhelle, the oldest, Kesmitas, and John Jacob." Captain Bull was probably Amos. At that time he was thirty-four years old.

English, deliver up all their prisoners within three months, cede to the crown the Niagara carrying place and allow the free passage of troops through their country, and renounce " all intercourse with the *Delawares* and *Shawanoes*," and assist the English in bringing them to punishment. As hostages, three of their principal chiefs were to await the complete fulfillment of the terms.

When the English under Bradstreet reached Niagara in August, he found no Indians in arms. There the *Senecas* met him, delivered up fourteen prisoners, and asked that the *Lenapes* and *Shawanoes* should be included in the treaty of April,[1] Johnson, who had arrived before Bradstreet, agreed to this on condition that those tribes delivered up their king and Squash Cutter, their chief warrior, and the *Senecas* left with him two of their chiefs as hostages for the fulfillment of the terms. With the *Ottawas*, *Chippewas*, *Hurons*, and other tribes under Pontiac, peace was also made, although Pontiac did not appear. The Indian country was made a part of the royal dominions; its tribes were bound to aid the English troops, and in return were promised assistance and protection; Indian murderers and plunderers were to be delivered up; all captives were to be set free and restored, and the families of English settlers assured of welcome.

Not less successful was the expedition under Boquet. A little below the mouth of Sandy creek, beneath a bower erected on the banks of the Tuscarawas, chiefs of the *Senecas*, the *Lenapes*, the *Shawanoes*, and the *Mahicans*, invited peace. The *Lenapes* delivered up eighteen prisoners, and eighty-three small sticks as pledges for the return of as many more. At the junction of the White Woman and the Tuscarawas, in the centre of the Indian villages, the *Shawanoes* accepted the terms of peace with dejected sullenness, and promised, by their orator, Red Hawk, to collect all captives from the lower towns and restore them in the spring.[2]

On the 27th of April, 1765, the pledges which had been given by the *Senecas* were redeemed by the surrender of the

[1] Stone, in his *Life and Times of Sir Wm. Johnson*, gives Bradstreet little cre- dit for his part in this transaction.
[2] *Bancroft*, v, 210, 221.

*Lenape* king, Long Coat, and his principal warrior, Squash Cutter, who in their turn became hostages for the Susquehanna clans. Captain Bull and two of his warriors were released, and the remaining prisoners, who had been sent to New York for security, were brought up and placed in charge of the commanding officer at Albany until the Susquehanna clans, to whom they belonged, should deliver up their prisoners according to promise. On the 19th of June the latter appeared with twenty-five persons, including even half-breeds, the children of intermarriages with the Indians. The exchange was made ; the hostage chiefs departed, and the war of ten years was closed.[1]

The withdrawal of the French brought with it the necessity of treaties with the tribes that had been in alliance with them, as well as changes in the policy of the English. The task was a difficult one. The attachment of the northern and western Indians to the French was strong ; the grievances of the *Senecas* and their *Lenape* allies were aggravated by the peace to which they had been compelled and in which they had been forced to concede that their lands were a part of the royal dominions. In regard to their territorial possessions, their decision in 1748 had grown into a positive policy, which the English were obliged to recognize on the very threshold of negotiations, as well as the wide-spread influence which it exerted. To treaties, submissions, and cessions, which recognized any other fact than that they were a free people — that they had independent lands, which were their ancient possessions — they would give no attention, while to proffered protection they replied that they wanted none so much as from the English themselves.[2]

---

[1] The treaty of peace was made with Killbuck or Bemineo, Long Coat or Anindamooky, and Squash Cutter or Yaghkapoose, on the part of the eastern Lenapes, and was ratified and confirmed by Turtle Heart or Aquarsqua, Wieweenoghwa, Tedabajhsika, Lenapes of the Ohio, and Benavissica, Manykypusson, Nanicksah, and Wabysequina, Shawanoes of the Ohio.—*Colonial History*, VII, 738.

[2] *Colonial History*, VII, 958. Colonel Bradstreet, in his "Thoughts on Indian Affairs," gives a different view of the policy of the tribes. He writes : "Of all the savages upon this continent, the most knowing, the most intriguing, the less useful, and the greatest villains, are those most conversant with the Europeans, and deserve most the attention of the government by way of correctio and these are the Six Nations, Shawanoes, and Delawares. They are well acquainted with the defenseless state of the inhabitants who live on the frontiers, and think they will ever have it in their power to distress and plunder them, and never cease raising the jealousy of the Upper Nations against us, by propagating amongst them

To appease their demands Johnson had proposed to them in 1765, to "make a line" which should be recognized alike by themselves and the English as a boundary beyond which neither should pass. The proposition was accepted, but its execution was delayed. Meanwhile the tribes remained morose and jealous and at times ready to take up the hatchet. Hostilities on the western border continued of frequent occurrence; the difficulties in Pennsylvania, were kept alive by the constantly increasing tide of European emigration. Connecticut determined to occupy the Wyoming valley, while the fanatics of the Canestogo massacre shot and scalped with unrelenting zeal the Indian hunters wherever opportunity offered. Smarting under these aggressions, the *Senecas*, in 1768, by a large belt said to the *Lenapes* and *Shawanoes*: "Brethren, these lands [1] are yours as well as ours; God gave them to us to live upon, and before the white people shall have them for nothing, we will sprinkle the leaves with blood, or die every man in the attempt." Finding that the matter could no longer be delayed, a conference was called at Fort Stanwix and the contemplated boundary line established.[2] In the name of the king, Johnson took a deed for the territory south and east of the Ohio. In addition to this deed, William Trent obtained title to a tract between the Kenawha and Monongahela; the proprietaries of Pennsylvania, one of the Wyoming lands, and George Croghan one confirmatory of two grants which the Indians had given him, in 1766,

such stories as make them believe the English have nothing so much at heart as the extirpation of all savages. The apparent design of the Six Nations is, to keep us at war with all savages but themselves, that they may be employed as mediators between us and them, at a continuation of expense, too often and too heavily felt, the sweets of which they will ever forget nor lose sight of, if they can possibly avoid it. That of the Shawanoes and Delawares is to live on killing and captivating and plundering the people inhabiting the frontiers; long experience has shown them they grow richer, and live better thereby, than by hunting wild beasts."—*Colonial History*, vii, 690.

[1] The reference is to lands then being occupied by the English along the Monongahela, and the Red Stone creek.

[2] This treaty was concluded Nov. 5th, 1768. By its terms all the lands north and west of the Ohio and Alleghany rivers to Kittaning; thence in a direct line to the nearest fork of the west branch of the Susquehanna; thence, following that stream through the Alleghanies, by the way of Burnett's Hills and the eastern branch of the Susquehanna and the Delaware into New York, to a line parallel with Nonaderha creek, and thence north to Wood creek, east of Oneida lake—was recognized as the territorial domain of the Six Nations, *Lenapes*, *Shawanoes*, etc.—*Colonial History*, viii, 135.

of thirteen hundred acres on the Alleghany river. The sum of
ten thousand dollars in goods and money was paid to the Six
Nations and their allies, and their possessions in the valley of
the Hudson, as well as of the Delaware, were known to them
no more.

Not only was the policy referred to, with its resultant boundary, developed by the war, but the position of the Indian nations was changed. As the representative allies of the English,
the confederated tribes still had a name, but in almost all other
respects their dominion and authority had shriveled up under
the touch of the contending civilizations as certainly as had that
of the nations which had earlier fallen under its malign influence.
Nominally united when the war closed, and maintaining a
recognized deference to the action and wishes of each other,
as they had during its continuance, they were nevertheless practically divided. The *Mohawks*, dwelling in the presence of
Johnson — his own children swelling their ranks[1]— reflected in
their action the wishes of the English government, or stirred
up the tribes to mischief with the expectation of rewards as
mediators; petted, and perhaps deservedly so, for services which
had cost them the loss of their ablest chief and a large number
of their best warriors, they were not the less debauched by
liquor, enfeebled by disease,[2] and shorn of their prestige ; while
the *Senecas*, more manly and generous, less contaminated by
civilization by their separation from its more immediate influence, dictated the policy and controlled all of active force that
remained among their ancient brethren. As a nation they never
again appeared in the field as contestants. Power and territory
alike fell from their grasp at Fort Stanwix.

Brighter was the record of the *Lenapes*, and their grand-child-
ren, the *Shawanoes* and *Mahicans* of the west, judged from the
standpoint of the success which had crowned their efforts. Entering upon the struggle as " poor women" striking their oppressors with " billets of wood," they emerged from it
" increased in interest and respect," in the opinion of their
enemies, " their conduct having restored them to the rank of

[1] It is said that Johnson had not less
than one hundred children by squaws.

[2] Johnson.—*N. Y. Colonial History*,
VII, 957.

32

men," and given to them an influence not only " very extensive,"[1] but destined in the future to embalm their names as the
most formidable of the original Indian nations of Hudson's
river. Their prowess vindicated in the field, their diplomacy
triumphant in council, their manhood wrung from the unwilling
hands of civilized and uncivilized foes, they gave to the conflicts
of the west an impetus which made their name national, and
grafted it forever upon the politics and history of their native
land.

Not lost to the records of this eventful period were the *Mahicans* and *Wappingers* of the Hudson. While floating fragments
from their ranks found new homes among the *Mohawks* and
*Senecas*, swelled the victorious clans of their brethren in the
west, suffered persecution for righteousness' sake at Gnadenhütten, or chanted with Montcalm the war songs of the French,
at Westenhuck, in the valley of the Housatonic, their ancient
council fire was kept brightly burning and their braves aided to
give to the English the supremacy of the continent. The
introduction among them of unselfish and devoted ministers of
the gospel had restored to them, in a great measure, their
ancient character, and made their influence felt in the camp and
in the field, so much so, indeed, that the *Mohawks* sent to their
schools their children for instruction, and the *Oneidas* were
proud to hail them as brothers. When the war came on,
Johnson made an effort to raise from their ranks a company to
aid in the expedition against Crown point,[2] failing only to permit
Governor Shirley to draw off with his expedition " nearly every
fighting man among them." [3] After the war they demanded
restitution from the *Abenaquis* for the loss of one of their
number, and delayed the consummation of peace with them
until 1762.[4] After the peace, they revived their claims to lands
in Albany county, as well as in Dutchess — in the former,
pressing even west of the Hudson, and in the latter, asserting
and clearly proving fraud in the sale of the tract now embraced

[1] Johnson.—*Colonial History*, vii, 953.     *Colonial History*, viii, 452.
[2] *Johnson Manuscripts*, ii, 86.     [4] A warrior was finally sent to them by
[3] *Stockbridge, Past and Present.* " They     the Abenaquis to compensate them for
served as a corps in the late war, and are     their loss.—*Johnson Manuscripts*, xxiv,
in number about three hundred."—*Tryon*,     125.

in the county of Putnam. Failing to secure redress, they attempted the forcible ejectment of the settlers, and compelled the interference of the military. Subsequently, Nimham, the *Wappinger* king, in company with chiefs from the *Mahicans* of Connecticut, visited England and received favorable hearing. Returning to America their claims were thrown into the courts and were there overtaken by the Revolution.

Still clinging to their ancient homes, at the close of the war, were considerable numbers of the *Esopus* and *Mahican* clans, then generally known as " domestic tribes." Of the former " Nachnawachena, alias Sanders, chief sachem, accompanied by sachems Hakawarenim, Qualaghquninjon, and Walagayhin, and twenty-three Indians besides squaws and children," came to conference at Kingston, September 7th, 1771.[1] They were then principally residents of the country back of the Shawangunk mountains, and without special usefulness in the contest which had decided the future rank of their brethren, the *Minsis,* in the west. Not the last, but the closing record of the English administration in reference to them is that by Governor Tryon, in 1774 : " The river tribes have become so scattered and so addicted to wandering, that no certain account of their numbers can be obtained. These tribes — the *Montauks* and others of Long island, *Wappingers* of Dutchess county, and the *Esopus, Papa-goncks,* etc., of Ulster county — have generally been denominated River Indians and consist of about three hundred fighting men. Most of these people at present profess Christianity, and as far as in their power adopt our customs. The greater part of them attended the army during the late war, but not with the same reputation of those who are still deemed hunters."[2]

[1] *Manuscripts of Sir Wm. Johnson,* XXIII, 4.    [2] *Colonial History,* VIII, 451.

## CHAPTER X.

The Indians and the War of the Revolution — The Destruction of the Six Nations — The last of the Mahicans.

HE hostility of the Indian tribes of the west to the colonists, in the war of the Revolution, had its origin mainly in the long catalogue of aggressive acts which the colonists themselves had committed, and against which the tribes had adopted a settled and well understood policy, involving resistance to further encroachments upon territory which they regarded as their especial domain. In their controversies in regard to these encroachments the Indians had learned to distinguish between the king of England and those whom they regarded as their oppressors, and to assume that while the latter were trespassers, the former was a just judge to whom they could appeal. The revision of the Wyoming deeds, and the establishment of the treaty line of 1768, they regarded as having been especially directed by the former, in acknowledgment of the justice of their claims, and this impression was strengthened by the policy which Johnson pursued, as distinguished from that which was sanctioned by colonial authority.[1]

Unfortunately the colonists made not only no effort to remove this impression, but, by their repeated violations of the treaty line, kept alive the irritations which its establishment was de-

---

[1] " His majesty, with great wisdom and discretion, was pleased to direct that (no settlements) should now be made below the great Kanhawa river, with which I acquainted the Indians, agreeable to my orders, but numbers of settlements had been made there previous to the cession. Attempts made since to form others on the Mississippi, and great numbers in defiance of the cession, or the orders of the government in consequence thereof, have since removed not only below the Kanhawa, but even far beyond the limits of the cession, and in a little time we may probably hear that they have crossed the Ohio wherever the lands invite them ; for the body of these people are under no restraint, and pay as little regard to government as they do to title for their possessions."— *Johnson, Colonial History* VIII, 460.

signed to remove. The Virginians did not cease to push their pioneers into the Ohio valley, while the Pennsylvanians, under Franklin, although acting with the consent of the tribes in interest, were not the less violators of the spirit of the treaty. The Virginians, however, openly disregarded the compact, and did not scruple to regard the Indians as legitimate prey for their rifles, or to commit a succession of outrages more cruel and unprovoked than any known to savage warfare. Retaliation followed, and what was known as Cresap's war was inaugurated. The immediate causes of this war may be briefly stated. In the spring of 1774, a party of land agents under the lead of Captain Michael Cresap, was sent out by the Virginians to locate and open up farms in the valley of the Ohio, near the present cities of Pittsburg and Wheeling. The Indians remonstrated with Governor Dunmore, but instead of heeding them, the latter sent word to Cresap that he must be prepared for hostilities. Determined to anticipate the Indians in the attack which appeared to be imminent, Cresap, on the twenty-sixth of April, declared war, organized his party and moved towards the Ohio where he killed two Indians, and, on the following day, surprised a party of *Senecas* and inflicted upon them the loss of one man.

Not satisfied with these achievements, the party pushed forward to attack the encampment of Logan, a *Mingoe* chief, near the mouth of Yellow creek. The expedition was abandoned without consummation, only to be transferred to others. Opposite Logan's encampment a trader named Baker had erected a cabin and engaged in the sale of rum. At this cabin a party of flying settlers met, among whom was one Daniel Greathouse who acted as their leader. Logan and his Indians, it is said, had determined to cut off Baker,[1] and that the latter,

[1] *Stone's Life and Times of Sir Wm. Johnson.* The attack, however, appears to have been wholly without justification. The following is the account given in *Colonial History*, VIII, 464: "Received information from Captain Crawford and one Mr. Nevill, from Virginia, that on their way to this place they met a number of inhabitants settled below this, moving off, among whom was a party who presented seven Indian scalps, and stated their having taken them in the following manner: That a number of Indians having encamped at the mouth of Yellow creek, they with one Grithouse had collected themselves at the house of one Baker opposite to the said Indian camp, and decoyed the Indian men, and two women over to their side of the river to drink with them, who, upon finding

warned by a friendly squaw to escape, invited the aid of Great-house, who organized a band of thirty-two men and crossed the river for the purpose of falling upon the Indians; but finding that they were too strong for him, retreated, and, with a show of friendship, invited them to an entertainment. Without suspicion of treachery, part of the Indians accepted the invitation, and while engaged in drinking — some of them in a state of intoxication — were set upon and butchered in cold blood. The Indians who had remained at their encampment, hearing the noise of the treacherous attack, ran to their canoes to rescue their friends. This movement had been anticipated, and sharp-shooters stationed in ambuscade, shot numbers of them in their canoes, and compelled the others to return. Logan's mother, brother and sister were among the slain.

These transactions were soon followed by another outrage, which, though of less magnitude, was not less atrocious. An aged and inoffensive *Lenape* chief, named the Bald Eagle, while returning from a visit to the fort at the north of the Kanhawa, was shot while alone in his canoe. Not satisfied with this cowardly act, the perpetrator of the murder seized the canoe, tore the scalp from the head of his victim, placed the body in a sitting posture in the canoe, and sent it adrift down the stream to bear to the friends of the venerated sachem the most exasperating evidence of the hostility which had been committed. At about the same time, Silver Heels, a favorite chief of the *Shawanoes*, was murdered by trespassers upon the Indian territory, and in less than a month forty victims were added to the rapacity of the whites.[1] These acts thoroughly aroused the tribes, and the *Lenapes* and *Shawanoes*, under Cornstalk, and the

them intoxicated, fell upon them and knocked them in the head, and scalped them; that soon after two other Indians came over to see what detained their friends, and were served in the same manner; that after this the Indians appeared uneasy, and six of their men were coming across the river to see after their people, who approaching near the shore, observed the white people lying in ambush for them, and, attempting to return to their camp, were fired upon and two of them were killed, who dropped into the river, and two others they observed fall dead in the canoe, and the fifth, upon their landing, they could discover very badly wounded so that he could scarce get up the bank."

[1] The very critical situation of Indian affairs, occasioned by the cruelties and murders committed by Cresap, who with some frontier banditti, causelessly murdered near forty Indians on the Ohio.— *Colonial History*, VIII, 471.

*Senecas* and *Mingoes* [1] led by Logan, threw themselves with fire and tomahawk upon the Virginia border.

The war was nominally concluded in October. Immediately on its outbreak Dunmore organized a force of three thousand men and marched to the Ohio country. One of the divisions of this force, under Colonel Lewis, reached the mouth of the Great Kanhawa on the sixth, and was there attacked, on the tenth, by one thousand warriors of the western confederacy, under Cornstalk, who had determined to anticipate his junction with the main army under Dunmore. The battle was a desperate one, and neither party could fairly claim the victory. The Virginians lost their commander, Colonel Lewis, one-half of their commissioned officers and fifty-two privates killed, while the Indians lost, in killed and wounded, two hundred and thirty-three. In the night the Indians retreated. Meanwhile Dunmore had pushed on to the Sciota, with the division under his command, and was there met by a flag of truce from the Indians proposing to treat for peace. Negotiations were opened, and a treaty concluded. [2] But the war did not stop. Boone and Bullit, and other pioneers, [3] provoked fresh hostilities and entailed upon the colonists the animosities which had been engendered in all the long struggle for the possession of the Ohio valley.

The French traders and priests who remained in the Indian country, moreover, contributed in no small degree to keep alive the hostile feeling which they had inculcated from the first hour of their presence in the Ohio valley. In the conflict which they saw was coming, they also saw the hope of a restoration to France of the territory which had been lost. Holding their head-quarters in the Spanish possessions of Louisiana, they in-

[1] The *Mingoes* were a mixed people formed mainly by the intermarriage of *Minsis, Senecas* and *Shawanoes*. They acknowledged the jurisdiction of, and were ruled by chiefs of the *Seneca* nation. (*N. Y. Colonial History*, VIII, 517). Brodhead states that the "Mingoes were the Andastes, or Gandastogues, or Conestogas who lived at Conestoga creek, where they were settled after their subjugation by the Iroquois" (Gallatin, 55), but such does not appear to be the fact, except as they were made so by the intermarriages of which Johnson speaks.

[2] Cornstalk conducted the negotiations on the part of the Indians. Logan was not present, but sent to the conference the famous speech which Jefferson preserved in his *Notes on Virginia*, and which has made the name of Logan a household word.

[3] *Daniel Boone, Colonial History*, VIII, 395.

vited the northern and western Indians thither and delivered to them speeches " setting forth the danger all their nations were in, from the designs of the English, who, they said, had it in view to possess all their country." [1] From them also came the invitation to the tribes to remove further down the Ohio, with a view to make their organization more compact and formidable, an invitation which Custalaga, a *Lenape* chief, with one hundred of his followers, accepted, and was very soon after followed by larger delegations,[2] animated by a common feeling of resistance. With the alliance of the *Shawanoes* and the *Mahican* clans, the *Lenapes* were now more powerful than the Six Nations themselves,[3] and, no longer taunted as women, but recognized as brothers by them, they prepared to contest the supremacy of the colonists.

The prejudice against the colonists, which was entertained by the western tribes, was, as has been already shown, equally bitter on the part of the *Senecas*, over whom Johnson with great difficulty maintained even a nominal control, and the feeling was largely shared by what were called the Upper nations of the confederacy. The *Mohawks, Oneidas* and *Tuscaroras* had less interest in the western controversy. Under the treaty of 1768, they had been paid for the lands which they claimed, not only in Pennsylvania, but for those embraced in the famous Kayaderossera patent on the Hudson,[4] so long a subject of complaint on the part of the *Mohawks*; besides, they were

---

[1] *Colonial History*, VIII, 396, 404, 507.

[2] *Colonial History*, VIII, 396. After the alliance of the colonists with France, this policy was reversed. On the 29th of August, 1779, Count Rochambeau issued to them a proclamation — through a delegation of Oneidas, Tuscaroras and Caughnawagas who visited him at Newport — in the following words : " The king of France, your father, has not forgotten his children. As a token of remembrance, I have presented gifts to your deputies in his name. He learned with concern, that many nations, deceived by the English, who were his enemies, had attacked and lifted up the hatchet against his good and faithful allies, the United States. He has desired to tell you, that he is a firm and faithful friend to all the friends of America, and a decided enemy to all its foes. He hopes that all his children, whom he loves sincerely, will take part with their father in the war against the English."

[3] " The worst circumstance is that these people have of late become more powerful by alliances, and the Six Nations less, so that their authority begins to be disputed at advantage." — *Johnson Manuscripts*, XXII, Nov. 29, 1772.

[4] This patent covered all the land lying between the Hudson and Mohawk rivers, extending from Coic falls, near the junction of those streams, to the third, or as it is now called, Baker's falls, on the Hudson, and contained about seven hundred thousand acres of land. — *Stone's Life of Johnson*, II, 299.

more immediately under the control of the English. The *Mohawks* had a blood alliance with Johnson ; the *Oneidas* and *Tuscaroras* had submitted themselves almost entirely to the guidance of the English ministers who had located among them, and their every-day associations were of a different nature from those of their more westward brethren. Practically, the confederacy was divided, although it still maintained the forms of unity and some of its spirit. While against the authorities of New York the more eastern tribes had no special complaint, their education, from the days of Stuyvesant, had been adverse " to the Bostonians," and the feeling was strengthened by the persistent determination of the Connecticut people to settle at Wyoming in defiance of the treaty of 1768, by which the rights of the proprietaries of Pennsylvania were secured. They hated them, too, upon general principles growing out of the extirminating policy of Church and his followers, and came to sympathize with the Indians in the French alliance and to encourage their hostilities.

The great strength of the control which the English had over them, however, lay in the personal associations of the *Mohawks* with the Johnson family. To create this influence Johnson had become an Indian ; his legitimate children had grown up with theirs, while those by his mistress, Molly Brant, eight in number, were " bone of their bone and flesh of their flesh."[1] Skillfully was this influence wielded by Johnson and the home government. The reduction of Canada had created the necessity for a reorganization of the Indian department. The Canada tribes, as well as those of the west, were too remote for that official intercourse to which they had become accustomed under the French, and required separate superintendence ; but it was also necessary that that superintendence should be conducted on a basis uniform with that which was applied to the confederated tribes. The materials for such an organization were already provided. George Croghan had filled the post of assistant to Johnson ; Daniel Claus and Guy Johnson, the sons-in-law of Johnson, were entirely familiar with the duties to be

[1] The children borne to him by Molly Brant, sister of the great chief, were made legitimate by marriage a short time before his death.

performed ; their interests were bound up in obedience to the directions of Sir William. To Croghan was assigned the charge of the Ohio country ; Col. Claus was sent to Canada, with his head-quarters at Montreal, while Guy Johnson was made deputy in charge of the Six Nations and the neighboring tribes, and remained at Johnson Hall.[1]

That there was plan and purpose in this arrangement, there is no reasonable doubt. It was no idle boast on the part of Johnson, when, in 1771, he wrote that he was confident that "in any event that might happen in Europe or in America," he could, from the measures he had taken and the influence which he possessed, secure and attach to the interests of the crown, " such a body of Indians as if not so numerous as those opposed," to those interests, would " give a severe check to their attempts."[2]  Nor were the expectations of the home government disappointed in the result, although the great force of the plan was lost by the death of Johnson in July, 1774.[3] When that event occurred, Guy Johnson at once assumed the duties of superintendent,[4] with all the prestige which his rela-

[1] *Colonial History,* vii, 579.

[2] *Documentary History,* ii, 983.

[3] Sir William Johnson was born in Ireland, about the year 1714. He was the nephew of Sir Peter Warren, the commodore who was distinguished in the attack on Louisburgh, Cape Breton, 1745. Sir Peter married a lady (Miss Watts) in New York, purchased large tracts of land upon the Mohawk, and about 1734, young Johnson was induced to come to America and take charge of his uncle's affairs in that quarter. He learned the Indian language, adopted their manners, and by fair trade and conciliatory conduct, won their friendship and esteem. He built a large stone mansion on the Mohawk, about three miles west of Amsterdam, where he resided for twenty years, previous to the erection of Johnson Hall at Johnstown, where he resided at the time of his death. He was never given credit for great military skill or personal bravery, and was more expert in intriguing with the Indians, than in leading disciplined troops boldly into action. For his success at Lake George, he was made major general and a knight.

His first wife was a Dutch girl, for whom, it is said, he gave five pounds for payment of her passage money to the captain of the emigrant ship in which she came to this country. By her he had one son, John, and two daughters who married respectively Daniel Claus, and Guy Johnson. When she was on her death-bed, Sir William was married to her in order to legitimate her children. After her death her place was supplied by Molly Brant, sister of Joseph, the Mohawk chief, by whom he had eight children. She was a very sprightly and beautiful squaw when he took her to his mansion as his mistress. Toward the close of his life he married her in order to legitimate her children. He died of disease of the heart, while attending the conference with the Indians stated in the text, July 11th, 1774, aged 60 years.— *Lossing* i, 232, 287 ; *Stone's Life and Times of Sir William Johnson, etc.*

[4] He was commissioned to fill the vacancy in September, but performed the duties of superintendent in the interim by virtue of his appointment as deputy.

tionship to his predecessors inspired, combined with the support
of Sir John Johnson, who succeeded to his fathers's title and
estate, and that of Molly Brant, and Thayendanegea, her
brother — the Joseph Brant of the Revolution — then a prominent chief of the upper Mohawk castle, who was made his
secretary.

Against these controlling influences the colonists could not
only array that which had been acquired by individuals through
personal intercourse with the Indians, and that which had been
gained by the labors of the Rev. Samuel Kirkland and the Rev.
James Dean, missionaries to the *Oneidas* and *Tuscaroras.*[1] The
extent of these influences was considerable—especially that exercised by the missionaries named—but nevertheless was entirely inadequate to compensate for that which was wielded by

[1] JAMES DEAN.—The history of this individual, and his agency in many of the events transpiring previous to and during the revolutionary war, would form a volume of deeply interesting and most thrilling incidents. He was a native of New England and educated with special reference to missionary labor among the Indians, with whom he lived many years from his youth. At the outbreak of the war he was stationed at Oghkwaga, where he made no attempt to conceal his views from the Indians. In 1774, he was employed by the Continental congress to visit the New York and Canada tribes to ascertain the part they would probably take in the contest. For this purpose he assumed the disguise of an Indian trader and, supplied with goods, accomplished the object of his mission. An adopted son of the Oneidas, and regarded by them with more than parental affection, his influence over them was especially conspicuous. He was subsequently appointed to the office of Indian agent, and during the whole war of the revolution he continued his services to the country in that capacity. A very considerable portion of the war he was stationed at Fort Stanwix, and by virtue of his office, superintended the intercourse with the Indians. At the close of the war the Oneidas granted him a tract of land two miles square, lying on the Wood creek west of Rome, to which he removed in 1784. Here he continued two years, when he effected an exchange with the nation for the tract of land lying in Westmoreland, known as Dean's patent, to which he removed, and where he continued to reside until his death in September, 1832.—*Stone's Life of Brant,* I, *Appendix.*

SAMUEL KIRKLAND. — This distinguished missionary was born at Norwich, Conn., 1742. After a special education for the work, he was sent to Oneida Castle, in 1766, and continued to labor among that tribe for forty years. During the revolutionary war he was in the pay of the United States, and in 1779, was brigade chaplain in General Sullivan's campaign against the Indians of western New York. After the peace he remained among the Oneidas, and in 1788, assisted at the great Indian council for the extinction of their title to the Genesee country. So sensible was the state government of the value of his services, that in the year 1789, it granted him a tract of land two miles square in the present town of Kirkland, whither he immediately removed, and where he subsequently made a liberal endowment of land for the purpose of founding a school which was originally called Hamilton Oneida Academy, subsequently incorporated under the name of Hamilton College. After a life of much public usefulness, he at length departed this life on the 28th of February, 1808.—*Note, Colonial History,* VIII, 631; *Jones's History of Oneida County.*

the Johnsons. Had Guy Johnson possessed the shrewdness and skill of his predecessor, the result, so far as the Six Nations were concerned, would not have been doubtful; but in that which he gained by his position, he was seriously compromised by the superior diplomacy of the colonists.

Both parties moved with caution. While Johnson was unremitting in his endeavors to preserve the good will and affection of the Six Nations, the colonists lost no time in instructing them in regard to the nature of the controversy, and in advising them to act as neutrals. With a very considerable portion of the Six Nations neutrality had long been an established policy, and gained for the colonists not only an attentive ear, but compelled Johnson to adopt it as the course which he wished them to pursue. To the declarations of Dean and Kirkland, and to the belts which the faithful *Mahicans* sent to all the tribes advising neutrality — that the " dispute did not concern the Indians ; that it arose from the crown's endeavors to obtain a large reimbursement for the expenses of the late war, which the colonists could not comply with, and therefore an army was sent to compel them" — Johnson found it necessary to reply that the " dispute was solely occasioned by some people who, notwithstanding the king's law, would not permit some tea to land, but destroyed it ;" that the matter was one with which they had " nothing to do," any more than they had " with the foolish people" who talked to them about that " which they themselves did not understand."[1] Thus urged, the Six Nations in general council at Onondaga, resolved to have " nothing to do with the axe, but to support their engagements."

This action left the Johnsons with nothing but their personal influence and official relations, but these they believed, and not without reason, were sufficient to control to a great extent the action of the tribes. The well-founded suspicions of the integrity of the Johnsons, which the colonists entertained, brought the issue to a culmination much sooner than they had intended. The committee of safety of Tryon county, early in 1775, set a strict watch upon their movements, and when, in May, Guy Johnson received secret instructions from General

[1] *Colonial History*, VIII, 538, 557.

Gage, requiring him to report himself at Montreal for instructions, he professed alarm for his personal safety and appealed
to his retainers among the Indians to induce the Six Nations
to take upon themselves his protection. Gathering together
a company of tories, among whom John and Walter N. Butler
were prominent, and accompanied by Brant and a portion of
the *Mohawks*, he fled to Oswego, where he held a conference
with the tribes, and from thence pushed on to Montreal, where,
in July, he met the Indians of the northren confederacy, seventeen hundred in number.[1] Whether his fears were well
founded or not, the movement was an adroit one. Wherever
he met the Indians he urged upon their consideration the attack
which had been made upon himself, and appealed to the memory
of his father-in-law, and to his associations with them, to protect Sir John, and to induce them to become his followers; yet
he still insisted that his mission was that of peace, and that the
Indians should maintain their neutrality.

Such was the condition of affairs when, in July, the Continental congress resolved to establish three departments of Indian
affairs, the northern, middle and southern, " with powers to
treat with the Indians in their respective departments, to preserve peace and friendship, and to prevent their taking any part in
the present commotion." [2]   In accordance with this resolution,
the commissioners for the northern department [3] held a council
with chiefs of the Six Nations at German Flats on the fifteenth
of August, but the attendance being limited, adjourned it to
Albany, where, on the twenty-fourth, its proceedings were concluded. At this conference the commissioners recited the
grievances of which the colonists complained, and against which
they had resolved to take up arms, and advised the Indians to
observe neutrality. "This is a family quarrel between us and
old England," said they; "you Indians are not concerned in
it. We don't wish you to take up the hatchet against the king's

[1] *Colonial History*, viii, 636.
[2] It was not until a year later that congress authorized the employment of Indians. Those who acted with the colonial forces prior to that time were enlisted
by the colonies in their independent capacity.

[3] The commissioners for the northern
department were Gen. Philip Schuyler,
Major Joseph Hawley, Turbot Francis,
Oliver Wolcott and Volkert P. Douw.
The department included the Six Nations
and all other tribes to the northward of
them.

troops; we desire you to remain at home, and not join either side, but keep the hatchet buried deep. In the name and behalf of all our people, we ask and desire you to love peace and maintain it, and to love and sympathize with us in our trouble, that the path may be kept open with all our people and yours, to pass and repass without molestation."

" You told us it was a family quarrel," said Abraham, the venerable chief of the upper Mohawk castle,[1] in reply; "and that we should sit still, and mind nothing but peace. Our great man, Colonel Johnson, did the same at Oswego; he desired us to sit still likewise. You likewise desired us that if application should be made to us by any of the king's officers, we would not join them. Now, therefore attend, and apply your ears closely. We have fully considered this matter. The resolutions of the Six Nations are not to be broken or altered.[2] When they resolve, the matter is fixed. This chain is the determination of the Six Nations not to take any part, but as it is a family affair, to sit still and see you fight it out. We beg you to receive this as infallible, it being our full resolution; for we bear as much affection for the king of England's subjects on the other side of the water, as we do for you upon this island. It is a long time since we came to this resolution. It is the result of mature deliberation. It was our declaration to Colonel Johnson. We told him we should take no part in the quarrel, and hoped neither side would desire it. The resolutions of the Six Nations are not to be broken." [3]

While there can be no reasonable doubt that the determination of the Six Nations was fairly expressed by the speaker, its announcement was not without qualifications. The Wyoming lands, he insisted, the tribes regarded as belonging to the proprietaries of Pennsylvania, and desired that the settlement which

[1] Abraham was the brother of Hendrik (*Colonial History*). He originally represented the lower Mohawk castle, and was known as Little Abraham. On the death of Hendrik, he became chief sachem of Canajoharie or the upper Mohawk castle; Young Abraham, as he was called, succeeded to the lower Mohawk castle, and Seth became chief of the Schoharies (*Colonial History*, vii, 115). He subsequently followed the fortunes of the Johnsons, but died soon after the opening of the Revolution.

[2] Referring to the action of the council at Onondaga.— *Colonial History*, viii, 556.

[3] Proceedings of conference.— *Colonial History*, viii, 605, etc.

they had made in 1768 should be held as valid against the Connecticut people.[1] The commissioners had expressed the determination of the colonists " to drive away, kill and destroy all who appeared in arms " against them. " We beg you to take care what you do," said Abraham ; " there are many around us who are friends to the king. As to your quarrels to the eastward along the sea coasts, do as you please. But it would hurt us to see those brought up in our bosoms ill-used. In particular we would mention the son of Sir William Johnson.[2] He was born among us, and does not intermeddle in public disputes. We would likewise mention our father the missionary who resides among the *Mohawks.* The king sent him to them, and if he was removed, they would look upon it as taking away one of their own body." Then the people of Albany had taken from them two pieces of land, " without any reward, not so much as a single pipe ;" they should be restored. " If you refuse to do this, we shall look upon the prospect to be bad ; for if you conquer, you will take us by the arm and pull us all off."

Whatever may have been the precise character of the instructions which Guy Johnson received from General Gage, there is no doubt in regard to those which were issued to him by the ministry, and which he received after his arrival in Montreal. These instructions were under date July 5th and July 24th. In the former he was advised to inform the Indians that in consequence of the " unnatural rebellion" which had broken out, the " immediate consideration" of the grievances of which they

[1] Connecticut claimed by virtue of the boundaries of its original charter. The deed which they had received was set aside in the agreement of 1768.

[2] John Johnson was the son of Sir William by his first wife. He was born in 1742, and succeeded his father to his title and estates in 1774. He was not as popular as his father, being less social and less acquainted with human nature. His official relations to the parent government, and his known opposition to the rebellious movements of the colonies, caused him to be strictly watched, and, as we have noted in the text, not without just cause. Expelled from his estate, his property confiscated, his family in exile, he became an uncompromising enemy to the patriots, and exerted his influence against them until the close of the war. Soon after the close of the war he went to England, and, on returning in 1785, settled in Canada. He was appointed superintendent and inspector general of Indian affairs in North America, and for several years he was a member of the legislative council of Canada. To compensate him for his losses, the British government made him several grants of lands. He died, at the house of his daughter, Mrs. Bowers, at Montreal, in 1830, aged 88 years.—*Lossing*, 1, 285.

had complained was defeated, but that they should ultimately be protected and preserved in all their rights ; while in the latter he was told that, as they had already "hinted that the time might possibly come when the king, relying upon the attachment of his faithful allies, the Six Nations, might be under the necessity of calling upon them for their aid and assistance," that time had now come ; that he should "lose no time in taking such steps" as might be necessary "to induce them to take up the hatchet against his majesty's rebellious subjects," and that he should "engage them in his majesty's service" upon such plan as would be suggested to him by General Gage. The course to be pursued in carrying out this plan was left to Johnson, but with the specific instruction that he should "not fail to exert every effort to accomplish it, and to use the utmost dilligence and activity in the execution of the order."[1]

Entering upon the duties assigned to him with a zeal sharpened by the seizure of his property in the Mohawk valley, Johnson nevertheless found his efforts to control the Six Nations obstructed by the action of the council of Onondaga in favor of neutrality, as well as by the success of the colonists in the reduction of Ticonderoga and Crown point, and although Brant and his *Mohawks* still adhered to him, his recruits were principally confined to enlistments from the Canada tribes. When Montgomery attacked Quebec, he claimed to have had over four hundred Indians in encampment, but of that number only ninety were participants in the engagement. The retreat of the Americans and the subsequent capture of Ethan Allen inspired his recruits for a short time, but by the middle of October scarce one of his dusky followers remained.

Even Brant was lukewarm and indifferent. The pledge of the tribes was sacred and could not be easily broken, even by one so firmly bound to the fortunes of the Johnsons. Besides, he was thoroughly schooled in the selfish politics of his predecessors, and would have positive assurances of compensation for his services. In this emergency, the plan resorted to in 1710 was adopted. Brant was sent to England ; was there feasted and honored as his predecessors had been, and like

[1] *Colonial History*, VIII, 596.

them returned to the tribes pledged to do the bidding of his royal master. Reaching Canada in the winter of 1776, he at once entered upon the work of organizing a force of Iroquois[1] to operate upon the borders of New York and Pennsylvania, in conjunction with the operations of the western confederacy. The field had been as well prepared for him as possible. Sir John Johnson, the last of the patrons of his family, had fled from his parole of honor, and taken refuge in Montreal, and whatever regard the confederates had for his father had been fully aroused, while the tories had been active in prejudicing the colonists.

In the spring of 1777, Brant appeared at Oghkwaga with a retinue of warriors. He had not yet committed any act of hostility within the borders of New York, yet none doubted his intentions. In June he ascended the Susquehanna to Unadilla, with about eighty warriors, and requested an interview with the Rev. Mr. Johnstone of the Johnstone settlement. He declared that his object was to procure food for his famished people, and that if it was not furnished, the Indians would take it by force. Mr. Johnstone sounded him in regard to his purposes, and the chief told him, without reserve, that he had made a covenant with the king, and was not inclined to break it. The people supplied him with food, but the marauders not satisfied, drove off a large number of cattle, sheep, and swine. As soon as they departed, not feeling safe in their remote settlement, the whites abandoned it, and took refuge in Cherry Valley. Some families in the neighborhood of Unadilla fled to the German Flats, and others to Kingston and Newburgh on the Hudson.

For the purpose of obtaining more positive information in regard to the intentions of the Indians, General Herkimer was instructed to visit Brant at Unadilla. Herkimer took with him three hundred Tryon county militia, and invited Brant to meet him. This the chief agreed to. It was a week after Herkimer arrived at Unadilla, however, before Brant made his

---

[1] "Joseph, since his arrival from England, has showed himself the most zealous and faithful subject his majesty can have in America, in Indian matters, and deserves to be noticed as such."— *Colonel Claus, Colonial History*, VIII, 724.

appearance.   He came accompanied by five hundred warriors.
Neither party had confidence in the other, and it was finally
agreed that their accompanying forces should encamp within
two miles of each other, and that the principals to the conference should, with a few of their followers, meet in an open
field.   These preliminaries being adjusted, the conference was
opened.   In reply to Herkimer's inquiries, Brant declared,
" that the Indians were in concert with the king, as their fathers
had been ; that the king's belts were yet lodged with them, and
they could not violate their pledge ; that Herkimer and his followers had joined the Boston people against their sovereign ;
that although the Boston people were resolute, the king would
humble them ; that General Schuyler was very smart on the
Indians at German Flats,[1] but at the same time was not able
to afford them the smallest article of clothing ; and finally,
that the Indians had formerly " made war on the white people
when they were all united, and as they were now divided, the
Indians were not frightened."   He also told Herkimer that a
path had been opened across the country to Esopus, for the
tories of Ulster and Orange to join them.[2]

A few days after this conference, Brant withdrew his warriors
from the Susquehanna, and joined Sir John Johnson and
Colonel John Butler, who had collected a body of tories and
refugees at Oswego,[3] preparatory to a descent upon the Mohawk and Schoharie settlements.   There Guy Johnson, and
other officers of the British Indian department, summoned a

---

[1] The conference of July, 1775.

[2] *Campbell's Annals of Tryon County.*
Claus tells the brazen story that Herkimer " had three hundred men with him
and five hundred more in the distance,"
and that " Brant, who had not two hundred men, after resolutely declaring that
he was determined to act for the king,"
obliged Herkimer to retreat "with mere
menaces, not having twenty pounds of
powder among his party." (*Colonial History*, VIII, 720.) It was by such stories
that the Indian ring managed to give a
consequence to the Six Nations which
they did not possess.

[3] In 1722, under the direction of Governor Burnet, a trading house was
erected at Oswego, on the east side of
the river.   In 1726, in order to prevent
the encroachments of the French, Governor Burnet erected old Fort Oswego,
on the west side of the river.   In 1755,
Fort Ontario was constructed, on the east
side of the river, under the direction of
Governor Shirley.   On the 14th of August, 1756, both these forts, with a garrison of 1600 men, and a large quantity
of ammunition, were surrendered to the
French, under Montcalm.   The forts
were returned to the English under the
treaty of peace of 1763.   They were surrendered to the United States, by the
British government, under the treaty
of 1794.

grand council of the Six Nations, who were invited to assemble " to eat the flesh and drink the blood of a Bostonian ;" in other words, to feast on the occasion of a proposed treaty of alliance against the patriots, who were denominated Bostonians as a special appeal to the prejudices of the Indians. There was a pretty full attendance at the council, but a large portion of the sachems adhered faithfully to their covenant of neutrality, and it was not until the British commissioners appealed to their avarice that their sense of honor was overcome. The contract was closed by the distribution of scarlet clothes, beads, and trinkets, in addition to which each warrior was presented a brass kettle, a suit of clothes, a gun, a tomahawk and a scalping knife, a piece of gold, a quantity of ammunition, and a promise of a bounty upon every scalp he should bring in.[1] Brant was acknowledged as a war captain, and soon after commenced his career of blood upon the borders.

Meanwhile the attention of the colonists had not been entirely devoted to the Six Nations. In April, 1774, the Provincial congress of Massachusetts sent a message to the *Mahicans* and *Wappingers*[2] at Westenhuck, apprising them of the gathering tempest, and expressing a desire to cultivate a good understanding with them. In reply, Captain Solomon Wa-haun-wan-waumeet visited Boston on the eleventh of April, and delivered the following speech :

" Brothers : We have heard you speak by your letter ; we thank you for it ; we now make answer.

" Brothers: You remember when you first came over the great waters, I was great and you was very little, very small. I then took you in for a friend, and kept you under my arms, so that no one might injure you ; since that time we have ever been true friends ; there has never been any quarrel between us. But now our conditions are changed. You are become great

[1] See *Life of Mary Jamison.* This pamphlet was written in 1823, and published by James D. Bemis, of Canandaigua, N. Y. She was taken a captive near Fort Duquesne (now Pittsburg) when a child, and was reared among the Indians. She married a chief and became an Indian in every particular, except birth. At the council here spoken of she was present with her husband.— *Lossing's Field Book of the Revolution,* I, 239.

[2] This message was addressed " To Captain Solomon Ahhannuauwaumut, chief sachem of the Moheakounuck Indians." He died in 1777.

and tall. You reach the clouds. You are seen all around the world, and I am become small, very little. I am not so high as your heel. Now you take care of me, and I look to you for protection.

" Brothers: I am sorry to hear this great quarrel between you and old England. It appears that blood must soon be shed to end this quarrel. We never till this day understood the foundation of this quarrel between you and the country you came from.

" Brothers: Whenever I see your blood running, you will soon find me about to revenge my brother's blood. Although I am low and very small, I will gripe hold of your enemy's heel, that he cannot run so fast, and so light, as if he had nothing at his heels.

" Brothers: You know I am not so wise as you are, therefore I ask your advice in what I am now going to say. I have been thinking, before you come to action, to take a run to the westward, and feel the mind of my Indian brethren, the Six Nations, and know how they stand — whether they are on your side or for your enemies. If I find they are against you, I will try to turn their minds. I think they will listen to me, for they have always looked this way for advice, concerning all important news that comes from the rising of the sun. If they hearken to me, you will not be afraid of any danger behind you. However their minds are affected you shall soon know by me. Now I think I can do you more service in this way, than by marching off immediately to Boston, and staying there; it may be a great while before blood runs. Now, as I said you are wiser than I; I leave this for your consideration, whether I come down immediately or wait till I hear some blood is spilled.

" Brothers: I would not have you think by this that we are falling back from our engagements. We are ready to do any thing for your relief, and shall be guided by your councils.

" Brothers: One thing I ask of you, if you send for me to fight, that you will let me fight in my own Indian way. I am not used to fight English fashion, therefore you must not expect I can train like your men. Only point out to me where your enemies keep and that is all I shall want to know."

Two days afterwards the congress made the following reply:

"Brothers: We this day, by the delegate from Stockbridge, first heard of your friendly answer to our speech to you by Captain William Goodrich, which answer we are told you made to us immediately by a letter, which we have not yet received. We now reply.

"Brothers: You say that you were once great, but that you are now little; and that we were once little and are now great. The Supreme Spirit orders these things. Whether we are little or great, let us keep the path of friendship clear, which our fathers made and in which we have both traveled to this time. The friends of the wicked counselors of our king fell upon us, and shed some blood soon after we spake to you last by letter. But we, with a small twig killed so many, and frightened them so much, that they have shut themselves up in our great town called Boston, which they have made strong. We have now made our hatchets, and all our instruments of war, sharp and bright. All the chief counselors, who live on this side the great water, are sitting at the grand council-house in Philadelphia; when they give the word, we shall all as one man, fall on, and drive our enemies out of their strong fort, and follow them till they shall take their hands out of our pouches, and let us sit in our council-house, as we used to do, and as our fathers did in old times.

"Brothers: Though you are small yet you are wise. Use your wisdom to help us. If you think it best, go and smoke your pipe with your Indian brothers toward the setting sun, and tell them of all you hear and all you see; and let us know what their wise men say. If some of you young men have a mind to see what we are doing, let them come down and tarry among our warriors. We will provide for them while they are here.

"Brothers: When you have any trouble, come and tell it to us, and we will help you."

The occasion for the services of the *Mahicans* was not long delayed. When the alarm came up from Lexington, a year later, they took the field, and participated in the battle of Bunker Hill on the seventeenth of June. From thence Captain Solomon, or Captain Hendrik as he was subsequently known, repaired with his warriors to the council at German

Flats, and, at its adjourned session at Albany, renewed the pledge of his people in language most eloquent. " Depend upon it," said the noble chieftain ; " depend upon it we are true to you, and mean to join you. Wherever you go, we will be by your sides. Our bones shall die with yours. We are determined never to be at peace with the red coats, while they are at variance with you. We have one favor to beg. We should be glad if you would help us to establish a minister amongst us, that when our men are gone to war, our women and children may have the advantage of being instructed by him. If we are conquered, our lands go with yours; but if you are victorious, we hope you will help us to recover our just rights."[1] Wherever the influence of the *Mahicans* could reach, it was exerted among their brethren of the west. Their fugitive clans at Oghkawaga, and their associates from the Esopus tribes,[2] refused for a time to take up the hatchet against the colonists, and held the *Tuscaroras* to neutrality ; while those among the *Lenapes*, east of the Alleghanies, as well as the domestic *Lenape* clans, joined them in an earnest support of the patriots. At White Plains, in October, 1776, their united war-cry, " Woach, Woach, Ha, Ha, Hach, Woach ! " rang out as when of old they had disputed the supremacy of the Dutch, and their blood mingled with that of their chosen allies.[3]

Active hostilities brought sifting time to the Six Nations. Notwithstanding the efforts of the Johnsons and the pleadings of Brant, they were not united in the alliance with the British,

[1] The *Mahicans* claimed several tracts of land, extending even west of the Hudson. Their principal claim, however, was for a portion of the Livingston patent and for lands at Westenhuck. The latter they claimed to have leased to the whites for a term of years, but had lost the papers. The matter has been before the legislature of New York several times, but like the claim of the Wappingers, has never been adjusted.

[2] " We, the head of this place, with our brethren the *Tuscaroras* and some of the *Onondagas* and *Mahicanders*, being assembled.      *      * We hope you will give no heed to the false reports that are going about, for we assure you,

brothers, that we are sincerely disposed to keep our covenant of peace with you our brethren." ( *Letter to Justices of Kingston signed by chiefs of Tuscarora aud Esopus Indians* ). See *Proceedings Provincial Convention of New York*, i, 803, 805 ; ii, 301, 419, 424. To what extent these Indians were compromised with Brant is not known, but it is quite certain that a large number of the Esopus Indians became his obedient followers.

[3] The Indians were stationed on Chatterton's hill, under Colonel Haslet, and were in the heaviest of the engagement on the 28th of October.— *Lossing's Field Book*, ii, 822.

although Brant doubtless drew recruits from all the tribes. The *Oneidas* and *Tuscaroras* consistently refused to join him; the *Onondagas* were not at first warmly enlisted in the movement; the *Mohawks* were divided.[1] So far as recognized tribal action was concerned, however, it soon became an established fact, that the *Mohawks, Cayugas, Onondagas*, and *Senecas*, had attached themselves to the king. Of the entire confederacy not more than eight hundred warriors took the field, under the British, at any time; but this number, added to those from the Canada tribes, and those whose hostilities in the west had never been suspended, constituted no inconsiderable portion of their forces. Could they have been regularly enrolled and disciplined, or could their services have been depended upon at any time, they would have constituted an effective body of men; but their modes of warfare would not admit of discipline, and their habits of living would not permit their attendance, in any considerable numbers, except at certain seasons of the year. That they were a scourge to the frontier settlements, is unquestioned; yet in no instance does it appear that they constituted the entire attacking force, but on the contrary that they were invariably led by tories, whose deeds of cruelty outrivaled savage ingenuity, and whose numbers, in most instances, was greater than that of the Indians.

The principal campaign in which the British Indians were engaged was that undertaken in 1777, to determine the control of the Hudson river. Sweeping down from Canada with his powerful army, Burgoyne recaptured Crown point and Ticonderoga, while his auxiliaries, the Indians and tories, attacked the defenses more remote from his route. Of these Fort Schuyler[2] was the first, against which Colonel Butler marched

[1] The reference is *not* to the lower Mohawk castle of which Little Abraham was chief sachem while his brother Hendrik lived, but to that known as the Praying Mohawks, at the mouth of Schoharie creek, which maintained at least a nominal alliance with the colonists, or rather observed the neutrality to which they had pledged themselves. General Sullivan, however, believed that they "were constantly employed in giving intelligence to the enemy, and in supporting their scouting parties when making incursions," and that "when the Mohawks joined the enemy," they were "left to answer those purposes, and keep possession of the land" of the tribe. By his direction they were subsequently taken prisoners and removed to Albany.—*Stone's Life of Brant,* II, 40.

[2] Originally Fort Stanwix. The present city of Rome, Oneida county, now covers

from Oswego with a motley crew of whites and Indians,[1] under the commands of John Johnson, Claus, and Brant, and
united with the forces under St. Leger.[2]   The siege commenced
on the fourth of August, when a few bombs were thrown into
the fort, while the Indians, concealed behind trees and bushes,
wounded several men who were engaged in raising the parapets.
Similar annoyances occurred on the fifth, but formidable operations were held in abeyance pending an attack upon a force of
colonists who were approaching, for the relief of the fort, under
General Herkimer.   To meet this force Butler and Brant were
dispatched, and  at Oriskany was fought the desperate engagement in which the heroic Herkimer gave up his life.

Meanwhile a successful sally from the fort had carried consternation and disgrace into the British ranks.   So impetuous
was this sally, that the camp of John Johnson and his Royal
Greens was seized ; its valorous commander fleeing without
his coat, and his tory confederates following at his heels.
Twenty-one wagon-loads of spoil, five British standards, the
baggage and papers of Johnson, and the clothing of his Indian
allies,[3] rewarded the victors.   The siege was continued until
the twenty-second, when an incident occurred which showed
the unreliability of the Indians, and defeated its further prosecution.   A half idiot, named Hon Yost[4] Schuyler, a nephew to
General Herkimer, who had been taken to Canada by Walter
Butler, burst into the British camp almost out of breath, and
delivered the story that the Americans, in numbers like the forest
leaves, were approaching ; that he himself had barely escaped
with his life, in testimony of which he appealed to his coat which

its site.   The old fort was erected during
the French and Indian war of 1755, and
subsequently became a point of much
importance in transactions with the Six
Nations.

[1] Johnson's Royal Greens.

[2] St. Leger's detachment was sent to
Oswego, there to unite with Butler's
refugees and Brant's Indians, and with
them to penetrate the country from that
point, capture Fort Schuyler, sweep the
valley of the Mohawk, and join Burgoyne
at Albany.

[3] Colonel Claus (*Colonial History*, viii,
721) gives the following particulars :

" During the action (at Oriskany), when
the garrison found the Indians' camp
(who went out against their reinforcements) empty, they boldly sallied out
with three hundred men and two field
pieces, and took away the Indians' packs,
with their clothes, wampum and silver
work, they having gone in their shirts,
or naked, to action. The disappoint-
ment was rather greater to the Indians
than their loss, for they had nothing to
cover themselves with at night, against
the weather, and nothing in our camp to
supply them."

[4] *Jan Joost*, John Justus.

bore the marks of several bullets. The Indians were thoroughly alarmed. St. Leger tried to pacify them, but, mourning the loss of over seventy of their number at Oriskany, and apprehensive of further disaster, they broke and fled towards their boats on Oneida lake, killing on their way thither many of their tory allies, and obliging St. Leger to write that they were " more formidable than the enemy they had to expect."[1]

But, while conducting the siege, they took occasion to chas-. tise the *Oneidas* who had refused to unite with them. After the battle of Oriskany, Brant and a party of his warriors fell upon the old Oneida castle, burned the wigwams, destroyed the crops, and drove away the cattle of his former confederates. No sooner had he retreated, however, than the *Oneidas* retaliated. The residence of Molly Johnson, at the Upper Mohawk castle, was ravaged, herself and family driven from home, and her cash, clothing and cattle taken. From thence the avengers visited the Lower castle, and drove the followers of Little Abraham, one hundred in number, to refuge in Montreal, laying waste their plantations. Molly fled to Onondaga, and besought vengeance for the indignities which she had suffered, but to her possessions she was never restored; the indignant *Oneidas* had blotted out forever the seats of power from whence her tribe had swayed the destinies of a once powerful people.[2]

In the meantime the battle of Bennington had been fought with disastrous results to Burgoyne, not the least of which was the pall which it threw over the spirits of his dusky allies, who now began to find their way back to Canada in large numbers. With his defeat at Stillwater, they were as thoroughly demoralized as they were at Fort Schuyler when frightened by an idiot boy. Within three days after that battle, one hundred and fifty warriors made their peace with General Gates, accepted the war-belt, partook of the feast, and joined the Americans. When the final surrender of the British army came, not an

[1] The story of Hon Yost is well told in *Lossing's Field Book.* Having lost their shirts the Indians evidently feared that they might lose their skins.
[2] *Colonial History*, VIII, 725. Johnson says (*ibid.*, 727), the destruction of the Mohawk castles occurred after the battle of Bennington, and that the fugitives fled to Burgoyne, but the account by Claus is the most probable.

Indian was found in its ranks.  For their conduct Johnson and Claus had many excuses to offer.  The latter charged that their "harsh and indiscreet treatment" by Major Campbell, caused the greatest part of them to quit Burgoyne; Johnson assumed that at Oriskany they were not adequately supported by St. Leger, and that had they been they "would have rendered more material service;" but the fact would seem to be .that they had acted in precise accordance with the course which they had pursued in the previous war with France, and were ready at all times to court the favor of the party which, for the time being, appeared the most successful.  The evidence of their moral greatness is yet wanting.

For border warfare, however, the Indians under Brant, who were principally composed of *Senecas, Onondagas, Cayugas* and *Mohawks*, were still a power in the hands of the tories, as their subsequent ravages in the Mohawk valley, and at Wyoming and Minnisink, in 1778-9, sufficiently attest.  The path which Brant had opened to the Esopus country, in the spring of 1777, became indeed a path of blood.  Rallying such warriors as could be induced to continue in the service of the crown, Colonel John Butler succeeded, in the spring of 1778, in organizing a force of five hundred Indians and six hundred tories, and with these made his appearance on the Susquehanna.  At Wintermoot's fort, on the third of July, the colonial militia, in inferior numbers, under Colonel Zebulon Butler, opposed his progress in a desperate conflict.  Retreating from thence to Fort Forty, and unable to rally the flying inhabitants to its defense, terms of capitulation were agreed to by which the valley of Wyoming was surrendered to the mercy of savage white men and half-civilized Indians.  Foremost in the frightful orgies which followed, was Catharine Montour, the Queen Esther of the *Senecas*, a half-breed,[1] who assumed the office of executioner, and, using a maul and a tomahawk, passed around the

[1] She was a native of Canada, and her father one of the French governors, probably Frontenac.  She was made a captive during the wars between the Hurons and the French and the Six Nations, and was carried into the Seneca country, where she married a young chief who was signalized in the wars against the Catawbas.  He fell in battle, about the year 1730.  Catharine had several children by him, and remained a widow.  Her superior mind gave her great ascendancy over the Senecas, and she was a queen indeed among them.—*Lossing*, 1, 257.

ring of prisoners, who had been arranged at her bidding, deliberately chanted the song of death and murdered her victims to its cadences in consecutive order. Forts, houses, barns, grain and cattle were destroyed. When Butler and his tories withdrew, the homes of five hundred settlers had been laid waste, their occupants made fugitives, their dead left unburied. Shielding their bloody work, with the name of Brant, and throwing the cause of the attack on the disaffection of the Indians at the occupation of the valley by the whites, Butler and his tories have been floated on the page of history as endeavoring to restrain the ravages which they had instigated. Stripped of their disguise, they now stand as the spoilers of an exposed settlement, without the excuse which a regularly constituted army might offer of harassing an enemy.[1]

Although Butler withdrew his followers from the valley almost immediately after the massacre, he nevertheless left behind him those who had personal grievances to avenge and mercenary rewards to secure. These were mainly fugitives from the Esopus clans at Oghkwaga, and tories, who, availing themselves of the withdrawal of Count Pulaski and his legion of cavalry from Minnisink, where they had been stationed for the protection of the frontier, made a descent, on the fourth of May, 1779, upon the settlers at Fantinekil in western Ulster, killing six of the settlers and burning four dwelling houses and five barns. Colonel Cortlandt's regiment, then stationed at Wawarsing, went in pursuit of the authors of the mischief, but without success. Scarcely had he turned back, before the town of Woodstock was attacked and several houses destroyed.

Reinforced by Brant in person, the war raged along the entire border. In July, Fantinekil was again visited, and the widow

---

[1] The story of Wyoming has been told in all its details by Minor and Stone, and others, and is repeated by Lossing in his *Field Book*. Notwithstanding the persistent efforts of the poet Campbell and that of the English historians to escape censure by blackening the name of Brant, the fact is pretty well established that he was almost entirely innocent of the excesses which were committed. Nor is there better ground for associating with the transaction the old dispute of the Lenapes. That question was satisfactorily settled by the treaty of 1768. The only question in dispute was that between the Connecticut company and the proprietaries of Pennsylvania, in which the Indians had no part, except as they were influenced by the contestants. The truth of Wyoming can only be written by an analysis of the actors in the massacre and their association with the proprietaries of Pennsylvania.

of Isaac Bevier and her two sons, and Michael Socks and his father, mother, two brothers, wife and two children, were massacred, and the house which they occupied given to the flames. At the house of Jesse Bevier the assailants were successfully resisted, although the building was set on fire and its inmates exposed to a terrible death. Alarmed, it is said, by a faithful dog, settlers two miles distant came to the relief of their friends. The tories fled without completing their work, only to reappear at Napanoch, where they burned the only house standing on the site of the present village of Ellenville. From thence they moved to Minnisink, where, on the night of July 19th, Brant, with sixty of his Indians, and twenty-seven tories disguised as savages, stole upon the little town, and, before the people were aroused from their slumbers, fired several dwellings. With no means of defense, the inhabitants sought safety in flight to the mountains, leaving all their worldly goods a spoil to the invaders. Their small stockade fort, a mill, and twelve houses and barns were burned ; several persons were killed and some taken prisoners. Orchards and farms were laid waste, cattle were driven away, and booty of every kind carried to Grassy brook on the Delaware, where Brant had his headquarters.

Alarmed by fugitives, Lieutenant Colonel Tusten, of Goshen, issued orders to the officers of his regiment to meet him at Minnisink the next day, with as many men as they could muster. In response to this call one hundred and forty-nine men were gathered in council with him the following morning. Tusten regarded the force as too small to attempt the pursuit of the invaders, but he was overruled, and the line of march taken up. On the twenty-first, Colonel Hathorn, of Warwick, joined the pursuers with a small additional force, and assumed the command. On the twenty-second, Hathorn pushed on to the high hills overlooking the Delaware, near the mouth of the Lackawaxen, where the enemy was discovered. Brant, who had watched the movement, ordered the main body of his warriors to an ambuscade in the rear of Hathorn's force, and when the latter, not finding his foes in front as he expected, attempted to return from the plain which he had reached, he was met by the fire of his wily antagonist.  A long and bloody conflict ensued.  Brant had the advantage of position and superior numbers; one-third of Hathorn's small force became detached; closer and closer the Indians and their white allies drew their circle of fire until Hathorn was hemmed within the circumference of an acre of ground, upon a rocky hill that sloped on all sides, where he maintained the conflict until the sun of that long July day went down.  With the gathering twilight the ammunition of the militia was exhausted, and, placing themselves in a hollow square, they prepared their last defense with the butts of their muskets. Broken at one corner, the square became a rout, and the flying fugitives were shot down without mercy.  Behind a rock on the field, Tusten dressed the wounds of his neighbors, while its shelter was also made the point from which a constant fire was kept up by a negro without his knowledge.  As the last shot fell from this retreat, the Indians rushed to the spot, killed Tusten and the wounded men in his charge, seventeen in number, and completed the bloody work which they had commenced.  Of the whole number who went forth to chastise the invaders, only about thirty returned to relate the scenes through which they had passed, and to graft forever their traditions of the carnage from which they had escaped upon the history of Orange county.

The attack upon Wyoming and the devastation which threatened the borders determined the action of congress.  In the spring of 1779, and while yet the incursions upon the frontiers of Ulster county were in progress, an expedition was organized to invade the Seneca country, in which the tories and Indians held their headquarters, with a view to chastise and disperse them.  This expedition moved in two divisions, the first under General Sullivan by the way of the Susquehanna and Wyoming; and the second under General James Clinton through the valley of the Mohawk.  The expedition was entirely successful.  At Tioga the divisions were united, and from thence moved into the heart of the Indian country, and marked their pathway with blazing Indian villages and blackened harvest fields. " The Indians shall see," said Sullivan, " that we have malice enough in our hearts to destroy everything that contributes to their support," and faithfully was that determination executed.  Catha-

rine Montour received in part the punishment she merited in
the destruction of her residence at Catharinestown ; Kendaia
was swept from existence ; Kanadaseagea, the capital of the
*Senecas*, near the head of the lake which bears their name, with
its sixty well built houses and fine orchards ; Kanandaigua, with
its "twenty-three very elegant houses, mostly framed, and, in
general, large," and its fields of corn and orchards of fruit, and
Genesee castle, the capital of the *Onondagas*, with its "one
hundred and twenty-eight houses, mostly large and very elegant,"
were alike destroyed.  Forty Indian towns were burned ; one
hundred and sixty thousand bushels of corn in the fields and
in granaries, were destroyed ; a vast number of the finest fruit
trees were cut down ; gardens covered with vegetables were
desolated ; the proud Indians, who had scarce felt the touch of
the colonists except in kindness, were driven into the forests to
starve and be hunted like wild beasts ; their altars were overturned,
their graves trampled upon by strangers, and their beautiful
country laid waste.

The punishment administered by Sullivan was indeed terrible,
but was it just ?  That the projectors of the expedition, including Washington, so regarded it, is well known ; that four of
the tribes had broken their pledge of neutrality and carried forward their revenges and prejudices to the account of the innocent, is also known.  That they were the victims of the wiles
of designing men — had learned their lessons of hatred in the
earlier controversies between the contending civilizations — was
as strongly urged in their behalf then as it can be now.  Had
they been without warning, the destruction of their towns would
have been without justification ; but they had been both warned
and entreated.  In December, 1777, congress had addressed
to them an earnest and eloquent appeal to preserve their neutrality, and refrain from further hostilities, to sit under the shade
of their own trees and by the side of their own streams and
"smoke their pipe in safety and contentment ; "[1] but they

<hr/>

[1] This address recognized the division
which then existed in the confederacy.
To the four hostile tribes, it said :

"Brothers, Cayugas, Senecas, Onondagas and Mohawks : Look well into your
hearts, and be attentive.  Much are you
to blame, and greatly have you wronged
us.  Be wise in time.  Be sorry for your
faults.  The great council, through the
blood of our friends who fell by your

would not listen, and grew bold in the supposed impossibility of being reached by the government. The visitation which they had provoked was a necessity.

The scourging army passed by the towns of the *Oneidas* and *Tuscaroras*, and struck its blows where chastisement was most deserved. A single village of the *Mohawks* was spared,[1] consisting of four houses, the occupants of which were made prisoners; but the torch was stayed by the entreaties of homeless frontier settlers who begged that they might occupy them until they could procure others, and to them was also given the grain, horses and cows, the stores and furniture, of the remaining followers of Little Abraham, who had found opportunity to make themselves obnoxious as informers, if not as active participants in the English cause. The council-seat of the traditional Atotarho was thrown down, and the council-fire of the nation, which had so long been kept burning at Onondaga, was put out never to be rekindled on its ancient hearth.

The offending tribes were astounded. The *Onondagas* flew to the *Oneidas* for relief; the *Senecas* and *Cayugas* joined the

tomahawks at the German Flats, cries aloud against you, will yet be patient. We do not desire to destroy you. Long have we been at peace; and it is still our wish to bury the hatchet, and wipe away the blood which some of you have so unjustly shed. Till time shall be no more, we wish to smoke with you the calumet of friendship at Onondaga. But, brothers, mark well what we now tell you. Let it sink deep as the bottom of the sea, and never be forgotten by you or your children. If ever again you take up the hatchet to strike us, if you join our enemies in battle or council, if you give them intelligence, or encourage or permit them to pass through your country to molest or hurt any of our people, we shall look upon you as our enemies, who, under a cloak of friendship, cover your bad designs, and like the concealed adder, only wait for an opportunity to wound us when we are most unprepared. Believe us who never deceive. If, after all our good counsel, and all our care to prevent it, we must take up the hatchet, the blood to be shed will lie heavy on your heads. The hand of the thirteen United States is not short. It will reach to the farthest extent of the country of the Six Nations; and while we have right on our side, the good Spirit, whom we serve, will enable us to punish you, and put it out of your power to do us farther mischief."

To the Oneidas and Tuscaroras no such warning words were necessary. "Hearken to us," said the address to them: "It rejoices our heart that we have no reason to reproach you in common with the rest of the Six Nations. We have experienced your love, strong as the oak; and your fidelity, unchangeable as truth. You have kept fast hold of the ancient covenant chain, and preserved it free from rust and decay, and bright as silver. Like brave men, for glory you despise danger; you stood forth in the cause of your friends, and ventured your lives in our battles. While the sun and moon continue to give light to the world, we shall love and respect you. As our trusty friends, we shall protect you, and shall at all times consider your welfare as our own."— *Stone's Life of Brant*, I, 292, etc.

[1] The castle of the Praying Maquas at the mouth of Schoharie creek.

*Mohawks* at Fort Niagara.[1]   Humbled, the former sent their chiefs to Fort Stanwix and asked, " Was the destruction of our castle done by design, or by mistake ?   If by mistake, we hope to see our brethren, the prisoners ; but if our brethren, the Americans, mean to destroy us also, we will not fly — we will wait here and receive our death."   " I know the agreement made four years ago with the Six Nations," replied Colonel Van Schaick ; " I also know that all of them, except the *Oneidas* and *Tuscaroras*, broke their engagements and flung away the chain of friendship.   The *Onondagas* have been great murderers ; we have found the scalps of our brothers at their castle.   They were cut off, not by mistake, but by design — I was ordered to do it, and it is done."   Trembling, the fugitives at Niagara, appealed to Haldiman, the governor of Canada : " The great king's enemies are many, and they grow fast in number.   They were formerly like young panthers ; they could neither bite nor scratch ; we could play with them safely ; we feared nothing they could do to us.   But now their bodies are become big as the elk, and strong as the buffalo ; they have also got great and sharp claws.   They have driven us out of our country for taking part in your quarrel.   We expect the great king will give us another country, that our children may live after us, and be his friends and children as we are."[2]

At Fort Niagara they perished in large numbers from diseases caused by the absence of accustomed food, and the exposures to which they were necessarily subjected.   But their hatreds grew with their misfortunes.   Red Jacket plead with them to make peace, without avail ; against the name of Washington they wrote that of Annatakaules, the destroyer of towns.   Still powerful for predatory warfare, they organized anew during the winter, and, with Corn-Planter in command of the *Senecas*, fell upon the *Oneidas* and *Tuscaroras* ; burned their castle, church, and village, and drove the offenders down upon the

---

[1] Fort Niagara was erected by the French in 1725, and was for many years the seat of the French missionaries.   The English captured it in 1759, when it was rebuilt and regarrisoned.   During the revolution, it was held by the British, and became the head-quarters of the Indians and tories.   It was surrendered to the United States in 1794.

[2] The authenticity of this document has been disputed.   The portion quoted, however, is a statement of facts, if not by the Indians themselves.—*Appendix Stone's Life of Brant.*

white settlements for protection.[1]   In May, in detached parties
they renewed their attacks upon the borders of Ulster county,
plundered the houses of Thomas and Johannes Jansen, in the
town of Shawangunk; killed a Miss Mack and her father, as
well as a young woman from New York then residing with
them, in one of the mountain gorges, and subsequently reached
the Hudson in an attack upon the settlement at Saugerties,
where they made prisoners of Captain Jeremiah Snyder and his
son Isaac, who were taken to Fort Niagara and from thence to
Montreal.   The convenient instruments of the tories, they
followed their footsteps wherever they were bidden.

In the meantime, Sir John Johnson, at the head of a band of
refugees and Indians, five hundred in number, stole through the
woods from Crown point and appeared at Johnson Hall.   His
purpose was to remove the treasure which he had buried on the
occasion of his first flight, and to punish some of his old neighbors.   In both he was successful.   Two barrels of silver coin,
the fruits of his father's honest traffic with the Indians, rewarded
him; his attendants lighted up the surrounding neighborhood
with blazing dwellings, and murdered the defenseless people.
The village of Caghnawaga[2] was given to the flames, and
along the Mohawk valley for several miles every building, not
owned by a loyalist, was burned, the cattle killed, and all the
horses that could be found taken away.   With many prisoners
and much booty, Johnson made good his retreat.

During the autumn more formidable operations were undertaken.   Sir John Johnson, with three companies of refugees,
one company of German Yagers, two hundred of Butler's
Rangers, and one company of British Regulars, with Brant and

---

[1] The fugitives collected together near Schenectady, where they remained until after the war, in active alliance with the colonists.

[2] This village took its name from that of the ancient Mohawk village called Gaudaouague; by the French, On-engioure, and by the Dutch, Kaghne-wage.   It was in this village that Father Jogues was so badly treated dur-ing eighteen months of captivity.   Its site is now covered by the village of Fonda, Montgomery county.   The Mo-hawks who originally occupied it were proselyted by the Jesuits and induced to remove to Canada, where they were established at a mission called by them-selves, in remembrance of their ancient village, Caghnawaga. (*Brodhead*, II, 129, 299.  *Ante*, p. 97).   At the time of its destruction it was occupied principally by German families from the Palatinate.

36

Corn planter and five hundred of their warriors, entered the Schoharie valley, and although not successful in reducing the block-houses which had been erected, nevertheless spread destruction along their pathway. Not a house, barn, or grain-stack known to belong to a whig, was left standing; one hundred thousand bushels of grain were destroyed in a single day. The houses of the tories were spared, but no sooner had the enemy retired than the exasperated whigs set them on fire, and all shared the common fate. The valley of the Mohawk was next visited. At Caghnawaga the buildings which had been left standing at the previous visitation, as well as those which had been rebuilt, were destroyed, and every dwelling on both sides of the river, as far up as Fort Plain, was burned. Murder and rapine attested alike the hatred of Johnson for his former neighbors and the vengeance of his dusky allies.

But the marauders were not permitted to again escape without molestation. Governor George Clinton, having received information from two *Oneidas*, of their movements, promptly marched to the relief of the district. A strong body of *Oneida* warriors, led by their chief, Louis Atyataronghta,[1] who had been commissioned a colonel by congress, joined him on his way. Near Fort Plain the opposing forces met; Brant and his Indians, in a thicket of shrub oaks, were supported by Johnson, while the right of the patriot line was held by the *Oneidas*. The defiant war-whoop of the opposing chiefs was echoed by their followers; supported by the militia, the *Oneidas* dashed forward; Brant gave way and fled, wounded in the heel, to the fording place near the old upper Indian castle, crossed the river and found refuge in the rear of the reserve forces of his friends. Johnson immediately made hasty retreat to his boats on Onondaga lake, and escaped to Canada by the way of Oswego, shorn of whatever prestige he had gained on his former raid.

Similar were the events of 1781. The devastations of the invading bands commenced again on the borders of Ulster. In August, a body of three hundred Indians and ninety tories fell

---

[1] It is said that he was the representative of three nations, having in his veins the blood of the French, the Indian, and the negro. His bravery was unquestioned.

upon the settlers in the Wawarsing valley and " burned and destroyed about a dozen houses, with their barns," and killed one of the inhabitants, " the rest having fled." Colonel Hardenburgh, with a force of only nine men, hastened forward to the aid of the settlers, and, throwing his men into a small stone house, checked the advance of the enemy. In their repeated attempts to dislodge him, thirteen of their number were left dead upon the field. Colonel Paulding's regiment of state levies, together with the militia, was soon on the ground, but not in time to punish the marauders, although they were pursued for seven days.

In October the Mohawk valley was visited by Major Ross and Walter N. Butler at the head of about one thousand troops, consisting of regulars, tories and Indians. The settlement known as Warren Bush was broken into so suddenly that the people had no chance for escape. Many were killed and their houses plundered and destroyed. Colonel Willett, informed of the incursion, marched with about four hundred men, including *Oneida* warriors, to the defense of the valley. He was joined by Colonel Rowley with the Tryon county militia, and the plan of attack agreed to. Rowley was sent to fall upon the enemy in the rear, while Willett was to attack them in front. The belligerents met a short distance above Johnson Hall, and a battle immediately ensued. Willett's militia broke and fled to the stone church in the village, but at that moment Rowley attacked the rear and soon compelled the enemy to retreat, leaving forty of their number killed and wounded and fifty prisoners. The pursuit was not taken up until the next morning, when it was continued until evening before the enemy were reached. A running fight then ensued ; Butler's Indians became alarmed at the havoc in their ranks and fled ; a brisk fire was kept up for some time by the tories, until Butler, who was watching the fight from behind a tree, exposed his head and fell under a quick ball from an *Oneida*, who knew him and who was watching his motions ; his troops fled in confusion ; the *Oneida* bounded across the stream that separated the contestants, and while Butler, yet living, cried for quarter, finished the work

which he had commenced, tore from his head the reeking trophy
which he sought, and bore it as a banner in the onward charge

of his comrades.  So perished
Walter N. Butler, the most
heartless of all the tories who
engaged in the border wars ; so
closed the attacks upon the
frontier settlements of New
York.

The gallantry of the *Oneidas*
and *Tuscaroras* during the war
was only exceeded by that of
the *Mahicans* and *Wappingers*.
Active in the campaign of
1777, the latter joined Washington again in the spring of 1778,
and were detached with the forces under Lafayette to check the
depredations of the British army on its retreat from Philadelphia.
At the engagement at Barren hill they defeated a company of
British troops, but not precisely in the manner of creditable warfare.  Stationed in a wood at a considerable distance from the
main army, they met the attack of the enemy by discharging
their muskets and uttering their hideous battle-cry.  "The result," says Sparks, "was laughable ; both parties ran off equally
frightened at the unexpected and terrific appearance of their
antagonists."[1]

But such was not their record in Westchester county, where
they first met the British, and where they were stationed soon
after the engagement at Barren hill.  In July, while Simcoe and
Tarleton were making some examinations of the country, the
*Mahicans* formed an ambuscade for their capture, and very
nearly succeeded in their purpose, the party escaping by changing their route.[2]  Their most distinguished service, however,
was performed in August.  While on a scouting expedition on
the thirtieth, Lieutenant Colonel Emerick met a body of them
under Nimham, the king of the *Wappingers*, and in the engage-

---

[1] *Sparks*, VII, 547.          [2] *Simcoe's Military Journal.*

ment which followed was compelled to retreat. On the following morning the whole of the British force at Kingsbridge was ordered out and the largest portion placed in an ambuscade, while Emerick was sent forward to decoy his assailants of the previous day. The plan failed, but an engagement was brought on, by Emerick's corps, on what is now known as Cortland's ridge, in the present town of Yonkers, which was one of the most severe of the war. The Indians made the attack from behind the fences, and in their first fire wounded five of their enemies, including Simcoe. Falling back among the rocks they defied for a time the efforts to dislodge them. Emerick offered them peace and protection if they would surrender; four of their number accepted the terms only to be hewn in pieces as soon as they reached his lines. The engagement was renewed; Emerick charged the ridge with cavalry in overwhelming force, but was stoutly resisted. As the cavalry rode them down, the Indians seized the legs of their foes and dragged them from their saddles to join them in death. All hope of successful resistance gone, Nimham commanded his followers to fly, but for himself exclaimed: " I am an aged tree; I will die here." Ridden down by Simcoe, he wounded that officer and was on the point of dragging him from his horse when he was shot by Wright, Simcoe's orderly. " The Indians fought most gallantly," is Simcoe's testimony; but the number engaged is not stated. Emerick reported that " near forty " of them " were killed or desperately wounded." If his previous statement is correct, that the number who had " just joined Washington " was " about sixty," over one-half must have fallen in the engagement.[1]

To their services in that and in other engagements the testimony of Washington is added.[2] Literally did they redeem the pledge which they had given at Albany, the pledge of Ruth: " Whither

[1] Near forty of the Indians were killed or desperately wounded, among them Nimham, a chieftain who had been to England, and his son (*Simcoe's Journal*). Bolton states that eighteen bodies were recovered from the field and buried in one pit. The loss of the British is said to have been five; but it was rare indeed that they made a correct return, and the number may have been much greater.

[2] " Head Quarters, Bergen Co.,
            September 13, 1870.
*To the President of Congress:*
   Sir: This will be presented to your excellency by Captain Hendriks Solomon of Stockbridge. He and about

thou goest I will go, and where thou lodgest I will lodge ; thy
people shall be my people, and thy God my God ; where thou
diest will I die, and there will I be buried." The privations
which the patriots suffered, they shared without a murmur ; in
their devotion they never wearied. When the tattered banners
of the struggle were folded away, they returned to their ancient
seats, and at the head waters of the Hudson again met the white
men, now their brothers by a holier covenant, as they had
met them in 1609, the sole representatives of the Indian tribes
of Hudson's river.

By the treaty of peace between the United States and Great
Britain — which was without stipulation in regard to the Indian
allies of the latter government — " the ancient country of the
Six Nations, the residence of their ancestors from the time far
beyond their earliest traditions, was included within the boundaries granted to the Americans." Nor was this their only loss ;
in their social and political condition they had been great
sufferers by their unfortunate alliance. The great body of the
*Oneidas* and *Tuscaroras* had been severed from the confederacy ;
the " eastern door " of their " Long House " had been broken
in and its ancient keepers, the *Mohawks*, made fugitives from
the seats of their fathers ; the alliance of the four tribes with
the crown had divested them of the respect of the victors ; their
towns had been destroyed and their fields wasted by the scourging army of Sullivan. When the war closed, the *Oneidas* and
*Tuscaroras* returned to their possessions, assured of the protection of their American allies ; the *Mohawks*, after brooding
awhile over their misfortunes, retired to the banks of the Ouise

twenty of his tribe have been serving as
volunteers with the army since the beginning of July. They have been generally attached to the light corps, and have
conducted themselves with great propriety
and fidelity. Seeing no immediate prospect of any operation in this quarter, in
which they can be serviceable, they are
desirous of returning home after receiv-
ing some compensation for the time, during which they have been with us, and
after having made a visit to Philadelphia,
I have thought it best to gratify them,
not only on account of being agreeable to
them, but because I have it not in my
power to furnish them with such articles
of clothing as they request, and which
they would prefer to money. Congress
will, I doubt not, direct such a supply as
they shall think proper. Captain Solomon, with part of these people was with
us in the year 1778. The tribe suffered
severely during that campaign, in a skirmish with the enemy, in which they lost
their chief and several of their warriors.
I have the honor to be
Yours, etc.,
GEO. WASHINGTON."

or Grand river, under the protection of the crown,[1] prepared to
renew the struggle whenever they should be bidden by those
whom they served; the *Senecas* relighted their council-fire, broken,
dispirited and divided.

New York was disposed to complete the work of disintegration and dispersion, which the war had developed, by expelling
the *Senecas*, *Onondagas* and *Cayugas* from all the country within
its bounds which had not been ceded by them under the treaty
of 1768; but congress adopted a more liberal policy, nevertheless one involving punishment. Commissioners on the part
of the United States met the representatives of the tribes at
Fort Schuyler in October, 1784, prepared to negotiate a treaty
based on a concession of territory. The *Mohawks* were not
represented; the *Senecas* asked delay until the tribes on the
Ohio could be summoned, but the commissioners would not
consent, nor would they recognize a unity that did not exist.
Red Jacket opposed the burial of the hatchet, while Cornplanter counseled peace, regarding the loss of territory,. on the
terms offered, as far better than the hazards of further war.
The efforts of the latter prevailed, and, on the twenty-second,
a treaty was signed by which the United States gave peace to
the *Mohawks*, *Senecas*, *Onondagas* and *Cayugas*, and received
them under their protection, on condition that all the prisoners
in their possession, white and black, should be delivered up.
The *Oneidas* and *Tuscaroras*, as well as all the tribes, were
secured in the possession of the lands they were then occupying,
with power to sell and relinquish, but at the same time gave up
all claims to the territory not in absolute occupation west of a
line beginning at the mouth of the Oyonwayea creek, flowing
into Lake Ontario four miles east of Niagara, thence southerly,
but preserving a line four miles east of the carrying path, to the
mouth of Tehoseroron or Buffalo creek; thence to the north
boundary of Pennsylvania; thence south along the Pennsylvania
line to the Ohio.

Had the tribes been permitted to follow their own inclinations,
this treaty would perhaps have been conclusive; but the Eng-

---

[1] At the close of the war the Mohawks were temporarily residing cn the Ameri- can side of the Niagara river, in the vicinity of the old landing place above

lish in Canada, and especially the tories, professing to believe that the contest between the colonies and the mother country had been postponed, not determined,[1] disseminated discontent and hastened to revive in the hearts of their allies the sacredness of the boundary line of 1768, and the policy upon which it had been based. The *Lenapes* and *Shawanoes* were encouraged to revolt ; Corn planter was driven from power by Red Jacket. Brant assumed the task of organizing formidable and active hostilities, and for that purpose visited England in 1785. On his return the tribes in interest opened communications with the American government, suggested that a grand council should be called, and that, pending its assemblage, and determination, surveyors and settlers should be restrained from passing beyond the Ohio.

The government, anxious to prevent hostilities, replied by sending instructions to General St. Clair, then governor of the north-western territory, to inquire particularly into the temper of the Indians, and if he found them hostile, to endeavor to hold as general a treaty with them as he could convene, and, if possible, satisfactorily extinguish their title to lands as far westward as the Mississippi. Under these instructions St. Clair concluded at Fort Harmer, on the ninth of January, 1789, two separate treaties ; the first, with the sachems of the Five Nations, the *Mohawks* excepted ; the second, with the sachems of the *Lenapes*, *Wyandots*, *Ottawas*, *Chippewas*, and other western clans represented. These treaties recognized the boundary line of 1784, but at the same time modified that treaty by conceding the right of the Indians to compensation for lands east of the line as far as the boundary of 1768.

At the negotiation of these treaties the fact became strikingly apparent that the confederate tribes were without agreement upon any line of policy,[2] Brant openly denouncing many of his

the fort. The governor of Canada subsequently assigned them lands on the Grand river about forty miles above Niagara Falls.—*Stone*, II, 239.

[1] Great Britain, it will be remembered, refused to negotiate a commercial treaty with the United States, or to surrender certain forts within the northern bound-

ary of the territory which had been relinquished. It was not until 1794, that a treaty was ratified covering these points, meanwhile the encouragement of the officers of the crown to the Indians was not disguised. See Johnson's letter in *Stone's Life of Brant*, II, 267.

[2] St. Clair writes : " A jealousy sub-

late allies as having " sold themselves to the devil." [1] Failing
to unite and wield the tribes to his purposes, he appealed to
the *Lenapes* and *Shawanoes* to take the offensive, with himself
and his associates as followers. The latter accepted the belt,
and began hostilities along the western border, then covering an
extent of four hundred miles. To restrain and punish the
insurgents General Harmer was sent out, in the autumn of
1790, with a force of fifteen hundred men, but suffered disaster
in a conflict near the junction of the St. Joseph and St. Mary
rivers ; and General St. Clair, with an expedition for a similar
purpose, was defeated and severely punished in November of
the following year. [2]

Encouraged by these successes, the *Lenapes* and their allies
resisted the overtures for peace which Captain Hendrik Aupaumut, the *Mahican* chief, conveyed to them, and, in council
at Miami Rapids, on the 13th of August, 1793, issued the declaration, that to them the money which the United States
offered for their lands was of no value, to most of them
unknown ; that no consideration whatever could induce
them to sell that from which they obtained sustenance for their
women and children ; that if peace was desired, justice must be
done, and to that end the money which was offered them should
be divided among the settlers who had invaded their country
and they be bidden to withdraw ; that they never made any agreement with the king by which their lands followed the fortunes
of his wars, nor would they now make a treaty which denied
to them the right to make " bargain or cession of lands whenever and to whomsoever they pleased ; " peace with them could
be had only on the basis that the Ohio should remain the
boundary line beyond which the white man should not come.
" We can retreat no further, because the country behind hardly
affords food for its present inhabitants ; we have therefore

sisted among them, which I was not
willing to lessen by considering them as
one people. They do not so consider
themselves ; and I am persuaded their
general confederacy is entirely broken.
Indeed, it would not be very difficult, if
circumstances required it, to set them at
deadly variance."—*Am. State Papers*, IV,
10.

[1] In other words, to the Yankees,
against whom he manifested at all times
the most intense hatred.

[2] *Stone's Life of Brant*, II, 308, etc.;
*Gallatin*, 50, 51, 68.

resolved to leave our bones in this small space, to which we are now consigned."

Thirteen tribes, the *Lenapes*, *Shawanoes*, *Minsis*, *Mahicans*, of the Delaware, *Nanticokes* and *Conoys*, the seven nations of Canada, the *Wyandots*, *Miamis*, *Chippeways* and *Pottawattamies*, and the *Senecas* of the Glaize, signed the declaration, and on the thirtieth of June following, sealed it with the blood of their bravest warriors in battle against General Wayne on the ground where St. Clair had been so disastrously defeated in 1791.[1]  From that field they retired crushed and broken, while fire and sword followed them in their retreat, and blazing villages and ruined fields convinced them that however just their cause, there was a limit to their powers of resistance.  Ruined in estate, and deserted by their English allies, with whom the United States had finally concluded definite treaty, they came up to a conference with Wayne, at Greenville, on the third of August, 1795, and accepted the terms of their conquerors.[2]

Full of interest as are the details of this struggle, they do not strictly pertain to the purpose of this work, the general facts sufficiently indicating the events attending the retreating footsteps of the once powerful occupants of the western valley of the Hudson.  Leaving the *Lenapes* and their grandchildren on the banks of the Mississippi, the warriors of the Six Nations, who, in small number, had participated in the contest, returned to the reservations which had been set apart for them by the legislature of New York, which in part they still occupy.[3] From their ancient dominions the *Mahicans* at Westenhuck removed, in 1785, on the invitation of the *Oneidas*, to a tract six miles square in the present towns of Augusta, Oneida county, and Stockbridge, Madison county.  Here they resided until 1821, when, with other Indians of New York, they purchased of the *Menominees* and *Winnebagoes*, a tract of land on the Wisconsin and Fox rivers in Wisconsin, and took up their residence there.[4]

[1] *Stone's Life of Brant*, ʉ, 382, etc.
[2] The loss inflicted upon the Americans during this war is officially stated at over two thousand men.
[3] *Census of New York*, 1855, appendix.

Only a comparatively small portion of the original reservations now remain in their possession.
[4] *Stockbridge, Past and Present*.

And there were other settlements. A band of *Montauks* of Long Island, *Mohegans* of Connecticut, and *Pequots* and *Narragansetts* of Massachusetts, under the leadership of Samson Occum, a *Mohegan* missionary, took up their residence in the Oneida country in 1788, and were confirmed on a reservation two miles in length by three in breadth, in the present town of Marshall, Oneida county, where, having no language in common, they adopted the English, and received the name of Brothertons. They subsequently removed to the west and settled in Wisconsin.

Similar was the course of the domestic clans of *Raritans*. From an early period a remnant of the tribe had occupied a reservation in the county of Burlington, New Jersey, where they were known as Brothertons. In 1802, they accepted an invitation from the *Mahicans* to unite with them, and, obtaining consent from the legislature, sold their lands and removed to the reservation of the latter. They were officially met by the authorities of New Jersey for the last time in 1832, when, reduced to about forty souls, they applied to the legislature for remuneration on account of their rights of hunting and fishing on unenclosed lands, which they had reserved in their various agreements with the whites, and the legislature promptly directed the payment to them of two thousand dollars in full relinquishment of their claims.[1]

[1] The application was made by *Shawuskukhkung* or Wilted Grass, a chief of the Delawares, who had been educated at Princeton at the expense of the Scotch Missionary Society. At the time of making the application he was seventy-six years of age. His address to the legislature, on the occasion, was as follows :

" MY BRETHREN.—I am old, and weak, and poor, and therefore a fit representative of my people. You are young, and strong, and rich, and therefore fit representatives of your people. But let me beg you for a moment to lay aside the recollection of your strength and of our weakness, that your minds may be prepared to examine with candor the subject of our claims.

" Our tradition informs us, and I believe it corresponds with your records, that the right of fishing in all the rivers and bays south of the Raritan, and of hunting in all unenclosed lands, was never relinquished, but on the contrary was expressly reserved in our last treaty, held at Crosswicks, in 1758.

" Having myself been one of the parties to the sale, I believe in 1801, I know that these rights were not sold or parted with.

" We now offer to sell these privileges to the state of New Jersey. They were once of great value to us, and we apprehend that neither time nor distance, nor the non-use of our rights, has at all affected them, but that the courts here would consider our claims valid were we to exercise them ourselves, or delegate them to others. It is not, however, our

On a small reservation on Long island the *Montauks* have still a representation, though with scarce a member of pure blood.   On the third of March, 1702, they made an agreement with the English in which the rights of each were definitely fixed, and resided in peace with their neighbors until after the revolution, when they made claim to lands which they had previously ceded, but without success.   The first to welcome Hudson's wandering bark, they are now the last representatives of the tribes which once held dominion on Sewanhackie.

Domestic clans or families of *Minsis* and *Mahicans* lingered

wish thus to excite litigation.   We consider the state legislature the proper purchaser, and throw ourselves upon its benevolence and magnanimity, trusting that feelings of justice and liberality will induce you to give us what you deem a compensation."

The whole subject was referred to a committee, before whom Hon. Samuel L. Southard voluntarily and ably advocated the claim of the Delawares; and at the conclusion of his speech remarked: "That it was a proud fact in the history of New Jersey, that every foot of her soil had been obtained from the Indians by fair and voluntary purchase and transfer, a fact that no other state in the union, not even the land which bears the name of Penn, can boast of."   The committee reported in favor of an appropriation of $2,000, which the legislature at once confirmed.   This was the crowning act of a series in which justice and kindness to the Indians had been kept steadily in view; and was thus acknowledged by the veteran chief in a letter to the legislature dated "Trenton, March 12, 1832:

"Bartholomew S. Calvin (his English name), takes this method to return his thanks to both houses of the state legislature, and especially to their committees, for their very respectful attention to, and candid examination of, the Indian claims which he was delegated to present.

"The final act of official intercourse between the state of New Jersey and the Delaware Indians, who once owned nearly the whole of its territory, has now been consummated, and in a manner which must redound to the honor of this growing state, and, in all probability, to the prolongation of the existence of a wasted, yet grateful people.   Upon this parting occasion, I feel it to be an incumbent duty to bear the feeble tribute of my praise to the high-toned justice which, in this instance, and, so far as I am acquainted, in all former times, has actuated the councils of this commonwealth in dealing with the aboriginal inhabitants.

"Not a drop of our blood have you spilled in battle — not an acre of our land have you taken but by our consent.   These facts speak for themselves, and need no comment.   They place the character of New Jersey in bold relief and bright example to those states within whose territorial limits our brethren still remain.   Nothing save benisons can fall upon her from the lips of a *Lenni Lenape*.

"There may be some who would despise an Indian benediction; but when I return to my people, and make known to them the result of my mission, the ear of the Great Sovereign of the universe, which is still open to our cry, will be penetrated with our invocation of blessings upon the generous sons of New Jersey.

"To those gentlemen, members of the legislature, and others who have evinced their kindness to me, I cannot refrain from paying the unsolicited tribute of my heart-felt thanks.   Unable to return them any other compensation, I fervently pray that God will have them in his holy keeping — will guide them in safety through the vicissitudes of this life, and ultimately, through the rich mercies of our blessed Redeemer, receive them into the glorious entertainment of his kingdom above."—*See note by W. J. Allinson, New Jersey Historical Collections.*

around their ancient seats for some years after the close of the revolution, but of them one after another it is written, "they disappeared in the night." In the language of Tamenund at the death of Uncas : " The pale faces are masters of the earth, and the time of the red men has not yet come again. My day has been too long. In the morning I saw the sons of *Unami* happy and strong ; and yet, before the night has come, have I lived to see the last warrior of the wise race of the *Mahicans.*"

APPENDIX.

# APPENDIX.

## I. BIOGRAPHICAL SKETCHES.

HE personal history of the early Indian kings and chiefs who held dominion in the valley of the Hudson, is involved in even greater obscurity than that which attaches to their contemporaries in other parts of the new world. Of MASSASOIT, MIANTONOMOH, UNCÁS, PHILIP, and other New England chiefs, and of POWHATTAN and POCAHONTAS of Virginia, there is some definite information; but of those who welcomed the emigrants from Holland, names alone survive. MONEMIUS and UNUWATS, whose castles Hudson visited, have no record except in the deed which they gave to their lands, while AEPJIN, king of the *Mahicans*, and GOETHALS, king of the *Wappingers*, float in an uncertain twilight which is scarcely relieved on the part of their contemporaries, KAELCOP and SEWACKENAMO of the *Minsis*, WYANDANCE, of the *Montauks*, and ORITANY of the *Hackinsacks*, by the stirring scenes in which they were participants. Even as late as 1710, when more definite records came to be written, there is no preservation of the lines of kings, nor is there positive identification of the *Mahican* and *Iroquois* sachems who then visited England. True, it is said that HENDRIK of the *Mohawks*, was one of the latter, and that ELOW-OH-KAOM, of the *Mahicans*, left a daughter who became the wife of UMPACHENEE, a chief subsequently known to the missionaries of Stockbridge; but as a rule, the declaration is not the mere creation of the poet SPRAGUE, that

> " The doomed Indian leaves behind no trace,
> To save his own or serve another race,
> With his frail breath his power has passed away,
> His deeds, his thoughts, are buried with his clay.
> His heraldry is but a broken bow,
> His history but a tale of wrong and woe,
> His very name must be a blank."

38

On the part of the *Lenapes* the name of TAMANY, or TA-
MANED has been preserved in a halo of traditionary glory.    He
was one of their sachems or kings, and lived possibly as late as
1680.    Heckewelder says:  "The fame of this great man
extended even among the whites, who fabricated numerous
legends respecting him, which I never heard, however, from
the mouth of an Indian, and therefore believe to be fabulous."
He is said to have been a resident of the present county of
Bucks, in Pennsylvania, and that he was buried near a spring
about three and a half miles west of Doylestown, in that county.
Heckewelder adds, that when Colonel George Morgan of
Princeton, visited the western Indians, by order of congress,
in 1776, he was so beloved for his goodness that the *Lenapes*
gave to him the name of their venerated chief.    Morgan brought
back to the whites such glowing accounts of the qualities of the
ancient chief, that, in the revolutionary war, he was dubbed a
saint, his name was placed on some calendars, and his festival celebrated on the first day of May in every year.    " On
that day a numerous society of votaries walked together in pro-
cession through the streets of Philadelphia, their hats decorated
with bucks' tails, and proceeded to a handsome rural place out
of town which they called a wigwam, where, after a long talk
or Indian speech had been delivered, and the calumet of friendship and peace had been smoked, they spent the day in festivity
and mirth.    After dinner Indian dances were performed, on the
green in front of the wigwam, the calumet was again smoked,
and the company separated."    " After the war," adds Thatcher,
" these meetings were broken up ; but since that time Tam-
many societies have sprung up in Philadelphia and New York,
which have excited no little influence in political circles."

ALLUMMAPEES, or *Sassoonan*, is the first ruling king of the
*Lenapes*, known to the records.    He was the associate, perhaps
the successor of *Tamany*.    In 1718, he headed the deputation
of Indian chieftains at Philadelphia, who signed an absolute
release to the proprietaries for the lands " situate between
Delaware and Susquehanna, from Duck creek to the mountains
on this side Lechay, which lands had been granted by their
ancestors to William Penn."    In 1728, he had removed " from

on Delaware to Shamokin." Conrad Weisser, the Indian interpreter, writes in 1747: "The Delaware Indians last year intended to visit Philadelphia, but were prevented by ALLUM-MAPEES' sickness, who is still alive, but not able to stir. They will come down this year, some time after harvest. ALLUM-MAPEES has no successor in his relations, and he will hear of none so long as he is alive, and none of the Indians care to meddle in the affair. *Shikellimy*[1] advises that the government should name ALLUMMAPEES' successor, and set him up by their authority, that at this critical time there might be a man to apply to, since ALLUMMAPEES has lost his senses and is incapable of doing anything." In 1747, the old chief took part in a treaty with the Moravians concerning the erection of a smithy at their town. In the fall of that year he deceased. Whatever he may have been in his earlier years, he was but little more than an intemperate imbecile at the time of his death. Weisser writes: "ALLUMMAPEES would have resigned his crown before now, but as he had the keeping of the public treasure (that is to say of the council-bag), consisting of belts of wampum, for which he buys liquor, and has been drunk for these two or three years almost constantly, it is thought he won't die so long as there is one single wampum left in the bag."[2]

TADAME was the successor of *Allummapees*. He held the crown until 1756, when he was "treacherously murdered, but by whom or for what cause," says Minor, "we find no record."[3] The probabilities are, however, that as he was active in the hostilities which had then been inaugurated with the English, his death was caused by some wretch of his own tribe for the purpose of obtaining the price which the governor of Pennsylvania had offered for his scalp.

TEEDYUSCUNG, the most distinguished of the modern *Lenape* kings, was the successor of *Tadame*. Major Parsons writes that he was "a lusty, raw-boned man, but haughty and very desirable of respect and command." Reichel, in his *Memorials of the Moravian Church*, adds: "According to his own state-

[1] *Shikellimy* was one of the viceregent Oneida chiefs, residing at Shamokin. He died in 1748.

[2] *Memorials of the Moravian Church*, i, 67.

[3] *History of Wyoming*.

ment, he was born about the year 1700, in New Jersey, east
of Trenton, in which neighborhood his ancestors of the *Unamis*
had been seated from time immemorial. Old Captain Harris,
a noted *Delaware*, was his father. The same was the father
also of Captain John of Nazareth, of young Captain Harris, of
Tom, of Jo, and of Sam Evans, a family of high-spirited sons
who were not in good repute with their white neighbors. The
latter named them, it is true, for men of their own people, and
TEEDYUSCUNG they named Honest John; yet they disliked
and then feared them, for the Harrises were known to grow
moody and resentful, and were heard to speak threatening words
as they saw their paternal acres passing out of their hands, and
their hunting-grounds converted into pasture and plowed fields."
When the Moravians appeared at Bethlehem, TEEDYUSCUNG
came to hear them; soon after professed conversion and was baptized. His conversion, however, was not proof against the
wrongs which his people had suffered, and when the offer of the
crown was made to him he readily accepted it, and became
their leader. At the conferences which he attended, says the
writer last quoted: " TEEDYUSCUNG stood up as the champion
of his people, fearlessly demanding restitution of their lands, or
an equivalent for their irreparable loss, and in addition the free
exercise of the right to select, within the territory in dispute, a
permanent home. The chieftain's imposing presence, his
earnestness of appeal, and his impassioned oratory, as he plead
the cause of the long-injured *Lenape*, evoked the admiration of
his enemies themselves. He always spoke in the euphonious
*Delaware*, employing this Castilian of the new world to utter
the simple and expressive figures and tropes of the native rhetoric with which his harangues were replete, although he was
conversant with the white man's speech. It would almost
appear, from the minutes of these conferences, that the English
artfully attempted to evade the point at issue, and to conciliate
the indignant chieftain by fair speeches and uncertain promises.
The hollowness of the former he boldly exposed, and the latter
he scornfully rejected; so that it was soon perceived that the
Indian king was as astute and sagacious, as he was unmovable
in the justice of his righteous demands. This conviction forced

itself upon his hearers, and then they yielded to the terms he laid down." He was the hero of the war of 1755, for while *Hendrik* boldly demanded the simple distribution of presents, TEEDYUSCUNG wrung the liberties of his people from both his civilized and uncivilized enemies.

In the spring of 1758, TEEDYUSCUNG removed to Wyoming, where, agreeably to his request and the conditions of treaty, a town had been built for him and his followers by the government of Pennsylvania. Here he lived not unmindful of his long cherished object, and here he was burned to death on the night of the 19th of April, 1763, while asleep in his lodge. "The concurrent testimony of his time agrees in representing him as a man of marked ability, a brave warrior, a sagacious counsellor and a patriot among his people. Although he was governed by strong passions, and a slave of that degrading vice which was the bane of his race, he was not devoid of feeling, but susceptible of the gentler influences of our nature. Numerous are the anecdotes extant, illustrating his love of humor, his ready wit, his quickness of apprehension and reply, his keen penetration, and his sarcastic delight in exposing low cunning and artifice." Stone adds: "In regard to the character of TEEDYUSCUNG, the sympathies of Sir William Johnson were with his own people ; yet in his correspondence, while he labored somewhat to detract from the lofty pretensions of the *Delaware* captain, the baronet conceded to him enough of talent, influence, and power among his people, to give him a proud rank among the chieftains of his race. Certain it is, that TEEDYUSCUNG did much to restore his nation to the rank of MEN."

NETAWATWEES, the successor of *Teedyuscung*, is spoken of in the highest terms by Loskiel and Heckewelder. Loskiel says: "This wise man spared no pains to conciliate the affection of all his neighbors. He sent frequent embassies to his grandchildren, admonishing them to keep the peace, and proved in truth a wise grandfather to them. He used to lay all affairs of state before his counsellors for their consideration, without telling them his own sentiments. When they gave him their opinion, he either approved of it, or stated his objections and amendments, always stating the reasons of his disapprobation.

Thus he kept them active, and maintained great respect. When the war of the revolution came on he did every thing in his power to preserve peace among the Indian nations. He, however, received a message from the *Hurons*, "that the *Delawares* should keep their shoes in readiness, to join the warriors." This message he would not accept, but sent several to the *Hurons* admonishing them to sit still, and to remember the misery they had brought upon themselves by taking share in the late war between the English and the French. These belts were carried to the chiefs of the *Hurons* in Fort Detroit, but as it was necessary to deliver them in the presence of the English governor, the latter, "to fulfill his duty, cut them in pieces, cast them at the deputies' feet, and commanded them to depart." He died at Pittsburg in 1776. Loskiel adds: "Ever since his sentiments changed in favor of the Gospel, he was a faithful friend of the brethren, and being one of the most experienced chiefs of his time, his council proved often very serviceable to the mission. The wish he uttered as his last will and testament, that the *Delaware* nation might hear and believe the word of God, preached by the brethren, was frequently repeated in the council by his successors, and then they renewed their covenant to use their utmost exertions to fulfill this last wish of their old, worthy and honored chief. Upon such an occasion Captain White Eyes, holding the Bible and some spelling books in his hands, addressed the council with great emotion and even with tears. My friends, said he, you have now heard the last will and testament of our departed chief. I will therefore gather together my young men and their children, and kneeling down before that God who created them, will pray unto him, that he may have mercy upon us and reveal his will unto us. And as we cannot declare it to those who are yet unborn, we will pray unto the Lord our God, to make it known to our children, and children's children." Heckewelder says: "All the surrounding nations appeared to have been sensible of his worth. While living, he often encouraged his people to adopt the way of living by agriculture, and finally become civilized. His ideas were, that unless the Indians changed their mode of living they would in time dwindle to nothing."

Captain WHITE EYES, or *Coquehageahton*, distinguished for his friendship for the Americans in the early stages of the revolution, was the successor of *Netawatwees*, but held the government only two years. On his death, in 1778, a regency took the direction during the minority of the lineal heir to the throne. On the death of the latter, in 1781, GELELEMAND, alias Killbuck, became king by election.

One of the earliest chiefs of the *Shawanoes*, of whom record has been preserved, was PAXINOS or *Paxinosa*, who came to the Minnisink country in 1692, and who appears, in the records of New York, as chief of the Minnisinks. He subsequently fell back with his people to the Delaware country, and next appears in the difficulties which grew out of the removal of the *Lenapes* to Wyoming. With a desire to strengthen themselves at the latter place, *Teedyuscung* and PAXINOS visited the "believing Indians" at Gnadenhütten, in 1752, and desired them to remove to the lands which they had selected, repeating as the order of the Six Nations : "They (the *Iroquois*) rejoice that some of the believing Indians have removed to Wyoming ; but now they lift up the remaining *Mahicans* and *Delawares* and settle them down in Wyoming, for there a fire is kindled for them, and there they may plant and think on God." About eighty of the converts accompanied the parties to Wyoming, but the remainder refused to do so, under the advice of the missionaries. In the spring of 1754, PAXINOS again appeared in the settlement, accompanied by twenty-three warriors and three *Iroquois* embassadors, and added to the order already quoted, that if the invitation was not heeded, "the great head (the *Iroquois*) would come down and clean their ears with a red-hot poker." Says Loskiel : "PAXINOS then turned to the missionaries, earnestly demanding of them not to hinder the Indians from removing to Wajomick, for that the road was free, therefore they might visit their friends there, stay with them till they were tired, and then return to their own country." On the 11th of February, 1755, PAXINOS "demanded an answer to the message he had brought last year," and was told that "the brethren would confer with the Iroquois themselves, concerning the intended removal of the Indians at Gnadenhütten to Wajomick." Loskiel adds : " PAXINOS, being only an embassador in this business, was satisfied, and even formed a closer acquaintance with the brethren.  His wife, who heard the gospel preached daily, was so overcome by its divine power, that she began to see her lost estate by nature, and earnestly begged for baptism.  Her husband, having lived thirty-eight years with her in marriage, to mutual satisfaction, willingly gave his consent, prolonged his stay at Bethlehem, was present in the chapel, and deeply affected when his wife was baptized by Bishop Spangenberg." The Indians did not remove, and, soon after PAXINOS' last visit, the Moravian settlement near Shamokin was attacked, and fourteen persons killed.  On the 24th of November, Shamokin shared the same fate.  Several persons were killed, and eleven belonging to the mission were burned alive ; and, on New Year's day the work of destruction was completed.  What connection PAXINOS had with these hostilities does not appear, but it is said that he sent his two sons to rescue brother Kiefer, if he should be in the hands of the enemy, and that that missionary was conducted by them to Gnadenhütten, showing that he must have been aware that the attack was contemplated.  He was present at the treaty with Johnson in 1756, and at Easton with *Teedyuscung* in 1757, on which latter occasion he was addressed by Governor Denny as " our hearty friend and a lover of peace."  Reichel says he removed with his family to the Ohio country in 1758, and that he was the last *Shawanoe* king east of the Alleghanies.  At the time of his removal he was an old man, and was doubtless soon after gathered to his fathers.  His son *Kolapeka* or *Teatapercaum*, alias Samuel, was a distinguished chief in the war of 1764.

Although perhaps not strictly a part of the history of the Indians of Hudson's river, the connection of the *Shawanoes* with the *Minsis* will permit the introduction of one or two of their more prominent chiefs.  BENEVISSICA represented them in the treaty at Fort Stanwix in 1764, and again in 1765.  In 1774, it is said that a belt was sent to NERERAHHE, a *Shawanoe*, " but he being a sachem, sent it to the chief warrior of his nation, SOWANOWANE."  Although it does not positively appear, there is some ground for the presumption that the latter was

none other than the famous CORNSTALK, who stood at the head
of the western confederacy in that year, and who held the command in the engagement with the forces under Dunmore and
Lewis at Point Pleasant. He was a man of more than ordinary
nerve and power, as well as one of the most eloquent of his
race. Says Stone: " Col. Wilson who was present at the
interview between the chief and Lord Dunmore, thus speaks of
the chieftain's bearing on the occasion : ' When he arose, he
was in no wise confused or daunted, but spoke in a distinct and
audible voice, without stammering or repetition, and with peculiar emphasis. His looks, while addressing Dunmore, were
truly grand and majestic, yet graceful and. attractive. I have
heard the first orators in Virginia, Patrick Henry and Richard
Henry Lee ; but never have I heard one whose powers of delivery surpassed those of CORNSTALK.' " After his treaty with
Dunmore he became a friend to the English, and to that friendship gave up his life. Learning that his people were determined
to make war upon the English, he visited the latter in 1777, at
the fort which they had erected at Point Pleasant to take advice.
The commandant of the fort detained him as a hostage, and
while thus detained he was joined by his son *Ellinipsico.*
Soon after the arrival of the latter, a white man named Gilmore
was killed near the fort. The cry of revenge was raised, and
a party of ruffians assembled, under the command of Capt.
Hall, who, instead of pursuing the guilty, fell upon the hostages
in the fort. Seeing that there was no escape for him, the old
chief addressed his son : " My son, the Great Spirit has seen fit
that we should die together, and has sent you to that end. It
is his will, and let us submit." CORNSTALK fell, perforated
with seven bullets, and died without a struggle, while his son
met his fate with composure and was shot on the seat upon
which he was sitting. " Thus," says Withers in his *Indian
Chronicles*, " perished the mighty CORNSTALK, sachem of the
*Shawanoes*, and king of the northern confederacy in 1774, a
chief remarkable for many great and good qualities. He was
disposed to be at all times the friend of the white man, as he
was ever the advocate of honorable peace. But when his
country's wrongs summoned him to battle, he became the

39

thunderbolt of war, and made his enemies feel the weight of his arm. His noble bearing, his generous and disinterested attachment to the colonies, his anxiety to preserve the frontier of Virginia from desolation and death, all conspired to win for him the esteem and respect of others ; while the untimely and perfidious manner of his death caused a deep and lasting feeling of regret to pervade the bosoms, even of those who were enemies to his nation, and excited the just indignation of all towards his inhuman murderers."

The most distinguished chief of the *Shawanoes*, of more modern times, was TECUMSEH, who, as Parton justly writes, "though not the faultless ideal of a patriot prince that romantic story represents him, was all of a patriot, a hero, a man, that an Indian can be." He was a cross-breed, the son of a *Shawanoe* by a *Creek* woman, and at a very early age gave evidence of superior abilities in the wars which were terminated by the treaty of 1794. Thoroughly indoctrinated in the policy of his people, and a willing student of the schools which demanded a line beyond which the whites should not advance to the hunting grounds of the west, the sale of the lands of his tribe on the Wabash, soon after Mr. Jefferson came into power, gave him great offense. About this time *Hendrik*, of the *Mahicans*, conceived the plan of uniting the tribes of the west for the better protection of their interests. TECUMSEH seized the idea quickly and perverted its purpose to the accomplishment of an organization which should have for its object the entire destruction of the whites, after the plan of his great prototype, King *Philip*. From tribe to tribe he passed, declaring : "The Great Spirit gave this great island to his red children ; he placed the whites on the other side of the big water ; they were not contented with their own, but came to take ours from us. They have driven us from the sea to the lakes ; we can go no further. They have taken upon them to say this land belongs to the *Miamis*, this to the *Delawares*, and so on ; but the Great Spirit intended it as the common property of us all." For four years he was engaged in the work of preparing the tribes for a general war. A silent man in the ordinary circumstances of life, he could employ more than the eloquence of Logan, and when descanting upon the Indian's wrongs, and the white man's encroachments.  General Harrison, who was long his patient and forbearing adviser, and then his conqueror, speaks of him as " one of those uncommon geniuses which spring up occasionally to produce revolutions, and overturn the established order of things.  If 'it were not for the vicinity of the United States, he would, perhaps, be the founder of an empire, that would rival in glory Mexico or Peru.  No difficulties deter him.  For four years he has been in constant motion.  You see him to-day on the Wabash, and in a short time hear of him on the shores of Lake Erie or Michigan, or on the banks of the Mississippi ; and wherever he goes he makes an impression favorable to his purposes."  Failing to accomplish his purpose, he accepted the overtures of the British and brought to their aid, in the war of 1812, two thousand warriors — an alliance more powerful than that which that government had ever been able to command even in the palmiest days of the Five Nations.  On the banks of the Thames, on the 5th of October, in an engagement which will forever occupy a prominent place in American history from its association with his fate, he gave up his life in endeavoring to promote the cause of those in whose selfish purposes he had no interest, but in whom he found what he believed to be the avengers of the wrongs of his people.  He is described as a person of erect, athletic frame, of noble, commanding appearance, and the air of a king.  When he arose before his savage audiences, his imposing manner created a feeling of awe; but when he kindled with his great subject, he seemed like one inspired.  His eye flashed fire, his swarthy bosom heaved and swelled with imprisoned passion, his whole frame dilated with excitement, and his strong untutored soul poured itself forth in eloquence, wild, headlong, and resistless.  When not addressing his clans, he was cold and haughty.  " His withering sarcasm," says Headley, " when Proctor proposed to retreat from Walden ; his reply to the interpreter, who, offering him a chair in the presence of Harrison, said, ' Your father wishes you to be seated,'—' My Father ! the sun is my father, and the earth my mother ; I will rest on her bosom '— reveal a nature conscious of its greatness."  And Parton adds : " If to conceive a grand, difficult, and unselfish project, to labor for years with enthusiasm and prudence in attempting its execution ; to enlist in it by the magnetism of personal influence great multitudes of various tribes ; to contend for it with unfaltering valor longer than there was hope of success ; and to die fighting for it to the last, falling toward the enemy covered with wounds, is to give proof of an heroic cast of character, then is the *Sha- wanoe* chief TECUMSEH, in whose veins flowed no blood that was not Indian, entitled to rank among heroes." [1]

The Six Nations were not without their great men, of whom King HENDRIK, or *Soi-en-ga-rah-ta,* who stood for so many years at the head of the *Mohawks,* was one. It is said that he was born in 1680, and that he was one of the chiefs who visited England in 1710.[2] His father was a *Mahican* chief, called by his people The Wolf, who, either by captivity and adoption became a member of the *Mohawk* family, or was attracted thither by the fair charmer who became his wife, herself the daughter of a king. In the right of his mother, HENDRIK became king. When about twenty years of age, and for half a century or more subsequently, he represented his people in council and in camp, coming down to the present time as a model of Indian courage and the embodiment of Indian eloquence. His greatest service to the English appears to have been performed in the battle under Johnson, at Lake George, in 1755, where he lost his life, and his greatest speech that which he delivered before the conference at Albany in 1754. That the reader may judge of its merits, without the trouble of reference, its most important parts are copied :

" Brethren : We return you all our grateful acknowledgments for renewing and brightening the covenant chain. This chain belt is of very great importance to our united nations, and all our allies ; we will therefore take it to Onondaga, where our council-fire always burns, and keep it so securely that neither thunder nor lightning shall break it ; there we will consult over

---

[1] *Parton's Life of Jackson ; Headley's Second War with England ; Drake's Life of Tecumseh ; Montgomery's Life of Harrison.*

[2] The statement of Governor Hunter ( *Colonial History,* v, 358), leaves no room to doubt that Hendrik was one of the chiefs named as parties to this expedition.

it, and as we have lately added two links to it, so we will endeavor to add as many more links to it as lies in our power; and we hope when we show you this belt again, we shall give you reason to rejoice at it, by your seeing the vacancies in it filled up. In the meantime we desire that you will strengthen yourselves, and bring as many into this covenant chain as you possibly can.

"We do now solemnly renew and brighten the covenant chain with our brethren here present, and all our other absent brethren on the continent.

"Brethren: As to the accounts you have heard of our living dispersed from each other, 'tis very true. We have several times endeavored to draw off those of our brethren who are settled at Oswegatchie but in vain, for the governor of Canada is like a wicked deluding spirit; however, as you desire we shall persist in our endeavors.

"You have asked us the reason of our living in this dispersed manner. The reason is, your neglecting us for these three years past. You have thus (taking a stick and throwing it behind his back), thrown us behind your back, and disregarded us, whereas the French are a subtle and vigilant people, ever using their utmost endeavors to bring our people over to them.

"Brethren: It is very true as you told us that the clouds hang heavy over us, and 'tis not very pleasant to look up, but we give you this belt to clear away all clouds, that we may all live in bright sunshine, and keep together in strict union and friendship; then we shall become strong and nothing can hurt us.

"Brethren: This is the ancient place of treaty, where the fire of friendship always used to burn, and 'tis now three years since we have been called to any public treaty here. 'Tis true there are commissioners here, but they have never invited us to smoke with them; but the Indians of Canada come frequently and smoke here, which is for the sake of their beaver; but we hate them. 'Tis your fault, brethren, that we are not strengthened by conquest, for we would have gone and taken Crown point, but you hindered us; we had concluded to go and take it, but we were told it was too late, and that the ice would not bear us; instead of this, you burnt your own fort at Saratoga and run away from it, which was a shame and a scandal to you. Look about your country and see; you have no fortifications about you, no, not even to this city; 'tis but one step from Canada hither, and the French may easily come and turn you out of your doors.

" Brethren : You desire us to speak from the bottom of our hearts, and we shall do it. Look about you and see all these houses full of beaver, and the money is all gone to Canada, likewise powder, lead and guns, which the French now make use of at Ohio.

" Brethren : The goods which go from hence to Oswego, go from thence to Ohio, which further enables the French to carry on their designs at the Ohio.

" Brethren : You were desirous that we should open our minds, and our hearts to you; look at the French, they are men, they are fortifying everywhere; but, we are ashamed to say it, you are all, like women, bare and open without any fortifications."

At the same conference, in subsequent session, he spoke as follows :

" Brethren : There is an affair about which our hearts tremble and our minds are deeply concerned; this is the selling of rum in our castles. It destroys many, both of our old and young people. We request of all the governments here present, that it may be forbidden to carry any of it amongst the Five Nations.

" Brethren : We are in great fears about this rum; it may cause murder on both sides. We don't want it to be forbid to be sold to us at Albany, but that none may be brought to our castles. The *Cayugas* now declare in their own name, that they will not allow any rum to be brought up their river, and those who do so must take the consequences.

" Brethren : We, the *Mohawks* of both castles, have also one request to make, which is, that the people who are settled round about us, may not be suffered to sell our people rum; it keeps them all poor, makes them idle and wicked; if they have any money or goods they lay it all out in rum; it destroys virtue and the progress of religion amongst us. We have a friendly request to make to the governor and all the commissioners here present, that they will help us to build a church at Canajoharie, and that we may have a bell in it, which, together with the putting a stop to the selling of rum, will tend to make us religious and lead better lives than we now do."

Comparisons, it is said, are odious; in this case they are not necessary in order to strip from history the high coloring which has been given to the eloquence of HENDRIK. Nor can it with truth be added that Aupaumut "for capacity, bravery and vigor of mind, and immovable integrity united, he excelled all the aboriginal inhabitants of whom we have any knowledge." Concede to him all that even charity demands for his race, he yet failed to rise to the greatness of *Massasoit, Uncas, Philip, Teedyuscung, Aupaumut, Pontiac,* or *Tecumseh.* He was less eloquent than *Logan* the *Oneida,* than *Aupaumut* the *Mahican,* than *Cornplanter* or *Red Jacket* of the *Senecas;* his bravery and his integrity were alike tarnished by his selfishness. That he was a great man among his people, " esteemed the bravest of the brave, among the *Iroquois,*" is true. The concurrent testimony of every traditionist awards to him great natural talents, judgment and sagacity. His death was heroic; his life, a criticism on the debasing influences of civilization upon his race.

THAYENDANEGA, or *Joseph Brant,* who is regarded as the successor of King *Hendrik,*[1] is said to have been the son of a *Mohawk* woman by a chief of the *Onondagas,* although there have been those who have regarded him as one of the illegitimate children of Sir William Johnson. He was born, says Stone, in the Ohio country, in 1742, where his father and mother were

[1] Speaking of the succession of kings, Schoolcraft remarks : " The son of the chief's oldest sister was the chief presumptive. Such was the Iroquois rule when King Hendrik fell at the battle of Lake George; he had a son of mature age, who made use of the memorable expression, on hearing his father's death, " No, he is not dead, but lives here," striking his breast. Yet he did not succeed his father in the Mohawk chieftaincy. It fell to his sister's son, Little Abraham, a mild and politic chief, who died at the era of the opening of the American revolution. On this, there was a vacancy which was supplied by the election of Joseph Brant, an entirely new man in the line of chiefs. It was the wise policy of Sir Wm. Johnson and his son, to lay the greatest stress on his tribal authority, and to strengthen it by every means, as the best and most direct way of exercising an influence over the tribes." (*Hist. Indian Tribes,* part IV, 481). In *Colonial History,* VIII, 53, Abraham is said to have been the great Hendrik's brother, not a son of the sister of that chief, as stated by Schoolcraft. But he was not the less the legitimate successor to the throne.

then temporarily residing, and where his father soon after died. His mother, on her return to Canajoharie, married an Indian called Carrihogo, or News Carrier, whose Christian name was Barnet or Bernard, which was subsequently contracted into Brant, by which name his step-son was also known, being first called Brant's Joseph, and subsequently, by inversion, Joseph Brant. His position as chief was mainly due to his associations with the Johnsons. His sister, Mary or Molly, was the concubine of Sir William, and as her brother was perhaps necessarily much in her company, Johnson sent him to Dr. Wheelock's school, and subsequently employed him as his secretary as an agent in public affairs. Throughout the revolution he was engaged in warfare chiefly upon the border settlements of New York and Pennsylvania, in connection with the Johnsons and Butlers. After the war he devoted himself to the social and religious improvement of the *Mohawks*, who were settled upon the Ouise or Grand river, in Upper Canada, upon lands granted to them by the governor of that province. He translated the Gospel of St. Mark into the *Mohawk* language ; and in many ways his exertions for the spiritual and temporal welfare of his people were eminently successful, and endeared him to his nation. He was far from being a great or an able chief, many of his contemporaries being his peers in courage and in native ability. His education and his association with the Johnsons gave him in prominence what he lacked in distinctive merit. He died at his residence at the head of Lake Ontario, November 24th, 1807, aged 65 years. One of his sons (John) was an officer in the British service, on the Niagara frontier in the war of 1812. (*Lossing*, 1, 257). Schoolcraft repudiates the claim set up by Stone that Brant was made the war chieftain of the confederacy. He asserts that no such office existed, and that Brant was simply a chief of the third and lowest class. (*Notes on the Iroquois*, 496). The authority which he exercised was undoubtedly by virtue of his commission from the British government. At no time was his course approved by the united voice of the confederacy in council at Onondaga.

LOGAN, who was regarded by Jefferson as the most eloquent of all the aborigines, " was the son of *Shikellimy*, alias *Swatane*, an *Oneida* chief of the *Oquacho* or Wolf tribe of Indians, who was in 1728, acting representative of the Five Nations, in business affairs with the proprietary government, and who was appointed their vicegerent, and in this capacity administered their tributaries within the province of Pennsylvania, with Shamokin for his seat.[1] His father was one of the earliest to encourage the introduction of Christianity by the Moravians. He was a great friend of the celebrated James Logan, who accompanied Penn on his last voyage to America, and who subsequently became distinguished in the colony for his learning and benevolence. Hence the name of his son. LOGAN married a *Shawanoe* woman and removed from his father's lodge to the Ohio country where he became a chief, and, from the fact of his intermarriage with the *Shawanoes*, a *Mingoe*. He was a friend of the white men, by education and association, and one of the noblest of his race, not only by right of birth, but in consideration of his own character. During the Indian wars connected with the contest with France, he took no part save in the character of a peace-maker. In the spring of 1774, a company of land agents and traders on the Ohio came in collision with the Indians, and in retaliation for the loss of two of their men, succeeded in killing LOGAN's entire family, including his youngest brother and his sister. For this and similar acts, LOGAN placed himself at the head of a band of Ohio *Senecas*, and, in company with the *Lenapes* and *Shawanoes* under *Cornstalk*, invaded the Virginia border with fire and tomahawk. At the treaty of peace with Dunmore, LOGAN was not present. On being visited for the purpose of securing his assent to the terms, he delivered the famous speech which Jefferson has preserved in his *Notes on Virginia*, and which has become familiar wherever the English language is spoken : " I appeal to any white man to say if he ever entered LOGAN's cabin hungry, and he gave him not meat ; if ever he came cold and naked and he clothed him not. During the course of the last long and bloody war, Logan remained idle in his cabin, an advocate for peace.

---

[1] *Memorials Moravian Church*, I, 83. *Shikellimy* is called a Cayuga chief, by some writers, and his son a Mingoe, but the testimony of Reichel seems clear that both were full-blooded Oneidas. *Shikellimy* had three sons, *John*, *James Logan*, and *John Petty*. He died in 1749.— *Loskiel*, II, 119.

Such was my love for the whites, that my countrymen pointed, as they passed, and said, ' Logan is the friend of the white men.' I had even thought to live with you, but for the injuries of one man.   Colonel Cresap, the last spring, in cold blood and unprovoked, murdered all the relations of Logan, not even sparing my women and children.   There runs not a drop of my blood in the veins of any living creature.   This called on me for revenge.   I have sought it ; I have killed many ; I have fully glutted my vengeance.   For my country, I rejoice at the beams of peace ; but do not harbor a thought that mine is the joy of fear.   Logan never felt fear.   He will not turn on his heel to save his live.   Who is there to mourn for Logan ?   Not one." Soon after the treaty at which this speech was delivered, LOGAN became intemperate, and on his return from one of his visits to Detroit was murdered in the woods.

Among the distinguished men of the Five Nations at an earlier period was GARANGULA, who was called "the pride of the *Onondaga* tribe," and whose speech in reply to M. de la Barre, the governor of Canada, in 1684, is quoted by Thatcher and Drake.   At the time of its delivery he was an old man, and disappears from history soon after.   A man of more activity was the warrior called by the English, BLACK KETTLE.   Colden speaks of him as a "famous hero ; " but few of his exploits have come down to the present time.   "It is only known," says Thatcher, "that he commanded large parties of his countrymen, who were exceedingly troublesome to the French.   In 1691, he made an irruption into the country around Montreal, at the head of several hundred men.   "He overran Canada (say the French annalists), as a torrent does the low lands, when it overflows its banks, and there is no withstanding it.   The troops of the stations received orders to stand upon the defensive ; and it was not until the enemy were returning home victorious, after having desolated the French possessions, that a force of four hundred soldiers was mustered to pursue them.   BLACK KETTLE is said to have had but half that number with him at this juncture, but he gave battle and fought desperately.   After losing twenty men slain, with some prisoners, he broke through the French ranks and escaped, leaving a considerable number of his

enemies wounded and killed." The story is no doubt exagge-
rated, but the courage and daring of the famous chief is well attested.
At a later period the names of SKENANDO, CORNPLANTER and
RED JACKET are prominent in Indian annals. The former
was of the *Oneidas*, and the author of this famous reply: " I am
an aged hemlock; the winds of an hundred winters have
whistled through my branches; I am dead at the top. The
generation to which I belonged has run away and left me."
He was one of the converts to the missionary, Kirkland; was
a warm friend of the Americans during the revolution, and died
in 1816, at the age of one hundred and ten years. CORN-
PLANTER was a *Seneca* half-breed, his father being a Dutch
trader. RED JACKET was a full-blooded *Seneca*. Both were
distinguished for their eloquence, and both were engaged in the
border wars of the revolution as inveterate enemies of the colonists. The former died in 1836, at the age of one hundred
and one years, and the latter in 1830, aged about ninety years.

PASSACONNAWAY, who was at the head of the *Pennacooks*
at the time of the discovery, was one of the most distinguished
men of the Indian nations. "His name," says Schoolcraft,
" is indicative of his warlike character —*Papisseconewa*, as written by himself, meaning The Child of the Bear." We first
hear of him in 1627 or 8. Thomas Morton, in his *New English Canaan*, thus speaks of him, being in this country at that
time : " That Sachem or Sagamore is a Powah of great estima-
tion amongst all kind of salvages, there hee is at their Revels
(which is the time when a greate company of salvages meete
from several parts of the country, in amity with their neighbors),
hath advanced his honor in his feats or jugling tricks (as I may
right tearmc them), to the admiration of the spectators, whom
hee endeavored to perswade that hee would goe under water to
the further side of a river to broade for any man to undertake
with a breath, which thing hee performed by swiming over and
deluding the company with casting a mist before their eyes that
see him enter in and come out ; but no part of the way he has
bin seene; likewise by our English in the heat of all summer,
to make ice appear in a bowle of faire water, first having the
water set before him, hee hath begunne his incantation accord-

ing to their usual custom, and before the same hath bin ended, a thick cloude has darkened the aire, on a sodane a thunder clap hath bin heard that has amazed the natives; in an instant hee hath showed a firme peece of ice to flote in the middest of the bowle in the presence of the vulgar people, which doubtless was done by the agility of Satan his consort."

But he was something more than a juggler; his ability as a warrior and as a ruler is acknowledged. Gookin wrote of him in 1675: "He lived to a very great age, as I saw him alive at Pawtucket when he was about one hundred and twenty years old." Schoolcraft argues that the time when Gookin saw him was in 1648, and hence that he was one hundred years old when the English first purchased land from him. He was converted by Eliot in 1648, and continued a professing Christian until the time of his death. In 1660, when about one hundred and thirty years old, he called his tribe around him and delivered his farewell speech. "The occasion," says Schoolcraft, "filled all with sorrow, in spite of Indian stoicism. PASSACONNAWAY was deeply affected, and his voice, tremulous with age and emotion, still was musical and powerful — a splendid remnant of that whose power and beauty, in the fullness and vigor of manhood, had soothed or excited the passions of assembled savages, and moulded them to suit the purposes of the speaker.

"Hearken," said he, "to the words of your father. I am an old oak, that has withstood the storms of more than an hundred winters. Leaves and branches have been stripped from me by the winds and frosts — my eyes are dim — my limbs totter — I must soon fall! But when young and sturdy, when no young man of the *Pennacooks* could bend my bow — when my arrows would pierce a deer at an hundred yards, and I could bury my hatchet in a sapling to the eye — no weekwam had so many furs, no poll so many scalp-locks as Passaconaway's! Then, I delighted in war. The whoop of the *Pennacook* was heard upon the Mohawk — and no voice so loud as Passaconaway's. The scalps upon the pole of my weekwam told the story of *Mohawk* suffering.

"The English came, they seized our lands; I sat me down at Pennacook. They followed upon my footsteps; I made war upon them, but they fought with fire and thunder; my young men were swept down before me when no one was near them.  I tried sorcery against them, but still they increased and prevailed over me and mine, and I gave place to them, and retired to my beautiful island of Natticook.  I, that can make the dry leaf turn green and live again; I, that can take the rattlesnake in my palm as I would a worm, without harm; I, who had communion with the Great Spirit, dreaming and awaking; I am powerless before the pale faces.  The oak will soon break before the whirlwind, it shivers and shakes even now; soon its trunk will be prostrate, the ant and the worm will sport upon it.  Then think, my children, of what I say; I commune with the Great Spirit.  He whispers me now.  'Tell your people, peace, peace is the only hope of your race.  I have given fire and thunder to the pale faces for weapons; I have made them plentier than the leaves of the forest, and still they shall increase! These meadows they shall turn with the plough, these forests shall fall by the axe, the pale faces shall live upon your hunting-grounds, and make their villages upon your fishing places.'  The Great Spirit says this, and it must be so.  We are few and powerless before them.  We must bend before the storm. The wind blows hard!  The old oak trembles!  Its branches are gone!  Its sap is frozen!  It bends!  It falls!  Peace, peace with the white man is the command of the Great Spirit, and the wish — the last wish of Passaconnaway."

The old chief did not die at that time, but his activity was so impaired that he abdicated his throne to his son *Wannalancet*. He died between 1663 and 1669 — the oldest, most learned, and most eloquent of his race.

Soquans and Minichque appear as representatives of the *Mahicans* on the Hudson in 1700.  The first was a speaker of more than ordinary merit, as his public addresses attest. Minichque is called the "great sachem" of his people, and great he certainly was in forgiving, upon his death-bed, his murderers, and praying that they might be spared the punishment due for the offense which they had committed.  There is a moral grandeur in this, the crowning act of his life, which appeals to every reasonable mind.  It is to be regretted that so little is known of his history.  There is no doubt he was one of the leaders of the *Mahicans* at the time the *Mohawks* appealed to the governor of Canada, to protect them against his nation,¹ and that he subsequently became firmly attached to the English government.  He was an intemperate man, but in this was no exception to his race ; he was beloved by his people for his greatness as a savage ; his dying wish associates with his memory one of the " attributes of the gods."

The " oldest man " among the *Mahicans,* when the New England missionaries first visited them, was Captain JOHN KONAPOT.  He was one of the signers to the deed to Parsons and his associates in 1724, and subsequently became an influential member of the mission church at Stockbridge.  Hopkins says of him : " KONAPOT, the principal man among the *Muhhe-kanok* of Massachusetts, was strictly temperate, very just and upright in his dealings, a man of prudence and industry, and inclined to embrace the Christian religion ; " and Sergeant adds : " He is an excellent man, and I do believe has the true spirit of Christianity in him."  He had from Gov. Belcher a commission as captain, and served his people and the Massachusetts government well and faithfully.  His son, JOHN KONAPOT, Jr., is said to have been the grandson of old King *Hendrik* of the *Mohawks.*  The date of his death is not given, but it probably occurred about 1750.

The most distinguished man of the *Mahicans* was Captain HENDRIK AUPAUMUT, subsequently known as Captain HENDRIK, who appears to have sustained the most important relation to his tribe and to the nation for nearly half a century.²  Of his birth and parentage nothing is known.  He is first

¹ *Brodhead,* II, 161.

² In 1771, Benjamin Kok-ke-we-nau-naut, called King Benjamin, being 94 years of age, resigned his office of sachem, and requested his people to elect a successor.  Solomon Un-haun-nau-waun-nutt was chosen.  He was acting in that capacity at the outbreak of the revolution and was addressed by the Massachusetts Convention. He died in February, 1777, while Benjamin lived until 1781, dying at the advanced age of 104 years.  After the death of King Solomon, the government, it is said, devolved upon Joseph Quan-au-kaunt (pronounced, by the English at least, Quinney-hong, and now generally spelled Quinney), who divided his power more equally with his counsellors — Peter Poh-quon-nop-peet (pronounced Ponkne-peet), Captain Hendrik Aupaumut and Captain John Konapot, Jr.  The wife of Captain Hendrik and the wife of King Solomon, were the sisters of King Joseph.—*Stockbridge, Past and Present.*

introduced as the speaker in the conference with the *Mohawk* embassadors during the war of 1746. At the conference in Albany, in 1754, he represented his tribe, and in response to the governor, delivered the following address:

"Fathers: We are greatly rejoiced to see you all here. It is by the will of Heaven that we are met here, and we thank you for this opportunity of seeing you altogether, as it is a long time since we have had such an one.

"Fathers: Who sit present here, we will just give you a short relation of the long friendship which hath subsisted between the white people of this country and us. Our forefathers had a castle on this river. As one of them walked out he saw something on the river, but was at a loss to know what it was. He took it at first for a great fish. He ran into the castle and gave notice to the other Indians. Two of our forefathers went to see what it was, and found it a vessel with men in it. They immediately joined hands with the people in the vessel and became friends. The white people told them they should not come any further up the river at that time, and said to them they would return back whence they came and come again in a year's time. According to their promise they returned back in a year's time, and came as far up the river as where the old fort stood. Our forefathers invited them on shore and said to them, here we will give you a place to make you a town; it shall be from this place to such a stream, and from the river back up to the hill. Our forefathers told them, though they were now a small people they would in time multiply and fill up the land they had given to them. After they went ashore some time, some other Indians who had not seen them before, looked fiercely at them, and our forefathers observing it, and seeing the white people so few in number, lest they should be destroyed, took and sheltered them under their arms. But it turned out that those Indians did not desire to destroy them, but wished also to have the white people for their friends. At this time, which we have now spoken of, the white people were small, but we were very numerous and strong. We defended them in that low state, but now the case is altered. You are numerous and strong; we are few and weak; therefore we expect you to act by us in these circumstances as we did by you in those we have just now related.   We view you now as a very large tree which has taken deep root in the ground ; whose branches are spread very wide.   We stand by the body of this tree and we look around to see if there be any who endeavor to hurt it, and if it should so happen that any are powerful enough to destroy it, we are ready to fall with it.

" Fathers : You see how early we made friendship with you. We tied each other in a very strong chain.   That chain has not yet been broken.   We now clean and rub that chain to make it brighter and stronger, and we determine on our part that it shall never be broken, and we hope you will take care that neither you nor any one else shall break it.   And we are greatly rejoiced that peace and friendship have so long subsisted between us.

" Fathers : Don't think strange at what we are about to say. We would say something respecting our lands.   When the white people purchased from time to time of us, they said they only wanted to purchase the low lands ; they told us the hilly land was good for nothing, and that it was full of wood and stones ; but now we see people living all about the hills and woods, although they have not purchased the lands.   When we inquire of the people who live on these lands what right they have to them, they reply to us, that we are not to be regarded, and that these lands belong to the king ; but we were the first possessors of them, and when the king has paid us for them, then they may say they are his.   Hunting now has grown very scarce, and we are not like to get our living that way.   Therefore we hope our fathers will take care that we are paid for our lands that we may live." [1]

In the war which followed, HENDRIK served the English faithfully, and returned to his people with honor.   In 1774, he represented his tribe at the Albany conference held by the commissioners of the Continental Congress, and there delivered one of the most eloquent speeches in the English language. " Depend upon," said he, " we are true to you, and mean to join you. Wherever you go, we will be by your sides.   Our bones shall

[1] *Colonial History*, VI, 881.

lie with yours. We are determined never to be at peace with the red coats, while they are at variance with you. We have one favor to beg: we should be glad if you would help us to establish a minister among us, that when our men are gone to war, our women and children may have the advantage of being instructed by them. If we are conquered, our lands go with yours; but if you are victorious, we hope you will help us to recover our just rights." And in this spirit himself and his people fought to make a free nation for white men.

Welcoming the missionaries among his people, HENDRIK impressed upon them a recognition of his worth even while refusing to unite with them, and in all his intercourse with them and with the authorities, won, by his demeanor and his integrity, the tribute due to royalty. Says his biographer: "He was often employed as an interpreter, and in this capacity his strong memory, his clear, lucid manner, and his mind-illumed face, as he conveyed the thoughts of a preacher to his people, are highly praised. His public speeches are spoken of as always remarkable for perspicuity and sound sense. 'I have,' says our informant, 'seen many Indian chiefs, but never his equal;'" testimony which is the more valuable, coming as it does from one who had no personal ends to serve by magnifying the consequence of the people among whom he labored, and who at one time had "the Great Hendrik" of the *Mohawks* among his pupils.

After the war of the revolution HENDRIK was frequently employed by the government on missions to the western Indians, and was an important agent in the negotiations with them. In 1810, says his biographer, Captain HENDRIK [1] was on the

---

[1] Captain Hendrik was employed in this capacity at the suggestion of the Rev. Mr. Kirkland, who wrote to General Knox, then secretary of war (April 22, 1791), as follows: "As I deprecate an Indian war from every principle of humanity and policy, permit me, sir, to suggest the idea of sending Captain Hendrik, one of the chiefs of the Stockbridge tribe to the westward. This tribe had formerly more influence with the Miamies, Shawanoes, Delawares and Chippewas, than all the Six Nations. Captain Hendrik is well acquainted with their customs and manners, and has since the war received several invitations to make them a visit. As you are in a measure a stranger to Captain Hendrik, allow me to say, from long personal acquaintance with him, that he is very little inferior to Cornplanter, who himself has a high esteem for the Stockbridge chief."— *Sparks' Life of Kirkland.*

White river, with his son Abner, and designed to have settled on the land given the *Mahicans* by the *Miamis.* Here he formed the plan of collecting all the eastern Indians in that region at a place where they might live in peace with the whites, and in fellowship with each other. Before *Tecumseh* began his labors, HENDRIK had sent a speech to his people on the subject, and was anxiously waiting for a reply, when his work was overtaken by the former and diverted into a gospel of hate. Then it was that the government paid to HENDRIK the highest compliment that could be given, by appointing him as the man most fit of all others to meet the eloquent chief of the *Shawanoes* on his own ground. For three years he followed the footsteps of *Tecumseh* and his brother, and so well and thoroughly did he combat their eloquence and their sophistry, that, had not the war of 1812 intervened, and the seductive influences of the British been given to the aid of the *Shawanoes,* they would have been powerless for evil. Of his labors in this field the Rev. John Sergeant writes : " It appears that through the judicious arrangements of Captain HENDRIK, the influence of the prophet is nearly at an end." His biographer adds : " Captain HENDRIK himself says that the head men of the various tribes do not join the prophet, but only the ignorant and unwary; that the message of the *Delawares* had already shut his mouth, and he believed that in the course of the next summer he would ' be brought down from the Wabash, to the ground from which his ancestors were created,' and so it proved. We find nothing, in the public histories of those times respecting Captain HENDRIK, but we do find that the battle of Tippecanoe was hazarded because the already waning power of *Tecumseh* required some desperate act ; and the eloquence of Captain HENDRIK, his influence as a Muh-he-ka-neew chief with the western Indians, and the information communicated by Mr. Sergeant, take us ' behind the scenes,' and show us at least one great cause of that waning. All due honor to the ' hero of Tippecanoe ; ' but let not the faithful *Mahican,* who, by sapping and mining, prepared the way for that victory, be forgotten." [1]

*Stockbridge, Past and Present; Stone's Life of Brant,* II, 307.

In the war of 1812, Captain HENDRIK joined the American army, was favorably noticed, and promoted to office. In all his public duties he never for a moment forgot his people, and one of his last acts was to write a history of his nation. In 1829, he removed to Green Bay, Wisconsin, where he was gathered to his fathers, the "noblest Roman of them all." What his namesake was to the English government, Captain HENDRIK was to the United States; what his namesake was not to his people, Captain HENDRIK was: an example of unselfish devotion and purity of character.

OCCUM, a *Mahican*, was the first educated and ordained Indian minister. He attended Dr. Wheelock's school at Lebanon, about the middle of the eighteenth century, embraced Christianity and was baptized by the mame of SAMSON. He began his labors as a teacher and evangelist among the *Montauks* on Long island, where he kept a school for some years. He was afterwards ordained by the Presbytery to preach the gospel, and became an efficient means of introducing Christianity to the Indian bands located at separate places in New England and New York. In 1755-56, he visited England, in company with the Rev. Mr. Whitaker, in order, by personal appeals, to solicit funds for the support of Dr. Wheelock's school. Not only was his mission successful, but, as he was the first Indian minister who had visited that country, he attracted special attention, and wherever he went crowds gathered to hear him. About 1786, he went to the country of the *Oneidas*, taking with him several Indians of kindred blood, who clung to him as their leader. He was subsequently joined by a number of *Mohegans* from the sea-coast of New England, and a few *Nanticokes*, *Narragansetts* and *Pequots*. Differences existing in their dialects, they agreed to drop them altogether, and adopt the English, taking the name of Brother-tons. He continued to devote himself to the interests of his people till age incapacitated him, and younger laborers stepped in. During his old age, he went to live with his kindred at New Stockbridge, where he died in 1792. Schoolcraft adds : " It is expressly stated by the New England clergy, to whom we are indebted for these notices, that his Christian and ministerial character were well approved, and that he was deemed to possess a peculiar fluency and aptness in teaching the Indians, over whom he exercised a happy influence. It is inferable, but not distinctly said, that the first or early period of his ministry formed the one of his most active usefulness; but his whole life, after his conversion, is to be regarded as a triumphant evidence of the power and endurance of the gospel truth in the Indian heart. Nor am I aware that we have a superior, if an equal, instance of an individual of the pure Indian blood having been ordained to the ministry who has left behind him so excellent a testimony of consistent usefulness. The foundation of the tribe of the Brothertons is a work due to his enterprise, foresight and exertions. The practical working of the plan which he introduced was excellent. The Brothertons continued to dwell together at their first location in Oneida county till they had well advanced in elementary education and the arts. At this period of their history, they sent delegates to Wisconsin to procure a cession of territory from the indigenous Indians of Fox river of that state, on the borders of Winnebago lake. Having disposed of their possessions in Oneida county, they in due time migrated to that location, where they now reside. By an act of congress, the Brothertons of Wisconsin were admitted to all the rights of citizens of the United States. They were also admitted, by a state act, to the rights of citizens of Wisconsin. The problem of their triple emancipation from barbarism, idleness, and political defranchisement, is thus completely worked out; and worked out in a practical way, in which the experience and wisdom of Occum and his clerical teachers of the olden time predicted, it could only be done." During his later years Occum's reputation passed under a cloud, and before his death he relapsed into some of the worst habits of his tribe; but this fact cannot detract from his personal worth or the excellence of his earlier life. Men can be found in all nations, whose record is marred by the weaknesses of age. "It is not conceived necessary to digress or deny the fact that Noah got drunk."[1]

---

[1] *History of Indian Nations,* part v, 518, etc.

The Moravian missionaries have preserved in their records the names and services of many of the Indian chiefs with whom they were associated, but none whose character is brighter than that of the *Mahican* chieftain, WASAMAPAH, or *Tschoop*, who, after his conversion was called *John*. He was the ruling chief at Shekomeko, in the present county of Dutchess. When first met by the missionary Rauch, he is described as the " greatest drunkard " among his people, and as being crippled by his vices. He became not only a convert, but an interpreter and a preacher of the word of life. Most eloquent is his own account of his conversion : " Brethren, I have been a heathen, and have grown old among the heathen, therefore I know how the heathen think. Once a preacher came and began to explain to us that there was a God. We answered : ' Dost thou think we are so ignorant as not to know that ? Go back to the place from whence thou camest ?' Then, again, another preacher came and began to teach us and to say, ' You must not steal, nor lie, nor get drunk,' etc. We answered : ' Thou fool, dost thou think we don't know that ? Learn first thyself, and then teach the people, to whom thou belongest, to leave off these things ; for who steal and lie, or who are more drunken than thine own people ?' and thus we dismissed him. After some time, Brother Christian Henry Rauch came into my hut and sat down by me. He spoke to me nearly as follows : ' I come to you in the name of the Lord of heaven and earth. He sends me to let you know that he is willing to make you happy, and to deliver you from the misery in which you are at present. To this end he became a man, gave his life as a ransom for man, and shed his blood for him.' When he had finished, he lay down upon a board, being fatigued with his journey, and fell into a sound sleep. I then thought, ' What kind of a man is this ? There he lies and sleeps ; I might kill him and throw him into the woods, and who would regard it ? But this gives him no concern ! However, I could not forget his words. They constantly recurred to my mind. Even when I slept I dreamed of that blood which Christ shed for us. This was something different from what I had ever before heard, and I interpreted Christian Henry's words to the other Indians."

WASAMAPACH removed from Shekomeko to the Delaware, in August, 1745. Here he acted as interpreter in the service held for the Indians on Sunday afternoon ; he also gave instruction in Mahican to a number of brethren and sisters who were designed for missionaries. On the organization of the refugees from Shekomeko into a Christian congregation, at Friedenshütten, on the 24th of July, 1746, he was appointed their teacher. Soon after the small pox broke out, and he became one of its victims, after an illness of seven days, during which he gave evidence of the thoroughness of his conversion. His death took place on the 27th of August, and his funeral on the 28th. Loskiel writes : " John was one of the first fruits. As a heathen he distinguished himself by his heathen and sinful practices, and as his vices became more seductive, on account of his natural wit and humor, so as a Christian he became a most powerful and persuasive witness of our Saviour among his nation. His gifts were sanctified by the grace of God, and employed in such a manner as to be the means of blessing both to Europeans and Indians. Few of his countrymen could vie with him in point of Indian oratory. His discourses were full of animation, and his words penetrated like fire into the hearts of his countrymen ; his soul found a rich pasture in the gospel, and whether at home, or on a journey, he could not forbear speaking of the salvation purchased for us by the sufferings of Jesus, never hesitating a moment, whether his hearers were Christians or Indians. In short, he appeared chosen by God to be a witness to his people, and was four years active in this service. Nor was he less respected as a chief among the Indians, no affairs of state being transacted without his advice and consent." And Bishop Spangenberg adds : " In his mien was the majesty of a Luther, a man whose mind grappled as by intuition the glorious mysteries of the gospel of Christ, and whose strength of will, inspired and sanctified by Christianity, at once triumphed over the vilest passions and most hideous vices by which the human heart can be deformed."

SHABASCH, the associate of *Wasamapah*, is also favorably spoken of by Loskiel. He became a convert and was baptized under the name of Abraham. He was appointed elder of the congregation at Shekomeko, and discharged its duties with credit. He subsequently accepted the chieftaincy of the *Mahicans* of the Delaware country and represented them in the conferences with Johnson, and also with the governor of Pennsylvania. He died in 1762, " much respected on account of his wisdom and grave deportment."

The *Wappingers* were not without their hero in the person of DANIEL NIMHAM, who, in 1765, is described as " a native Indian and acknowledged sachem or king of a certain tribe of Indians known and called by the name of *Wappingers*." He appears to have taken up his residence at Westenhuck in 1746, and to have subsequently taken part in the war of that period and also of that of 1754. The proceedings to which he was a party for the recovery of the lands of his people, would occupy a volume. The facts stated in the case, as reported by the lords of trade, on the hearing of NIMHAM, who visited England, for that purpose, are " that the tract of land, the property and possession whereof is claimed by these Indians, and their title disputed, is situated between Hudson's river and the line which divides the province of New York from that of Connecticut, extending in length from east to west about twenty miles, and in breadth from north to south about sixteen miles, and containing about two hundred and four thousand and eight hundred acres of land; that they continued in the uninterrupted possession of these lands, and in the actual improvement and settlement of the same, by themselves and their tenants, until the commencement of the late war (1755), when the head sachem, accompanied by all the males of that tribe able to bear arms, went into your majesty's service under Sir William Johnson, and the residue removed to Stockbridge, for their greater convenience and accommodation; that whilst the said sachem and his people were fighting under your majesty's banner, all this tract of land was taken up by persons claiming under a grant thereof made by the governor of New York to one Adolph Phillipse in 1697, and afterwards purchased by him of the ancestors of the said Indians, which purchase they allege, was not a purchase of the whole tract comprehended in the grant

of 1697, but only of a small part of it;[1] that finding themselves
by these claims likely to be dispossessed of their patrimonial
lands, they chose a guardian of their rights, and proceeded to
try their claim in various suits and actions in the courts of law
of New York ; that judgment having been given against them
on those several suits and actions (in the trial of which they
state great prejudice and partiality), they applied by petition in
February, 1765, to the lieutenant-governor and council, and
had a hearing upon their case ; that in the proceedings before
the lieutenant governor and council they were treated with great
supercilious neglect, the claims of their adversaries countenanced
and supported with apparent partiality, and a decision given
against them upon the evidence of a deed of purchase of these
lands from their ancestors, which deed they suggest to have
been fraudulent and counterfeit." It subsequently appeared
that Phillipse obtained his patent five years before he made his
purchase, in violation of the laws of the province, and there is
very little reason to doubt that he then obtained it from self-
constituted proprietors to cover a most nefarious transaction.
That NIMHAM and the *Wappingers* were unlawfully deprived
of the lands embraced in the present county of Putnam, may
be regarded as certain.[2]

NIMHAM's tragic death, in Westchester county, has already
been referred to. The following account of the engagement
in which he sealed his devotion to the cause of the colonists
with his life, is from the pen of those against whom he fought,[3]
American historians refusing, apparently, to do justice to the
memory of one who was wronged in his life and in his death :

" Lieut. Col. Simcoe, returning from head-quarters, the 30th
of August, heard a firing in front, and being informed that
Lieut. Col. Emerick had patrolled, he immediately marched to
his assistance. He soon met him retreating ; and Lieut. Col.

---

[1] The reference is to the Canopus'
lands included in the manor of Cortlandt.

[2] Phillipse did not live to enjoy his ill-
gotten lands. On his death they became
the property of his father, and afterwards
of his heirs. John Jacob Astor subsequently purchased the reversionary interest
of the heirs, for $100,000, and ten years
afterwards received from the state of New
York $500,000 in six per cent stocks for
the title which he had acquired.

[3] *Simcoe's Military Journal.*

Emerick being of opinion the rebels were in such force that it would be advisable for him to return, he did so. Lieut. Col. Simcoe understood that NIMHAM, an Indian chief, and some of his tribe, were with the enemy; and by his spies, who were excellent, he was informed that they were highly elated at the retreat of Emerick's corps, and applied it to the whole of the light troops at Kingsbridge. Lieut. Col. Simcoe took measures to increase their belief; and, ordering a day's provisions to be cooked, marched the next morning, the 31st of August, a small distance in front of the fort, and determined to wait there the whole day, in hopes of betraying the enemy into an ambuscade. His idea was, as the enemy moved upon the road, to advance from his flanks; and he meant to gain the heights in the rear of the enemy, attacking whomsoever should be within reach by his cavalry and such infantry as might be necessary. In pursuance of these intentions, Lieut. Col. Emerick with his corps was detached from the Queen's Rangers and Legion, as Lieut. Col. Simcoe thought fully instructed in the plan; however, he most unfortunately mistook the nearer house for the one at a greater distance, the names being the same, and there he posted himself, and soon after sent from thence a patrol forward upon the road, before Lieut. Col. Simcoe could have time to stop it. This patrol had no effect, not meeting the enemy; had a single man of it deserted, or been taken, the whole attempt had, probably, been abortive. Lieut. Col. Simcoe, who was half way up a tree, on the top of which was a drummer boy, saw a flanking party of the enemy approach. The troops had scarcely fallen into their ranks when a smart firing was heard from the Indians, who had lined the fences of the road, and who were exchanging shots with Lieut. Col. Emerick, whom they had discovered. The Queen's Rangers moved rapidly to gain the heights, and Lieut. Col. Tarleton immediately advanced with the Hussars and the Legion of cavalry; not being able to pass the fences in his front, he made a circuit to return further upon their right; which, being reported to Lieut. Col. Simcoe, he broke from the column of rangers, with the grenadier company, and, directing Major Ross to conduct the corps to the heights, advanced to the road, and arrived without being perceived, within ten yards

42

of the Indians.  They had been intent on the attack on Emerick's corps and the Legion ; they now gave a yell and fired upon
the grenadier company, wounding four of them, and Lieut. Col.
Simcoe.  They were driven from the fences ; and Lieut. Col.
Tarleton, with the cavalry, got among them, and pursued them
rapidly down Cortlandt's ridge.  That active officer had a narrow escape ; in striking at one of the fugitives, he lost his
balance and fell from his horse ; luckily the Indian had no bayo-
net, and his musket had been discharged.  Lieut. Col. Simcoe
joined the battalion and seized the heights.  A captain of the
rebel light infantry and a few of his men were taken ; but a
body of them, under Major Stewart, who afterwards was distinguished at Stony Point, left the Indians and fled.  Though
the ambuscade, its greater part, failed, it was of consequence.
Near forty of the Indians were killed or desperately wounded ;
among others NIMHAM, a chieftain who had been to England,
and his son ; and it was reported to have stopped a large number
of them, who were excellent marksmen, from joining General
Washington's army.  The Indian doctor was taken ; and he
said that when NIMHAM saw the grenadiers close in his rear,
he called out to his people to fly, ' that he himself was old and
would die there.'  He wounded Lieut. Col. Simcoe, and was
on the point of dragging him from his horse, when he was
killed by Wright, his orderly Hussar.  The Indians fought most
gallantly ; they pulled more than one of the cavalry from their
horses.  French, an active youth, bugle-horn to the Hussars,
struck at an Indian, but missed him ; the man dragged him
from his horse, and was searching for his knife to stab him,
when, loosening French's hand, he luckily drew out a pocket
pistol, and shot the Indian through the head, in which situation
he was found.  One man of the Legion Cavalry was killed,
and one of them and two of the Hussars, wounded."

The battlements of the Hudson,—

> " The mountain columns
> With which earth props heaven,"—

the early home of the patriot chief, are the monuments to his
memory ; the eternal flow of the Mahicanituk his requiem.

## II. LANGUAGE.

THE early Dutch writers resolved the various dialects which they met among the Indians into " four distinct languages, namely: *Manhattan, Minqua, Savanos,* and *Wappanoos.*" With the *Manhattan* they included the dialect spoken in the neighborhood of Fort Amsterdam, "along the North river, on Long island, and at the Neversink ; with the *Minqua,* the *Senecas* and other inland tribes." The *Savanos* was the dialect of the south, and the *Wappanoos* that of the east. The progress of the inquiry resulting in this classification was slow. Wassanaar writes, in 1621 : "'Tis worthy of remark, that so great a diversity of language exists among the numerous tribes. They vary frequently not over five or six miles ; forthwith comes another language ; they meet and can hardly understand one another. There are some who come sixty miles from the interior, and cannot well understand those on the river." Michaëlius, writing in 1628, says: "Their language methinks is entirely peculiar. Many of our common people call it an easy language, which is soon learned, but I am of a contrary opinion. For those who can understand their words to some extent and repeat them, fail greatly in the pronunciation and speak a broken language, like the language of Ashdod. For these people have different aspirates and many guttural letters which are formed more in the throat than by the mouth, teeth, and lips, which our people not being accustomed to, guess at by means of their signs, and then imagine that they have accomplished something wonderful. It is true, one can learn as much as is sufficient for the purposes of trading, but this occurs almost as much by signs with the thumb and fingers as by speaking. It also seems to us that they rather design to conceal their language from us than to properly communicate it, except in things which happen in daily trade ; saying that it is sufficient for us to understand them in those : and then they speak only half their reasons with shortened words ; and frequently call a dozen things and even more by one name ; and all things which have only a rude resemblance to each other they frequently call by the same name. In truth it is a made up childish language : so that even those who can best of all speak with the Indians and get along well in trade, are nevertheless wholly in the dark and bewildered when they hear the Indians speaking with each other by themselves." A'nother writer says : " The language of this people is very various ; they are very difficult for strangers to learn as they are spoken without any principles." And Van der Donck, writing in 1656, concludes : " Their languages and dialects are very different, as unlike each other as the Dutch, French, Greek and Latin are. Their declensions and conjugations have an affinity with the Greek and accord to it. Their declensions, augmentations, cases and adverbs, are like the Greek ; but to reduce their language to any of ours, would be impossible, for there is no resemblance between the same. Before we have acquired a knowledge of any of their languages or dialects, we know no more of what they say than if a dog had barked."

While these sturdy Dutch linguists were plodding over the subject, the Rev. John Eliot, of Massachusetts, had grasped the hidden key of the language and proclaimed that it had principles and form ; that even that which Michaëlius denominated "shortened words" was made in accordance with rules, and that in the observation of that writer of the fact that they frequently called " a dozen things and even more by one name," he had simply failed to note the inflections which constituted an important principle of the language. But notwithstanding the publication of Eliot's grammar in 1666, and the observations of the Jesuit and Moravian priests, it was not until 1819 that Du Ponceau, after a thorough comparison of the writings of his predecessors, was enabled to announce the proposition : " That the American languages in general use are rich in words and in grammatical forms, and that, in their complicated construction, the greatest order, method, and regularity prevail." It remained, however, for subsequent writers, and especially for Gallatin [1] and Schoolcraft, to elucidate fully the grammatical

---

[1] *A Synopis of the Indian Tribes within the United States east of the Rocky Moun-*    *tains, etc., by Hon. Albert Gallatin,* 1836.

structure of the languages and define the characteristic features of the several dialects.

According to these writers there were but two generic Indian languages, the *Algonquin* and the *Iroquois;* but these two were divided into tribal dialects and groups with distinctive characteristics. While each *Iroquois* tribe had its dialect, the generic language, as spoken by the Five Nations of New York, differed in many respects from that spoken by the southern and western *Iroquois* families. The *Algonquin* was represented by equally distinct tribal and general types. Edwards says that the *Mahican* was spoken " by all the Indians throughout New England ; " that though each tribe had "a different dialect," the language was "radically the same." Yet the *Algonquin* of the *Mahicans* was essentially different from the *Algonquin* of the *Lenapes.* Loskiel explains this more fully : " Though the three tribes of the *Delawares* have the same language, yet they speak different dialects. The *Unamis* and *Wunalachtikos*, who formerly inhabited the eastern coast of Pennsylvania and New Jersey, nearly agree in pronunciation ; but the dialect of the *Monsys*, who formerly lived in Menissing, beyond the Blue mountains, differs so much from the former, that they would hardly be able to understand each other, did they not keep up a continual intercourse. The language of the *Delawares* has an agreeable sound, both in common conversation, and public delivery. The dialect spoken by the *Unamis* and *Wunalachtikos* is peculiarly grateful to the ear, and much more easily learnt, by an European, than that of the *Monsys*, which is rougher and spoken with a broad accent. However, the *Monsy* dialect is a key to many expressions in the *Unamis* and *Wunalachtikos*. The latter have a way of dropping some syllables, so that, without a knowledge of the former, it would be impossible either to spell their words or guess their meaning.

"Several other languages derive their origin from the *Delaware*, and this proceeds chiefly from the vicinity or connections of the different nations and tribes. For instance, the language of the *Mahikans* is nearly related to the *Monsy* dialect, these two nations having formerly been neighbors in the province of New York. The *Shawanose* is also related to the *Monsy*, but more to the *Mahikan;* only the former generally place the accent upon the last syllable.   The *Ottawa* is nearly related to the *Shawanose,* but the *Chippewa* more immediately to the *Delaware.* The language of the *Twichtwees* and *Wawiachtanos* resembles the *Shawanose;* in dialect the *Kikapus, Tukachohas, Moshkos,* and *Karhaski,* differ from the *Delaware* in proportion to their distance from each other, but all are nearly related."

The *Algonquin* dialects spoken in the valley of the Hudson, at the time of the discovery, were at least six in number : The *Manhattan,* the *Wappanoo,* the *Mahican,* the *Minsi,* the *Unami* and the *Unalachtin.*   It is stated that the *Mahicans* conquered the territory which they occupied, mixed with their own 'the dialect of the people whom they had subdued and formed that subsequently spoken by themselves.   It is also said that the *Wappanoos* overran the old *Manhattans* and created another mixed dialect, while the third type was found among the natives of Long Island, in which perhaps many of the essential features of the *Manhattan* were preserved.   Of the three types on the west, the *Unami* and the *Unalachtin* are classed as *Delaware* as distinguished from the *Minsi.*   The *Mahican* has been preserved, partially at least, as has also to some extent the Long Island,—the latter extending along the east side of the river as far as the Highlands, where it met the *Wappanoos,* which has been preserved as spoken by its more eastern families in the *Massachusetts;* but the dialects on the west, as they were modified by association with those on the east, and the dialects of the east as modified by association with those on the west, are lost except as they live in geographical names, which resist established rules of interpretation, or are approximately preserved as they were spoken elsewhere, modified by different associations.   How widely they differed, can be inferred from Loskiel's statement that the *Minsi* of the Hudson resembled the *Mahican* and the *Shawanoe* and was scarce understood·by its more western families — how widely they differ in the imperfect forms in which they have been preserved, a few words from each will sufficiently illustrate.   Man, in Long Island, is *run; wonnun* (white man) in Wappinoo or Massachusetts, *wosketomp;* in Mahican *neemanoo;* in Delaware and Minsi, *lenno.* Mother, in Long Island, is *cwca;* in Massachusetts, *okaooh;*

in Mahican, *okegan;* in Minsi, *guy;* in Delaware, *gahowes.*
Stone, in Long Island, is *sun;* in Massachusetts, *hussun;* in Ma-
hican, *thaunaumka;* in Minsi, *achsun;* in Delaware, *akhsin*
(stone), *pemapukhk* (rock). Earth, in Long Island, is *keagh;* in
Massachusetts, *ahke;* in Mahican, *akek;* in Minsi, *achgi;* in
Delaware, *aki, akhki.*

But while the peculiar dialects of the valley have been lost,
or have at best an imperfect preservation, the principles upon
which they were based have been written. Gallatin says:
" The fundamental characteristics of the Indian languages of
America appear to be a universal tendency to express in the
same word, not only all that modifies or relates to the same
object, or action, but both the action and the object ; thus con-
centrating in a single expression a complex idea, or several ideas
among which there is a natural connection. All the other features of the language seem to be subordinate to that general
principle. The object in view has been attained by various
means of the same tendency and often blended together : a
multitude of inflections properly so called ; a still greater number of compound words, sometimes formed by the coalescence
of primitive words not materially altered, more generally by the
union of many such words in a remarkably abbreviated form,
and numerous particles, either significative, or the original
meaning of which has been lost, prefixed, added as terminations,
or inserted in the body of the word." An extreme illustration
of this principle is furnished by Mather, in the compound phrase
" Kummogkodonattoottummooetiteaongannunnonash," which is
presumed to imply, " our question." Edwards illustrates it in a
simpler form in the *Mahican.* "If a man hold out *his* hand
to an Indian to know the name, he may receive the answer
" knish" — *thy* hand ; but if he touches the hand of the *Indian,*
he is told " nnisk"— *my* hand ; and in either case he will infer
that he has received the Indian word for hand, simply, when
there is no such word in the language." Schoolcraft, in his
treatise,[1] explains this principle more fully and defines the idioms
and structure of the language. From this treatise the annexed
synopsis is made, presuming that those having occasion to do so,

[1] " *An Essay on the Grammatical Struc-    of Indian Tribes,* part ii, 353, etc.
ture of the Algonquin Language.*" —History*

or whose curiosity prompts them to the study, will consult the original.

### *Grammar of the Algonquin Language.*

1. *Alphabet.* The *Algonquin* possesses all the vowel sounds as heard in far, fate, fall ; met, meet ; shine, pin ; not, note, move ; put, nut. It has two labials, *b* and *p; * five dentals, *d, t, s, z,* and *j* or *g,* soft ; two nasals, *m* and *n;* and two primary gutturals, *k* and *g,* hard. The letters *f, r, v,* are wanting. The sound of *x* is also believed to be wanting in all the *Algonquin* dialects but the *Delaware* and *Mahican* of the Hudson valley, in which it is fully heard in Coxsackie, and in a few of the earlier geographical terms of New Jersey, the sound of *r* is represented in *ah.* Thus an alphabet of five vowels and thirteen consonants is capable of expressing, either simply or in combination, every full sound of the *Algonquin* language. In this estimate of primary sounds, the letters *c,* and *q,* and *y* as representing a vowel sound, are entirely rejected. The soft of *c* is *s,* the hard, *k.* The sound of *g* is always that of *k.* In the formation of words the vowelic, diphthongal and mixed sounds are syllabic. The following table represents the elementary syllables on the primary vowel sounds :

| (1) | | (2) | | (3) | | (4) | |
|---|---|---|---|---|---|---|---|
| AI as A in Fate. | | A as in Father. | | A as in Fall. | | A as in Hat | |
| | | | | | | only uttered with a consonant following. | |
| Aib | Bai | Ahb | Bah | Aub | Bau | | |
| Aid | Dai | Ahd | Dah | Aud | Dau | Ab | |
| Aig | Gai | Ahg | Gah | Aug | Gau | Ad | |
| Aih | Hai | Ah | Hah | Auh | Hau | Ag | |
| Aik | Kai | Ahj | Jah | Auj | Jau | Ah | |
| Ail | Lai | Ahk | Kah | Auk | Kau | Aj | |
| Aij | Jai | Ahl | Lah | Aul | Lau | Ak | |
| Aim | Mai | Ahm | Mah | Aum | Mau | Al | |
| Ain | Nai | Ahn | Nah | Aun | Nau | Am | |
| Aip | Pai | Ahp | Pah | Aup | Pau | An | |
| Ais | Sai | Ahs | Sah | Aus | Sau | Ap | |
| Ait | Tai | Aht | Tah | Aut | Tau | As | |
| Aiw | Wai | Ahw | Wah | Auw | Wau | At | |
| Aiz | Yai | Ahz | Zah | Auz | Yau | Au | |
| Aizh | Zhai | | | Auzh | Zhau | Az | |

| (1) | (2) | (1) | (2) |
|---|---|---|---|
| EE as in me | E as in met | I as in Fine. | I as in Pin. |
| Eeb   Bee | Eb | Bi | Ib |
| Eed   Dee | Ed | Di | Id |
| Eeg   Gee | Eg | Gi | Ig |
| Eeh   He | Eh | Hi | Ih |
| Eej   Jee | Ej | Ji | Ij |
| Eel   Lee | Ek | Ki | Ik |
| Eek   Kee | El | Li | Il |
| Eem   Mee | Em | Mi | Im |
| Een   Nee | En | Ni | In |
| Eep   Pee | Ep | Pi | Ip |
| Ees   See | Es | Si | Is |
| Eet   Tee | Et | Ti | It |
| Eew   Wee | Eu | Wi | Iw |
| Eez   Zee | Ez | Yi | Iz |
|  |  | Zi |  |

| (1) | (2) | (4) |  |
|---|---|---|---|
| O as in Note | O as in Move. | O as in Not. | U as in But. |
| Bo | Oob   Boo | Ob | Ub |
| Do | Ood   Doo | Od | Ud |
| Go | Oog   Goo | Og | Ug |
| Ho | Ooh   Hoo | Oh | Uh |
| Jo | Ooj   Joo | Oj | Uj |
| Ko | Ook   Koo | Ok | Uk |
| Lo | Ool   Loo | Ol | Ul |
| Mo | Oom   Moo | Om | Um |
| No | Oon   Noo | On | Un |
| Po | Oop   Poo | Op | Up |
| So | Oos   Soo | Os | Us |
| To | Oot   Too | Ot | Ut |
| Wo | Oow   Woo | Ow | Uz |
| Yo | Ooy   Yoo | Oy |  |
| Zo | Ooz   Zoo | Oz |  |

Diphthongal sounds are heard in limited classes of words, ending in *ia*, *io*, and *ou*. The nasal sounds, which abound in the language, are chiefly confined to the letter *n*, and the combination *ng*. The gutturals are mostly formed by the letters *gh* and *kh*. The hard sound of *g* has its expression in the half utterance

43

of *k* by which it is followed, as in the attempt to pronounce *gk*. The combinations of *ch*, *sh*, and *zh*, are common, as are also those of *bw*, *dw*, *gw*, and *hw*. *Ai* expresses the sound of *a* as in fate ; *ah* the sound of *a* as in father ; *au*, as in fall, auction, and *au* in law ; *ee* is the sound of *e* as in feel ; *ia*, as the sound of *i* in media ; *oi*, the sound of *o* in voice ; *aiw*, *ouw* and *eow* appear in converting verbs indicative into different moods ; *ih*, the sound of *i* suddenly stopped off ; *ooh*, the sound of *o* suddenly stopped off ; *uh*, the sound of *u*, roughly aspirated, and also *ugh* ; *ch*, as in English, also, *sh* and *zh* ; *bw* as in bwoin ; *gw* as in gwiuk ; *hw* as in mohwa ; *kw* as in wewukwun ; *mw* as in wa-mwa ; *ny* as in nyau ; *tshw* as in tshwe — tshwees-ke-wa, a snipe.

2. *Substantives.*    In a general survey of the language there is perhaps no feature which obtrudes itself so constantly to view, as the principle which separates all words, of whatever denomination, into animates and inanimates, as they are applied to objects in the animal, vegetable, or mineral kingdom. This principle has been grafted upon most words, and carries its distinctions throughout the syntax. It is the gender of the language ; but a gender of so unbounded a scope, as to merge it in the distinctions of a masculine and feminine, and to give a two-fold character to the parts of speech.

Nouns animate embrace the tribes of quadrupeds, birds, fishes, insects, reptiles, crustacea, the sun, moon, and stars, thunder, and lightning ; for these are personified, and whatever possesses animal life, or is endowed, by the peculiar opinions and superstitions of the Indians, with it.    In the vegetable kingdom their number is comparatively limited, being chiefly confined to trees, and those only while they are referred to as whole bodies, and to the various species of fruits, seeds, and esculents.    It is to be remarked, however, that the names for animals are only employed as animates, while the objects are referred to as whole and complete species ; but the gender must be changed when it becomes necessary to speak of separate members. Man, woman, father, mother, are separate nouns, so long as the individuals are meant ; but hand, foot, head, eye, ear, tongue, are inanimates. Buck is an animate noun, while his entire carcase is referred to, whether living or dead ; but neck, back, heart, windpipe, take the inanimate form. In like manner eagle, swan, dove, are distinguished as animates ; but beak, wing, tail, are arranged with inanimates. So oak, pine, ash, are animates ; branch, leaf, root, inanimates.

No language is perhaps so defective as to be totally without number. But there are few which furnish so many modes of indicating it as the *Algonquin.* There are as many modes of forming the plural as there are vowel sounds, yet there is no distinction between a limited and an unlimited substantive plural ; although there is, in the pronoun, an *inclusive* and an *exclusive* plural. Whether we say man or men, two men or twenty men, the singular *inin-e,* and the plural *ininewug,* remain the same. But if we say we, us or our men (who are present), or we, us, or our Indians (in general), the plural we, and us, and our — for they are rendered by the same form — admit of a change to indicate whether the objective person or persons be *included* or *excluded.* This principle forms a single and anomalous instance of the use of particular plurals ; and it carries its distinctions, by means of the pronouns, separable and inseparable, into the verbs and substantives, creating the necessity of double conjugations and double declensions, in the plural forms of the first person. Thus the term for Our Father, which, in the inclusive form, is *Kosinaun,* is, in the exclusive, *Nosinaun.*

The general plural is variously made. But the plurals making inflections take upon themselves an additional power or sign, by which substantives are distinguished into animates and inanimates. Without this additional power, all nouns plural would end in the vowels *a, e, i, o, u* ; but to mark the gender, the letter *g* is added to animates, and the letter *n* to inanimates, making the plurals of the first class terminate in *ag, eeg, ig, og, ug,* and of the second class in *an, een, in, on, un.* Ten modes of forming the plural are thus provided, five of which are animate, and five inanimate plurals. A strong and clear distinction is thus drawn between the two classes of words, so unerring indeed, in its application, that it is only necessary to inquire how the plural is formed to determine whether it belong to one or the other class.

Where a noun terminates with the vowel in the singular, the addition of the *g*, or *n*, shows at once both the plural and the gender.   In other instances, as in *peena*, a partridge ; *seebe*, a river ; it requires a consonant to precede the plural vowel, in conformity with a rule previously stated.   Thus *peenai-wug ;* and *seebe-wŭn*.   Where the noun singular terminates in the broad instead of the long sound of *a*, as in *ogimau*, a chief ; *ishpatinau*, a hill, the plural is *ogim-aug*, *ishpatinaun*.   But these are mere modifications of two of the above forms, and are by no means entitled to be considered as additional plurals.

Comparatively few substantives are without number.   There is, however, one exception from the general use of number. This exception consists of the want of number in the *third person* of the declensions of animate nouns, and the conjugation of animate verbs.   Not that such words are destitute of number, in their simple forms, or when used under circumstances requiring no change of these simple forms — no prefixes and no inflections.   But it will be seen, at a glance, how very limited such an application must be in a transpositive language.

Distinctions of number are founded upon a modification of the five vowel sounds.   Possessives are likewise founded upon the basis of the vowel sounds.   There are five declensions of the noun to mark the possessives, ending, in the possessive, in *am*, *eem*, *im*, *om*, *um*, *oom*.   Where the nominative ends with a vowel, the possessive is made by adding the letter *m*, as in *mai-mai*, a woodcock, *ne maimaim*, my woodcock, etc.   Where the nominative ends in a consonant, as in *ais*, a shell, the full possessive inflection is required, making *nin dais-im*, my shell. In the latter form, the consonant *d* is interposed between the pronoun and noun, and sounded with the noun, in conformity with a general rule.   Where the nominative ends in the broad, in lieu of the long sound of *a*, as in *ogimau*, a chief, the possessive is *aum*.

It is a constant and unremitting aim in the Indian languages, to distinguish the actor from the object ; partly by prefixes, and partly by inseparable suffixes.   That the termination *un* is one of these inseparable particles, and that its office, while it confounds the number of the third person, is to designate the object, appears probable, from the fact that it retains its connection with the noun, whether the latter follow or precede the verb, or whatever its position in the sentence may be.

In tracing the operation of the rule through the doublings of the language, it is necessary to distinguish every modification of sound, whether it is accompanied, or not accompanied, by a modification of the sense. The particle *un*, which thus marks the *third person and persons*, is sometimes pronounced *wun*, and sometimes *yun*, as the euphony of the word to which it is suffixed may require. But not the slightest change is thereby made in its meaning.

Substantives require, throughout the language, separable or inseparable pronouns, under the form of prefixes. Inflections of the first and second persons, which occupy the place of possessives, and those of the third person, resembling objectives, pertain to words which are either primitives, or denote but a single object, as moose, fire. There is, however, another class of substantives, or substantive expressions, and an extensive class — for it embraces a great portion of the compound descriptive terms — in the use of which no pronominal prefixes are required. The distinctions of person are, exclusively, supplied by pronominal suffixes. Of this class are the words descriptive of country, place of dwelling, field of battle, place of employment, &c. Thus, *Aindaud*, home or place of dwelling, in the substantive singular, is *Aindauyaun*, my home ; *Aindau-yun*, thy home; *Aindau-d*, his home. And the substantive plural is *Aindau-yaun-in*, my homes ; *Aindau-yun-in*, thy homes ; *Aindau-yaung-in*, our homes, &c.

Substantives have modifications by which locality, diminution, a defective quality, and the past tense are expressed ; by which various adjectives and adverbal significations are given ; and finally the substantives themselves converted into verbs. Such are, also, the modes of indicating the masculine and feminine (both merged in the animate class), and those words which are of a strictly *sexual* character, or are restricted in their *use* to males or females.

That quality of the noun which, in the shape of an inflection, denotes the relative situation of the object by the contiguous position of some accessory object, is expressed, in the English language, by the prepositions *in, into,* at or *on.* In the Indian they are denoted by an inflection. Thus the phrase, in the box, is rendered, in the Indian, by one word, *mukukoong;* the termination *oong* denoting the locality, not of the box, but of the object sought after. Generally, the inflection is employed when there is some circumstance or condition of the noun either concealed, or not fully apparent. The principal local inflections are *ing* and *oong,* which become *aing* and *eeng* as the terminal vowel of the noun may require. *Ishkodai,* fire ; *Ishkod-aing,* in or on the fire ; *Sebe,* river ; *Sebeeng,* in or on the river ; *Kon,* snow ; *Kon-ing,* in or on the snow ; *Azhibik,* rock ; *Azhibik-oong,* in or on the rock, &c.

The local form pertains either to such nouns of the animate class as are in their nature inanimates, or at most possessed of vegetable life. There is another variation of the local form of the noun, indicative of locality in a more general sense. It is formed by *ong* or *nong,* frequent terminations in geographical names. Thus, from *Ojibwai* (Chippewa) is formed *Ojibwainong,* place of the Chippewas. The termination *ing* is also sometimes employed, as *Monomonikaun-ing,* in the place of wild rice, &c.

The diminutive forms of the noun are indicated by *ais, ees, os,* and *aus,* as the final vowel of the word may require. Thus, *Ojibwai,* a Chippewa, becomes Ojibw-*ais,* a little Chippewa ; *Amik,* a beaver, Amik-*os,* a young beaver ; *Minnis,* an island, Minnis-*ais,* a small island ; *Shomin,* a grape, Shomin-*ais,* a little grape ; *Ossin,* a stone, Ossin-*ees,* a small stone ; *Sebe,* a river, Seb-*ees,* a small river ; *Negik,* an otter, Negik-*os,* a small otter ; *Wakiegun,* a house, Wakieg-*aus,* a small house. These diminutives, as far as they can be employed, supersede the use of adjectives, and are happily employed by the Indian in expressing ridicule or contempt. When applied to animals, or to inorganic objects, their meaning, however, is very nearly limited to an inferiority in size or age. Sometimes both the local and diminutive inflections are employed. Thus the word *minnisain-sing* signifies, literally, in the little island.

The syllable *ish,* when added to a noun, indicates a bad or dreaded quality, or conveys the idea of imperfection or decay.

The sound of this inflection is sometimes changed to *eesh*, *oosh*, or *aush*. Thus *Eckwai*, a woman, becomes Eckwai-*wish*, a bad woman ; *Nebi*, water, becomes Nebe-*esh*, strong water ; *Webeed*, a tooth, becomes Webeed-*aush*, a decayed or aching tooth. The rule is nearly universal that the final sound of *sh*, in any of its forms, is indicative of a faulty quality.

Substantives have, therefore, a *diminutive* form, made in *ais*, *ees*, *os*, or *aus* ; a *derogative* form, made in *ish*, *eesh*, *oosh*, or *aush* ; and a *local* form, made in *aing*, *eeng*, *ing*, or *ong*. By a principle of accretion, the second and third may be added to the first form, and the third to the second.

While substantives have their primitive and derivative forms, they also appear as compounds. Among the primitives may be found dissyllables and possibly trisyllables ; but as a principle, all polysyllabic words, all words of three syllables, and most words of two syllables, are compounds.

3. *Adjectives.* It has been remarked, that the distinction of words into animates and inanimates, is a principle intimately interwoven throughout the structure of the language, constituting indeed its fundamental principle. In the plural only of the substantive is the adjective indicated. One set of adjective symbols express the ideas peculiarly appropriate to animates, and another set is exclusively applicable to inanimates. Good and bad, black and white, great and small, handsome and ugly, have such modifications as are practically competent to indicate the general nature of the objects referred to, whether provided with, or destitute of, the vital principle. And not only so, but by the figurative use of these forms, to exalt inanimate masses into the class of living beings, or to strip the latter of the properties of life.

Examples illustrating this principle are quoted, and explained in complex and simple forms. Of the latter, it is said : Ask a Chippewa the name for a rock, and he will answer, *auzhebik*. Ask him the name for red rock, and he will answer, *miskwaubik* ; for white rock, *waubaubik* ; for black rock, *mukkuddawaubik* ; for bright rock, *wassyaubik* ; for yellow rock, *ozahwaubik* ; for green rock, *ozahwushkwaubik* ; for smooth rock, *shoishkwaubik*, etc., compounds in which the words, red, white, black yellow, etc., unite with *aubik*.

Let this mode of interrogation be continued, and extended to other adjectives, or the same adjectives applied to other objects, and results equally regular and numerous will appear. *Minnis,* we shall be told, is an island ; *miskominnis,* a red island ; *mukkuddaminnis,* a black island, etc. *Annokwut,* is a cloud ; *miskwaunakwut,* a red cloud ; *waubahnokwut,* a white cloud, etc. *Neebẹ* is the specific term for water, but is not generally used in combination with the adjective. The word *goma,* like *aubo,* appears to be a generic term for water or potable liquids. Hence, *gitshee,* great, *gitshig-guma,* great water ; *minno,* good, *minwau-guma,* good drink, etc. *Baimwa* is sound ; *baimwawä,* the passing sound ; *minwäwä,* a pleasant sound ; *mudwayausshkau,* the sound of waves dashing on the shore. These examples might be continued ad infinitum. Every modification of circumstances, almost every peculiarity of thought, is expressed by some modification of the orthography. Enough has been given to prove that the adjective combines itself with the substantive, the verb, and the pronoun ; that the combinations thus produced are numerous, afford concentrated modes of conveying ideas, and oftentimes happy terms of expression.

Varied as the adjective is in its changes, it has no comparative inflection. A Chippewa cannot say, that one substance is hotter or colder than another ; or of two or more substances unequally heated, that this or that is the hottest or coldest, without employing adverbs or accessory adjectives. And it is accordingly by adverbs and accessory adjectives that the degrees of comparison are expressed. *Pemnaudizziwin* is a very good substantive expression, indicating *the tenor of being or life.* *Nem bimmaud-izziwin,* my tenor of life ; *Ke bimmaud-izziwin,* thy tenor of life. To form the positive degree, *minno,* good, and *mudjee,* bad, is introduced between the pronoun *d* and the verb, thus : *Ne minno pimmaud-izziwin,* my good tenor of life ; *Ne mudjee pimmaud-izziwin,* thy bad tenor of life. To cᵒnstitute the comparative degree, *nahwudj,* more, is prefixed to the adjective. When the adjective is preceded by the adverb, it assumes a negative form.

4. *Pronouns.* Pronouns are buried, if we may so say, in the structure of the verb. In tracing them back, to their primitive

forms, through the almost infinite variety of modifications which they assume in connection with the verb, substantive, and adjective, it will facilitate analysis to group them into preformative and subformative classes; terms which have already been made use of, and which include the pronominal prefixes and suffixes. They admit of the further distinction of separable and inseparable pronouns. By separable is intended those forms which have a meaning by themselves, and are thus distinguished from the inflective and subformative pronouns, and pronominal particles; significant only in connection with another word.

Of the first class are the personal pronouns *nee* (I), *kee* (thou), and *wee*, or *o* (he or she), which are declined, to form the plural persons, by *neen owind, keen owau, ween owau.* The plural of the possessive mine, or my, in the inclusive, is made by *k* the pronominal sign of the second person, and the usual substantive inflection in *win*, with a terminal *d.* The letter *o* is a mere connective, without meaning. The second person is rendered plural by the particle, *au* instead of *win.* The third person has its plural in the common sign of *w.* The examples cited embrace the mode of distinguishing the person, number, relation, and gender — or what is deemed its technical equivalent, i. e., the mutations words undergo, not to mark the distinctions of sex, but the presence or absence of vitality; and also the inflections which the pronouns take for tense, or rather, the auxiliary verbs, have, had, shall, will, may, etc. This class embraces the preformative or prefixed pronouns.

The inseparable suffixed or subformative pronouns are: *yaun*, my; *yun*, thy; *id* or *d*, his or hers; *yaung*, our (ex.); *yung*, our (in.); *yaig*, your; *waud*, their. These pronouns are exclusively employed as suffixes; and as suffixes to the descriptive substantives, adjectives, and verbs. Relative pronouns are very limited. Demonstrative pronouns, both animate and inanimate, are found in many forms

The *Algonquin* language is in a peculiar sense a language of pronouns. Originally there appear to have been but three terms, answering to the three persons, I, thou, or you, and he or she. By these terms, the speaker or actor is clearly distinguished ; but they convey no idea of sex, the word for the third person in which we should suspect it, being strictly epicene.    In a class of languages strongly transitive, the purposes of precision required another class of pronouns, which should be suffixed to the end of verbs, to render the object of the action as certain as the actor is.    The language being without auxiliary verbs, their place is supplied by the tensal syllables, *ge*, *gah*, and *guh*, which have extended the original monosyllables into trisyllables.    This is the first step on the polysyllabical ladder.    To make the suffixed or objective pronouns, they appear to have availed themselves of a principle which they had already applied to nouns — namely, the principle of indicating, by the letters *g* or *n* added to the plural terms, the two great divisions of creation, on which the whole grammatical structure is built — namely, the genderic classes of living or inert matter. As these alphabetical signs, *g* and *n*, could be applied to the five terminal vowel sounds of all nouns and all verbs (for they must, to be made plural or conjugated, be provided with terminal vowels, where they do not, when used disjunctively, exist), there is naturally a set of five vital or animate and five non-vital or inanimate plurals.    Ten classes of nouns and ten classes of verbs are thus formed.    But as the long vowels in *au* and *oan* require three more varieties of numerical inflection in each of these vowels, the respective number of plural terms is eight, and the total sixteen — sixteen modes of making the plural, and sixteen conjugations for the verb.    This is productive of a variety of terminal sounds, and appears at the first glance to be confused, but the principle is simple and easily remembered ; so easily, that a child need never mistake it. The terminal *g* or *n* of each word denotes *in all positions*, the two great genderic classes of nature, which are the cardinal points of the grammar.

Agreeably to data furnished, the regular plurals are respectively *ag*, *eg*, *ig*, *og*, *ug*, and *ain*, *een*, *in*, *on*, *un*, with the additional *aug*, *eeg*, and *oag*, in the vital, and *aun*, *een*, and *oan*, for the long vowels, in the non-vital class.    Only two ideas are gained by thirty-two numerical inflections, namely, that the objects are vital or non-vital.

The pure verbs, the noun-verbs, the adjective-verbs, and the propositional, adverbial, and compound terms and declensions, are made plural precisely as the nouns, regard being always had to the principles of euphony, in throwing away or adding a letter, or giving precedence to an adjective inflection. The suffixed pronouns are required to be put at the end of these plurals, where they will not always coalesce without inserting them before the sign of the epicene or anti-epicene.

· These suffixed plural inflections, as before indicated, are *yaun,* *yun,* *id,* or simply *d*—*I, you, he, she;* which are changed to plurals personal by the usual inflections of the letter *g,* making them *yaung,* we, us, our (ex.) ; *yung,* we, us our (in.), and *yaig* for ye. The vital particle are, is placed before *d* for the pronoun they.

As the pronouns are made plural precisely as the nouns, for distinction's sake, the numerical inflections *aig, aug, eeg, ig, og, oog, ug,* may be employed to express the various senses of we, they, them, and us, ours, theirs. These fourteen suffixed pronouns enable the speaker to designate the objective transitive persons, and to designate the reflex action in the first plural, which is uniform.

The anti-epicene suffixed pronouns for the same persons, are *ain, een, in, on, aun, un, aim, eem, im, om, oam, um ;* with such changes in their adjustment as usage and the juxtaposition of consonants have produced.

5. *Verbs.* The whole stock of verbs in the Indian vocabulary is grouped with five epicene and five classes of anti-epicene conjugations. The conjugations embrace not only the natural verbs in common use, but they provide for all the nouns and noun-adjectives of every possible kind ; for these, it must be remembered, can all be converted, under the plastic rules of the language, into verbs.

With a formidable display of vocal terms and inflective forms, there is, therefore, a very simple principle to unravel the lexicography, namely, fidelity to the meaning of primary and vowelic sounds. If we compare this principle to a thread, parts of which are white, black, green, blue and yellow, the white may stand as the symbol of five vowelic classes of words in *a,* the black in *b*; the green in *c*; the blue in *d*; and the yellow in *e*. It creates no confusion to the eye to add, that there is a filament of red running through the whole series of colored strands, whereby five additional distinctions are made, making ten in all. These represent the two great classes of sounds of the *Algonquin* grammar, denoting what has been called the epicene and anti-epicene scheme.

If we would know to what class of conjugations a word belongs, we must inquire how the plural is made. It will be borne in mind that all verbs, like all substantives, either terminate in a vowel sound, or, where they do not, that a vowel sound must be added in making the plural, in order that it may serve as a coalescent for the epicene *g* or the anti-epicene *n*. Thus man, *inine*, is rendered men, *ininewug*, not by adding the simple epicene plural *ug*, but by throwing a *w* before it, making the plural in *wug*. So *paup*, to laugh, is rendered plural in *wug*, and not *ug*; whilst *minnis*, an island, *sebens*, a brook, and all words ending in a consonant, take the regular anti-epicene plural in *un*. The rule that in syllabication a vowel should follow a consonant is indeed universal.

The arrangement of the vowelic classes is so important to any correct view of the grammar of the language, and is, at the same time, so regular, euphonious, and philosophical, that it will impress it the better on the mind, by presenting a tabular view of it.

### CORRESPONDING CLASSES OF VERBS.

#### *Epicene Substantives.*

|   | | | PLURAL INFLECTIONS. |
|---|---|---|---|
| 1. | Words ending in | a | äg |
| 2. | " " " | e | ëg |
| 3. | " " " | i | ïg |
| 4. | " " " | o | ög |
| 5. | " " " | u | üg |

#### *Anti-epicene Substantives.*

|   | | | |
|---|---|---|---|
| 1. | Words ending in | a | än |
| 2. | " " " | e | ën |
| 3. | " " " | i | ïn |
| 4. | " " " | o | ön |
| 5. | " " " | u | ün |

*Epicene Verbs.*

CLASS OF CONJUGATIONS.

| | | | | | | | | |
|---|---|---|---|---|---|---|---|---|
| 1. | Verbs ending in | . | . ä or äg | . | . | . in class | a |
| 2. | " " " | . | . ë or ëg . | . | . | " | e |
| 3. | " " " | . | . ï or ïg | . | . | " | iᵛ |
| 4. | " " " | . | . ö or ög . | . | . | " | o |
| 5. | " " " | . | . ü or üg | . | . | " | u |

*Anti-Epicene Verbs.*

| | | | | | | | | |
|---|---|---|---|---|---|---|---|---|
| 1. | Verbs ending in | . | . ä or än | . | . | . in class | a |
| 2. | " " " | . | . ë or ën . | . | . | " | e |
| 3. | " " " | . | . ï or ïn | . | . | " | i |
| 4. | " " " | . | . ö or ön . | . | . | " | o |
| 5. | " " " | . | . ü or ün | . | . | " | u |

6. *Radices.* The *Algonquin* language is founded on roots or primary elements having a meaning by themselves. As *waub*, to see; *paup*, to laugh; *wa*, to move in space; *bwa*, a voice. The theory of its orthography is to employ these primary sounds in combination, and not as disjunctive elements, which has originated a plan of thought and concords quite peculiar. It is evident that such particles as *ak*, *be*, *ge*, were invested with generic meanings before they assumed their concrete forms of *ak-e*, earth; *ne-be*, water; *ge-zis*, sky. Without attention to this theory of radices, and to the word-building principle of the language, — to this constant capacity of incremental extension, and to the mode of doubling, triplicating, and quadruplicating ideas, it is impossible to analyze it — to trace its compounds to their embryotic roots, and to seize upon those principles of thought and utterance, by attention to which, there has been created in the forests of America, one of the most polysyllabic and completely transpositive modes of communicating thought that exists.

Humboldt applies the term "agglutinated" in defining the structure of the language. If by agglutination be meant accretion, and the adhesive principle be its syntax, the term is certainly appropriate. Whatever is agglutinated in the material world requires gluten to attach piece to piece, and its analogy in the intellectual process of sticking syllable to syllable, and word to word, is the accretive principle; and this syllabical gluten is precisely that to which the closest attention is required to trace its syntax.

7. *Word-Building.* The accretive system upon which the language is based is most clearly illustrated by analysis. *Waub* is, apparently, the radix of the verb, to see, and of the word, light. *Waubun* is the east, or sunlight, and, inferentially, place of light. *Aub* is the name of the eye-ball, hence *ai-aub,* to eye, or to see with the eye-ball. *Ozh* appears to be the root of every species of contrivance designed to float on water. *Wa-mit-ig-ozh,* the people of the wooden-made vessel — this is the *Algonquin* term for a Frenchman. *Ozh,* vessel ; *mitig,* trees or timbers, and *wa,* a plural phrase indicative of persons. It is said the Indian must have had a term for grape, before he made the compound term for wine, since the meaning of the latter is grape-liquor. *Aubo* in the *Algonquin,* means a liquid or liquor. *Shomin,* is a grape — but this is itself a dual compound. *Min,* in the same language, means a berry. The primordial root of the word is *Sho.* Hence the terms :

| | | |
|---|---|---|
| A Radix . . . . *Sho* . . . . . A grape. |
| A Radix, . . . *Min.* . . A berry. |
| Undecided, . . . *Aubo* . . . A liquor. |
| A compound of        Shominaubo.        Wine, that is grape- |
| four syllables.                          berry liquor. |

The word *Mishimin* means an apple. It is compounded from *Mish,* the primordial root, and *Min,* a berry, with the short sound of *i* thrown in for euphony. The principle of euphony requires a vowel to be interposed where two short words meet, which would bring two consonants (as in this case) together, and a consonant in expressions which would bring two vowels together. The enlargement of the word into the class of trisyllables, in all these cases, brings only *sound* into the new compound, without any enlargement of the sense. By joining the word *aubo* to this dualistic term, we have the Indian name for cider.

| | | |
|---|---|---|
| Radix, . . . . . *Mish* . . . Apple. |
| Connective, . . . . *i* |

Radix, . . . . . *Min* . . . Berry.
Undecided, . . . . *Aubo* . . Liquor.
Compound of four syllables. *Mishiminaubo.* Apple-berry liquor.

The term for rum is *ishkoda wabo.* Ishkoda is itself a compound word, *koda* signifies a plain or valley, and *ish*, fire, and is employed perhaps to denote quality and prostration ; *w* is a coalescent and *aubo*, liquor — five syllables, fire-liquor. The word for mechanical, and all classes of implements, is *Jĕgun.* To break up (any inanimate substance), is *Pegoobidön.* Land or earth is *Akki* ; *Akkum*, surface of the earth. Hence, *Pegoo-kumibeéjegun*, a plough or breaking-up-land instrument. *Wassa-au* is light ; *Biskoona*, flame. Hence, *Was-ko-nen-jegun*, a candle or light flame instrument.

Not only verbs and substantives are thus compounded and lengthened out in their syllabical structure, but adjectives admit of similar forms. Thus from the adjective radix *misk*, there is formed a variety of dual and trial compounds, which are in daily vocal use.

| | | | | |
|---|---|---|---|---|
| *Misquee,* | Blood. | From *misk*, red, and *nebee*, water. | | |
| *Misqueewon,* | Bloody. | " | " | *won*, a substance. |
| *Misqueengua,* | A blush. | " | " | *equa*, a female. |
| *Misquawauk,* | Red cedar. | " | " | *auk*, a tree. |

From the word *Minno*, good, is derived.

| | | |
|---|---|---|
| *Minnomonedo,* | . . | A good God, or an heavenly spirit. |
| *Minnoinnini,* | . . | A good man. |
| *Minnoequa,* | . . | A good woman. |

From the word *Mudjee*, or *Matchee*, as it is usually written, is formed :

| | | |
|---|---|---|
| *Matcheemonedo,* . | . . | A bad spirit of demon of evil. |
| *Matcheinnini,* | . . | A bad man. |

One of the most striking sources of Indian compounds is that derived from men's and women's names. The open firmament of heaven is the field from which these names are generally derived. They are, consequently, sublime or grandiloquent in phraseology ; sometimes poetic, always highly figurative, and often bombastic or ridiculous. The following examples of the personal names of each sex will denote this :

| | |
|---|---|
| *Au be tub gee zhig,* . . . | Centre of the sky. |
| *Baim wa wa,* . . . | The passing thunder. |
| *Cheeng gaus sin,* . . . | The noise of wind. |
| *Esh ta nak wod,* . . . | Clear sky or cloudless sky. |
| *Mo kau ge zhig,* . . . | The sun bursting from a cloud. |
| *Ning au be un,* . . . | The westerly wind. |
| *O zhau wus co ge zhig,* . . | The blue sky. |
| *Pa bau ge me wong,* . . | The showers. |
| *Sa sa gun,* . . . . | Hail. |
| *Waub un nung,* . . . | The morning star. |

Males have two and sometimes three names, but generally two, one of which may be called his baptismal name, and the other that which he has acquired from some incident or circumstance. The former is studiously concealed, and never revealed by the Indian bearing it ; the latter is the familiar cognomen. It is characteristic of female names, that they denote the gender in their terminal syllable *qua.* The following will sufficiently illustrate the manner in which they are compounded:

| | |
|---|---|
| *Au zhe bik o qua,* . . . . | Woman of the rock. |
| *Baim wa wa ge zhig a qua,* . . | Woman of the thunder-cloud. |
| *Cheeng gosh kum o qua,* . . . | Woman of the sounding footsteps. |
| *Ke neance e qua,* . . . . | Little rose-bud woman. |
| *Mau je ge zhik o qua,* . . . | Woman of the zenith. |
| *O gin e bug o qua,* . . . . | Woman of the rose. |
| *O buh bau mwa wa ge zhig o qua,* | Woman of the murmuring of the skies. |

The formation of geographical names is no exception to the rule. *Wombi,* in the Natick, or Massachusetts dialect,— which the *Wappingers* are presumed to have spoken,— means white ; *ic,* or *ik,* is a termination for *azhebik,* a rock or solid formation of rocks. Hence Wombic, the Indian name for the White mountains of New Hampshire. In the Algonquin, *monaud* signifies bad ; *nok* and *nac,* in the same language, is a term indicative of rock or precipice. Hence Monadnock, a detached

mountain of New Hampshire, whose characteristic is thus
denoted to consist in the difficulty or badness of its ascent.
The Delawares denominate their river *Lenapehituk*. Of this
term *Lenape* is their own proper name, *ituk* is a local phrase.
The Mahicans gave to their river a name similarly constituted
in *Mahicanituk*. The particle *na* in the Chippewa, indicates,
in compounds, " fairness, abundance, excellence, something
surpassing." *Amik*, is a term for a beaver, and *ong* denotes
place. Thus *Namikong*, the name for a noted point on Lake
Superior, means a surpassing place for beavers. The name
*Housatonick* is a trinary, which appears to be composed of *wassa*,
bright, *atun*, a channel or stream, and *ick* from *azhebic*, rocks ;
i. e., " Bright stream flowing through rocks." While it is
perhaps impossible to translate many of the local and geographical names which are found in the valley of the Hudson, from
the fact that the language was a mixture of Algonquin, Manhattan, Wappenackie, Mahican, Minsi and Iroquois, their formation was in accordance with the concrete principle, and in
many cases the root terms are easily detected.

Connected with this branch of his subject, the author intro-
duces a plan of a system of geographical names, founded
on the aboriginal languages, which gives to the investigation a
practical form, and, if adopted, would enrich our own language
as well as preserve the original. He says :

" It is found that many aboriginal terms which are graphically
descriptive in the native dialects, fail in the necessary euphony
and shortness necessary to their popular adoption. The principles of the polysynthetic languages embrace the rule of concen-
trating, in their compounds, the full meaning of a word upon a
single syllable, and sometimes a single letter. Thus in Alon-
quin, the particle *be* denotes water ; *wa*, inanimate motion ; *ga*,
personal action ; *ac*, a tree ; *hic*, a rock or metal. The syllable *ti*, in Iroquois, constantly means water ; *tar*, a rock ; *on*, a
hill ; *nec*, a tree. In the Natick or Massachusetts dialect, as
given by Mr. Eliot, the negative form of elementary words is
*matta ;* the local inflection *ett ;* the adjective great, *missi ;*
black, *mooi ;* white, *wompi*.

45

" The Indian languages also contain generic syllables or particles in the shape of inflections to nouns and verbs ; in the Algonquin, *abo*, a liquid ; *jegun*, or simply *gun*, an instrument ; *jewun*, a current ; *wunzh*, a plant ; *ong* or *onk*, a place, &c.

" By these concentrations, descriptive words become replete with meanings ; but it requires a very nice collocation and adjustment of syllables to attain the requisite degree of euphony, for the adoption of such compounds by foreign ears. Generally, words of three syllables recommend themselves to the English ear for quantity, in geographical names adopted from an Indian language, as heard in Oswego, Chicago, Ohio, Monadnock, and Toronto. In the terms suggested in the following lists of words, intended to be introduced into our geographical nomenclature, the principles of elision and concentration referred to, have been applied. The root-forms carry the entire signification to which they are entitled, in the elementary vocabulary, after they have been divested, by analysis, of their adjuncts. Thus, in the Algonquin, the syllable *ac* stands for land, earth, ground, soil ; *be*, for water, liquid ; *bic*, for rock, stone, metal, hard mineral ; *co* for object ; *ke* for country, precinct, or territory ; *os* for pebble, loose stone, detritus ; *min*, good ; *ia*, the term for a beautiful scene ; *na*, a particle, which, in compound words, denotes excellence ; *oma*, a large body of water ; *non*, a place ; *gan*, a lake ; *coda*, a plain or valley ; *oda*, a town, village, or cluster of houses, &c.

" By adding the primary syllable of a word, as conveying the entire signification of the word, and employing it as a nominative to other syllables, which are also made use of in their concentrated forms, a class of words is formed, which are generally shorter than their parent forms, more replete in their meanings, and securing, at the same time, a more uniformly euphonious pronounciation. Quantity and accent being thus at command by these elisions and transpositions, the number of syllables of which a new class of words shall consist, is a question to be predetermined. Expletive consonants, harsh gutturals, and double inflections, the pests of Indian lexography, are dropped, and the selections made from syllables which abound in liquid and vowel sounds. For it should be the object to preserve, as new elements in this peculiar branch of American literature, not the harsh and barbarous, but the soft and sonorous sounds.

1. *Terms from the Algonquin.* " As a basis for these terms, we take, from the vocabulary of analyzed words, the primary terms *ad, ab, os, wud, pat, mo, at, seeb, gon, pew, chig, naig, ag, mon, tig, cos, pen, mig, won;* meaning respectively deer, home, pebble, mountain, hill, spring, channel or current, river, clay-land, iron, shore, sand, water's edge, corn, tree, grass, bird, eagle, rose-bud. Subjecting these nominatives to the adjective expression *ia*, signifying beautiful, fair, admirable, and placing the particle *nac*, land, earth, soil, in the objective, and changing the latter for *gan* a lake; *bee*, water; *min*, good; *na*, excellent; *ma*, large water; *ock*, forest; we have the following trisyllabic terms:

| | | |
|---|---|---|
| Deer, . . . . | *Ad* . . . | *Ad ia nac.* |
| Home, . . . | *Ab* . . . | *Ab ia nac.* |
| Pebble, . . . | *Os* . . | *Os ia nac.* |
| Mountain, . . | *Wud* . . | *Wud ia nac.* |
| Hill, . . . . | *Pat* . . | *Pat ia nac.* |
| Spring, . . . | *Mo* . . | *Mo ia nac.* |
| Current, . . . | *At* . . | *At ia nac.* |
| River, . . . | *Seeb* . . | *Seeb ia nac.* |
| Clay-land, . . . | *Gon* . . | *Gon ia nac.* |
| Iron, . . . | *Pew* . . | *Pew ia nac.* |
| Shore, . . . . | *Chig* . . | *Chig ia nac.* |
| Sand, . . . | *Naig* . . | *Naig ia nac.* |
| Beach, . . . . | *Ag* . . | *Ag ia nac.* |
| Corn, . . . | *Mon* . . | *Mon ia nac.* |
| Tree, . . . . | *Tig* . . | *Tig ia nac.* |
| Grass, . . . | *Cos* . . | *Cos ia nac.* |
| Bird, . . . . | *Pen* . . | *Pen ia nac.* |
| Eagle, . . . | *Mig* . . | *Mig ia nac.* |
| Rose-bud, . . . | *Won* . . | *Won ia nac.* |

" By reversing the action of the verb, or noun nominative, a new set of phrases is created, by which the meaning is changed from deer-land, home-land, &c., to land of deer, land of home, &c. The number of the objective syllables is as various as the objects in nature. The whole class of animals, birds, rep-

tiles, insects, fishes; the wide-spread phenomena of the
heavens, of the forests and of the waters, supply words which
are susceptible of being employed in the construction of new
terms. Not only can the objective be exchanged for the nominative, but the qualifying word admits of many euphonious ex-
changes, and it may itself be employed as an objective, and the
nominative itself thrown in the body of the terms as a qualifying syllable; producing a set of words like those heard in Peoria
and Kaskaskia, where the terminal syllable, *ia*, denotes fair or
beautiful. In these terms the syllable *os*, denoting pebble or
drift, is the adjunct noun.

| | | |
|---|---|---|
| *Adósia* . . . | Fair deer land, . . | From *Adic.* |
| *Abósia,* . . | Fair home land, . . | " *Abia.* |
| *Patósia,* . . | Fair hill, . . . . | " *Ishpatina.* |

" If the terminal *ome* or *oma*, as it is heard in Gitchig-oma,
be employed, we have a set of terms denoting water prospects.

| | |
|---|---|
| *Min-ó-ma,* . . . . . | Good water. |
| *Mos-ó-ma,* . . . . . | Moose water. |
| *Mon-ó-ma,* . . . . . | Spirit water. |
| *Mok-ó-ma,* . . . . . | Spring water. |
| *Ac-ó-ma,* . . . . . | Rock water. |

" The particle *na* as heard in Namikong, denotes excellent,
abundant, surpassing. By taking this for the objective syllable,
and retaining the same nominative, and the same qualifying
syllable made use of above, the resulting terms are as follows:

| | | | |
|---|---|---|---|
| *Min-iá-na,* . . . . | Good, fair and excellent. | | |
| *Ack-iá-na,* . . . | " | " | land. |
| *Tig-iá-na,* . . . . | " | " | trees. |
| *Mon-iá-na,* . . . . | " | " | spirits. |

2. *Terms from the Iroquois.* The syllables *co*, a cascade; *ti*,
water; *tar*, rock; *on*, hill; *asto*, a defile, are selected as ex-
hibiting the transpositive capacities of this language.

" Termination in *atea*, a valley or landscape.

| | |
|---|---|
| *Co-at-at-ea,* . . . | Valley below falls. |
| *Ti-at-at-ea* . . . | Well watered valley. |

*Tar-at-at-ea,* . . . Rocks of the valley.
*On-at-at-ea,* . . . Hills of the valley.
*As-to-at-ea,* . . . Narrow pass of a river in the valley.

"Terminations in *oga*, a place, change these terms to "place of water and rocks," "place of hills and rocks," "place of the watery vale," etc. Terminations in *io*, beautiful: Co-i-o, beautiful falls; Te-i-o, beautiful waters; On-ti-o, beautiful hills; Tar-i-o, beautiful rocks; Os-i-o, beautiful view."

Examples of transpositions and elisions are abundantly furnished, but sufficient have been quoted to illustrate the principle and direct attention to the subject. Instead of Smith's corners, Johnson's mills, and a class of local terms without significance, might be introduced Na-pee-na, abounding in birds; Al-gan-see, water of the plains; I-ós-co, water of light; I-é-nia, wanderer's rest; Was-sa-han-na, bright river; Sho-min-ac, grape-land; Mon-á-kee, spirit land; Tal-lú-la, leaping waters; Os-sé-go, beautiful view; Bis-có-da, beautiful plain, terms of appropriate and permanent import. For private residences or country seats, no class of terms could be applied more expressive or more American. The titles of the old world certainly need not be copied when those that are fresh and fragrant await adoption.

### *Dialectic Vocabularies.*

Dialectic vocabularies, while not without their value for comparative purposes and for supplying primitive terms, afford but little aid in other respects. As a general rule, those which have been preserved are composed of words spoken in different localities and at different periods, and frequently mislead the inquirer. Those having occasion to do so, will consult them in their most complete form in *Schoolcraft's History*, and in *Gallatin's Synopsis*. The table annexed is introduced as simply illustrative.

## Comparative Vocabulary.

| | OLD ALGONQUIN. | LONG ISLAND. | MASSACHUSETTS. | MAHICAN. | DELAWARE. | MINSI. | SHAWANOES. | CHIPPEWAY. | MOHAWK. |
|---|---|---|---|---|---|---|---|---|---|
| God, | Kitchi manittoo | manto | manittoo; manit | { manito-a spirit, / pautaumomvoth, } | manitto | | wishemenetou | ketche manito | lawaneeu. |
| Man, | alissinap | run | wosketomp | neemanaoo | *liinnu; lenno | lenno | illeni | | oonguich. |
| Woman, | ickweh | squah | mittamwosses | pghainoom | *hokkua²a²; okhqueh | ochqueu | equiwa | | o-oonhechlien. |
| An Indian, | | ichun | aberginian | | lenape | | clanematethalene | | guihhoonwih. |
| House, Hut, | wikiwam | weecho | wekit; wetu | weekuwuhm | wiquóäm | wichquoam | wiggewoam | wakyigun | canuchsha. |
| Fire, | skootay | shut | nootae; nootau | stauw | *taande; tendeu | tendeu | scoote | ishkodai | ocheerle. |
| Water, | nipi | nup; niep | nippe | nbey | bee; mbi | niby | neppee; nûpee | neebi | oochnekanus. |
| Earth, | ackey, ackwin | keagh | ohke | akek | *ha²a²kke; aki; akhki | achgi | assiskee; ake | ahke | oohunjah. |
| River, | sipin | seepus | sepu | sepoo | *kittuun; sipu | sipu | sepi | seebi | kaihunhatate. |
| Stone, | assin | sun | qussuk; hussun | thaunaumku | akhsin | achsin | seegonah | { cssin-(stone),... / azhibik-(rock), } | oonoyah. |
| Tree, | meteeh | peuoye | mehtug | machtok | mihktuk | michtuk | touane | metik | kerllitle. |
| White, | wabi | wampayo | wompi | waupaaeek | *opeek; wape; wapsu | opeh | opee | { wawbishkaw-(inan) / wawbizze-(animate) } | curlagu. |
| Black, | mackatey | shickayo | moo-i | n'sikkayóoh | *siitke; nesgissit | nesgeek | mukkoote | mukkudaiwa | cahoonge. |
| Red, | miskwey | squayo | mishque | m chgaju | *mokkee; makhget | machksu | m'shwûâhwee | miskwa | ooqunchtarla. |
| Valley, | | | { ooneuhkoi; / oonouwohkoai, } | | *indatatakushaak; | | naiskgúiee | tahwattenaug | chechuloom wakoo. |
| Hill, | | | wadchuemes | gh'aukoock | { pakhsajek, / wakhtshutit, } | | moqueghke | ishpatinah | onondate. |
| Mountain, | | | wudchue; wadchu | w'chu | *ohee; wakhtshuh, | | missiwagewee | wudju | yoonoondoo waunuh. |
| Island, | minnis | | menohhannet | mnauhan | *menatey; menokhtey, | Minnis | menathee | minnis | cawaynoote. |
| Beaver, | amik | | tummunk | amisque | *nakuee; ktemaque, | | amaquah | ahmik | chinneetoo. |
| Bear, | mackwah | | mosq | mquoh | mak'hk, | | mukwquah | mukwquah | ooguharlee. |
| Wolf, | mahingan | | { mukquooshim; / mukquoshin, } | | { tumme; m'tummeu; / wiekhtiheu, } | | m'waiwah | micengun | ahgiohhoo. |
| Partridge, | pileysiwey | apacus | | pahpahcogh | *pupikuiis; popocus, | | kokolahsothah | pinai | oohquaizun. |
| Turkey, | | nahiam | nahenan | | tshikenum, | | pelewa | mezissa | skahwurlowurnee. |
| Fish, | kikons | operamac | nahmos | namassak | *namiis; namoes, | namees | amatha | kikon | keiyunk. |

*West New Jersey dialect as distinguished from Pennsylvania.

### III. GEOGRAPHICAL NOMENCLATURE AND TRADITIONS.

N addition to the geographical terms which have been given in the body of this work, there are many to which reference may very properly be made, as well as traditions " which take the form of history," from their very general acceptance as such. It is to be regretted that the orthography of most of the Indian geographical terms is so badly rendered in the official records as to make interpretation almost impossible, even where the dialect has been preserved, and especially is it to be regretted that the dialects themselves have not been preserved with more of their original character. As an almost universal rule, however, the statement may be accepted as a fact that the Indians had little of poetry in their composition, and that, while many of their terms can be made poetical, they were originally of the plainest and simplest descriptive equivalents. A black hill or a red hill, a large hill or a small one, a small stream of water or a larger one, or one which was muddy or stony, a field of maize, or of leeks, overhanging rocks or dashing waterfalls (*patternack*),— almost invariably denoting some physical peculiarity, or some product of the soil. Their commemorative terms were few.

*Manhattan* has already been explained as signifying island, or, in its plural form, islands; as applied to the people, "the people of the islands." The extreme point of land between the junction of East and North rivers, of which the battery is now a part, was called *Kapsee*, and is still known to many persons as the Copsie point. The term appears to have denoted a " safe place of landing," formed by eddy waters. *Sappokanikan*, a point of land on the Hudson below Greenwich avenue, is supposed to indicate, " the carrying place," from *sipon*, river, and *ounigan*, a portage. The Indians carried their canoes either over the point or across the island to East river, at this place, to save the trouble of paddling down to the foot of the island and then up the East river. (*O'Callaghan*). Corlear's hook was called *Naghtognk*, according to Benson. The name is also given as *Rechtauck;* from *reckwa*, sand. A tract of meadow land on the north end of the island, near Kingsbridge, was called *Muscoota*, that is " meadow or grass land." (*Benson.*) *Warpoes* was a term bestowed on a piece of elevated ground, situated above and beyond the small lake or pond called the *kolck;* the latter occupying several acres in the neighborhood of the present halls of justice in Centre street. Many of the streets of the city are laid out upon the old Indian paths. This is true of Broadway from the battery to the Park, where the Indian paths forked, one running east to Chatham square, and the other west to Tivoli garden, etc. This would lead to *Warpoes* by paths on the east and west side of the kolck. At or beyond *Warpoes* the paths again forked, one leading to *Sappokanikan* on the Hudson, and the other to *Naghtognk* or Corlear's hook. The island was not a place of permanent abode of the Indians, but was only occupied during certain seasons. It was sold to Minuet, the first director-general of the Holland government, in 1624, and was then estimated to contain about twenty-two thousand acres. The price paid to the Indians was sixty guilders, or about twenty-four dollars.

Staten island bears different names in different deeds. In the deed to Michael Pauw, in 1631, it is called *Matawucks,* and in that to Capellen, in 1655, *Eghquaous.* DeVries says that it was called *Monocknong,* and that the clan occupying it were *Monatons.* The deed to Capellen states that it was jointly owned by the *Raritans* and the *Hackinsacks.* Governor's island was called by the Indians, *Pagganck;* Bedloe's island, *Minnisais;* Ellis' island, *Kioshk;* and Blackwell's island, *Minnahanock,* the latter signifying "at the island," or "the island home." "The word is a compound of *Menahan,* an island, and *uck,* locality." (*O'Callaghan*).

On the point of land now öccupied by Fort Schuyler is located a tradition which Judge Benson relates in his *Memoirs of New York.* Directly opposite the fort are the famous stepping stones,[1] consisting of a number of rocks which project

[1] On a map descriptive of the battle near Lake George, in 1755, Stepping Stones is also applied to the palisades on the Hudson.—*Documentary History,* iv, 259.

in a line.from the Long Island shore, and show their bare tops at low water. " An Indian origin," says Benson, " is asserted for this name, and a tradition vouched as authority." It is said, that at a certain time the evil spirit set up a claim against the Indians, to Connecticut, as his peculiar domain ; but they being in possession, determined, of course, to try to hold it. The surface of Connecticut and Long Island were then the reverse of what they are now. The latter was covered with rocks ; Connecticut was free from them. The Indians first tried to negotiate with his majesty ; offering to retire from the land, provided they were permitted to girdle the trees and remove their property. No answer was made to the proposition, and both parties appealed to arms. The arch-leader took the field alone ; and being an overmatch for the Indians in skill and spirit, he at first advanced on them ; but, they having provided there should be constant reinforcements on their march, thereby preserving their corps entire, and harassing him incessantly, giving him no rest night nor day, he was obliged finally to yield to vigilance and perseverance, and fall back. He retired collected, and, as usual, gave up the ground only inch by inch ; and though retiring, still presenting a front whenever attack threatened. He kept close to the sound to secure his flank from attack on that side ; and having reached the point, and the water becoming narrow, and the tide running out, and the rocks showing their heads, he availed himself of them, and stepping from one to the other effected his retreat to Long Island. He at first betook himself, silent and sullen, to Coram, in the middle of the island ; but it being in his nature not to remain idle long, and rage being superadded, soon roused him and ministered to him the means of revenge. He collected all the rocks in the island in heaps at Cold Spring, and throwing them in different directions, to different distances across the sound in Connecticut, covered the surface of it with them as we now see it."

This tradition was given to the first settlers at Cold Spring, and the last Indians who remained there not only undertook to show the spot where his majesty stood, but insisted that they could still discern the prints of his feet. A projecting point of land on the neck is still called Satan's Toe.

46

Among the natural curiosities of Long Island is *Ronconcoa lake*, lying upon the boundary line which divides the four towns of Smithtown, Setauket, Islip, and Patchogue. This lake is of great depth and for a long time was supposed to be unfathomable. It has an ebb and flow in its waters at different periods ; and was early made the theme of Indian story and tradition. They regarded it with a species of superstitious veneration, and although it abounded in a variety of fish, they, at the early settlement, refused to eat them, believing they were superior beings and placed there by the Great Spirit.

About thirty miles from Brooklyn and midway between the north and south sides of the island, is a hill known as *Manetta*, a corruption of the original name, which was *Manitou*, or the hill of the Great Spirit. The tradition is, that many ages since, the aborigines residing in those parts suffered extremely from the want of water. Under their suffering they offered up prayers to the Great Spirit for relief. That in reply to their supplications, the Great Spirit directed their chieftain should shoot his arrow in the air, and on the spot where it fell they should dig, and would assuredly discover the element they so much desired. They pursued the direction, dug, and found water. There is now a well situated on this rising ground ; and the tradition continues to say, that this well is on the very spot indicated by the Good Spirit. The probabilities are that the hill takes its name from the fact that it was used as the place of general offering to the Great Spirit.

*Canoe Place*, on the south side of the island, near Southampton, derives its name from the fact, that more than two centuries ago a canal was made there by the Indians, for the purpose of passing their canoes from one bay to the other, that is across the island from *Mecox* bay to *Peconic* bay. Although the trench has been in a great measure filled up, yet its remains are still visible, and partly flowed at high water. It was constructed by *Mongotucksee*, or Long Knife, who then reigned over the nation of *Montauk* — a chief of gigantic form, proud and despotic in peace, and terrible in war. But although a tyrant of his people, he protected them from their enemies, and commanded their respect for his savage virtues. He sustained his power not less by the resources of his mind than by the vigor of his arm. An ever watchful policy guided his councils. Prepared for every exigency, not even aboriginal sagacity could surprise his canton. To facilitate communication around the seat of his dominion — for the purpose not only of defense but of annoyance — he constructed this canal, which remains a monument of his genius. The praises of *Mongotucksee* are still chanted in aboriginal verse to the winds that howl around the eastern extremity of the island.

Long Island, as already stated, was called *Sewanhackey.* Among the localities, *Occopoque* (Riverhead), takes its name from *accup*, a creek. The Indian village of *Accopogue* was situated on the creek which enters Little Peconic bay on the north side. *Nepeage* was the name of the peninsula which unites Montauk to the western part of East Hampton, and is supposed to mean " water land," from *nepe*, water, and *eage*, earth or land. (*O'Callaghan.*) *Montauk*, the name for the east end of the island, is from *mintuck*, a tree, in the Narragansett dialect. The place abounded with trees, according to Thompson. (*Ibid.*) *Namke*, from *namaas*, fish and *ke*, place was the name of the creek near Riverhead. (*Ibid.*) *Mereyckawick* (Brooklyn), is from *me*, the article in the Algonquin ; *reckwa*, sand, and *ick*, locality, "the sandy place." The name was probably applied, at first, to the bottom land or beach. Wallabout bay was called " the boght of Mareckawick." (*Ibid.*) *Huppogues*, in Smithtown, is an abbreviation of *sumhuppaog*, the Narragansett word for beavers. (*Rhode Island Historical Collections*, 1, 95.)

Bolton, in his *History of Westchester County*, has preserved many of the Indian names in that district. To the Spuyten Duyvel creek he assigns the term, *Papirinimen.* O'Callaghan gives the same name to a tract " on the north end of the island of Manhattans," about 228th street, between Spuyten Duyvel creek on the west and Harlem river on the east. Saw mill creek was called *Neperah*, from *nepe*, water, and gave its name to the Indian village of *Nappeckamak*, which stood on the site of the present village of Yonkers, literally "the rapid water settlement." In an obscure nook on the Hudson, west of the *Neperah*, is a large rock which was called *Meghkeekassin*, or

*Amackassin,*[1] or "the great stone," to which it is said the Indians paid reverence as an evidence of the permanency and immutability of their deity.

No Indian name more frequently occurs in the history of the county than that of *Weckquaesgeek*, nor one the precise location of which there is more difficulty in determining. O'Callaghan says: "This tract is described as extending from the Hudson to the East river. The name is from *wigwos*, birch bark, and *keag*, country —" the country of the birch bark." Bolton gives the name to an Indian village which occupied the site of Dobbs' ferry, which he denominates "the place of the bark kettle." In *Albany Records*, III, 379, is this entry: "Personally appeared *Sauwenare*, sachem of Wieckqueskeck, *Amenameck* his brother, and others, all owners, etc., of lands situated on North river called *Wieckquaeskeck*, and declared that they had sold the same to Wouter Van Twiller in 1645." In a deed to Frederick Phillipse, April 12, 1682, the bounds of the tract conveyed are given as, "southerly to a creek or fall called by the Indians Weghquegsike," and in another deed the tract is described as "a piece of land lying about *Wighquaeskeek*," and in still another the creek is called *Weghqueghe*. Bolton says the creek was called *Wysquaqua*.

The Indian name for Tarrytown was *Alipconck*, "the place of elms." Sing-Sing takes its name from an Indian village called *Ossing-sing*, from *ossin*, a stone, and *ing*, a place, the "place of stones," or "stone upon stone." (*Bolton*.) In a deed to Philip Phillipse, 1685, it is said, "a creek called *Kitchawan*, called by the Indians *Sinksink*." Bolton, however, gives the name of *Kitchawonck* to the Croton river. The site of the present village of Peekskill was called *Sackhoes* and was occupied by an Indian village known by that name. Teller's point was called *Senasqua*. Tradition weaves the story that the forms of the ancient warriors still haunt the surrounding glens and woods of this district, and the Haunted Hollow, and the sachems of Teller's point, have become household words in the neighborhood. Another tradition tells us that a desperate conflict was

---

[1] In one of the Phillipse Deeds, it is described as "a great rock called by the Indians *Sigghes*."

once held here by the *Kitchawongs* against their enemies, and that the mound near the entrance to Teller's point was erected over the dead who fell on that memorable occasion.

Anthony's nose was called *Kittatenny*, à Delaware term signifying "endless hills."[1] *Poconteco* river, called also *Pekanteco* or *Pereghanduck*, is presumed to express in its name the dark river; from *pohkunni*, dark, inde. *pecontecue*, night. The stream may have been densely overshadowed by trees. (*O'Callaghan.*) Bolton says the name signifies "a run between two hills." The Dutch styled it "Sleepy Haven kil," hence the origin of the present term Sleepy Hollow applied to the valley. *Sacrahung*, or mill river, takes its name from *sacra*, rain. Its liability to freshets after heavy rains, may have given origin to the Indian name. (*Ibid.*) *Quinnahung*, a neck of land at the mouth and west side of the Bronck river,— from *quinni*, long, and *unk*, locality. (*Ibid.*) *Aquehung*, "the place of peace,"—from *aquene*, peace,— was the name given to the place occupied by Jonas Bronck in commemoration of the peace which was there concluded with the Indians in 1643. (*Ibid.*) The Indian name for the Bronck tract, however, was *Ranachque* or *Raraque*. The tract commonly called by the English the "White Plains," was known to the Indians as *Quaroppas*. Verplanck's point was called *Meahagh*, and the lands immediately east, *Appamaghpogh*. *Poningo*, the name of the residence of one of the chiefs of the *Siwanoys*, embraces the tract of land now included in the towns of Rye and Harrison. Rye Neck was called *Apawquammis*. The town of Morisania was known as *Ranachque* or *Raraque*. The towns of New Castle and Bedford occupy a tract called *Shappequa*, a name now applied to the Shappequa hills, and destined to be remembered from its recent association with the name of Mr. Horace Greeley. The west neck adjoining New Rochelle was called *Magopson*. The Byram river was known by the name of *Armonck*, and the meadows bordering it *Haseco* and *Miosehassaky*. Harlem river was called *Muscoota*; Blind brook, *Mockquams*, and the high ridge east of it, *Enketaupuenson*; Beaver dam or Stony Brook, *Pockestersen*, and Delancey's neck, *Waumainuck*. A tract called *Rippowams*

---

[1] The name is applied to the entire range both in New Jersey and New York.

fell to the share of the people of Stamford, Conn., in 1655. It extended eighteen miles north and south, and eight miles east and west.

In the town of Carmel, in the county of Putnam, is located Lake *Macookpack*, now *Mahopack*, a term probably signifying simply a large inland lake, from *ma* large water and *aki* land. The same name was applied to what is now known as Copake lake in Columbia county. The lake is nine miles in circumference, and is situated about eighteen hundred feet above the level of the sea. On one of the islands of the lake is what is called the Chieftain's rock, on which was held, according to tradition, the last council of the tribe. This council was for the purpose of considering the proposition of the English to buy their lands and remove the tribe to the far west. Canopus, the aged sachem of the tribe, urged his followers to reject the proposal ; to rally to the defense of their empire, and the graves of their fathers. His impassioned eloquence determined the council against the proposition. JOHN W. LEE, Esq., of New York, has thrown this legend into the following verse :

"Once the airy curtain lifted, and the shadows rolling back,
Shadows of the years that hover o'er the lake of Mahopac —
Showed me Indian warriors gathered in the wooded island dell,
Which the rocks, all worn and moss-clad, and the waters guarded well.
    *    *    *    *,    *    *    *    *    *    *

Then upon the ledge above them, rose an aged, yet stalwart form,
Like some monarch of the forest, bending never to the storm,
Rose the CHIEFTAIN OF THE ISLAND, with that bearing of a king,
Which the pride of birth may strive for, but the SOUL alone can bring.

Turned his eagle gaze upon them, and with voice as clarion clear,
Waked the dreamers, and the waiting, wearied MAIDEN sleeping near :
"Rouse, Mahicans ! sons of heroes ! keep your ancient honor bright !
I have seen you in the battle — ye were lions in the fight.

" I have seen you in the council, when the watch-fire lit the glen,
And the clouds of war hung o'er us — ye were all undaunted then ;
When the faggots blazed around you, all defiant in your pain;
I have heard you chant your death-song — chieftains, NOW be men again !

"Snake or traitor hissed that whisper : ' Sell your forests, there is rest
On the banks of the Mississippi, on the prairies of the west.'
Who the craven counsel uttered ?   Let him in the fire-light stand !
Nay, he dares not.   Crouching coward ! palsied be thy trembling hand !

" When the pale-face, rushing on thee, grasps thy hatchet and thy bow !
Hark, the Spirit ! ' Stand, Mahicans ; guard your forests, meet the foe !'
By the memory of our empire ; by the mounds along the bank,
Where our fathers hear the moaning of the river Kicktawanc !

" Brothers ! gird ye for the struggle ; breast to breast, and eye to eye,
Let us swear the oath of glory — one to conquer, one to die !
Sound once more your ancient war cry !   Sound it from the mountain's
     steep,
Where the eagle hath her eyrie, and the rocks their vigils keep.

" Twice ten thousand shouts shall answer from the river to the sea !
Dare, nor falter !   Fear is failure.   Craven-hearted, will ye flee?
Go ! yet on the darkening future, read the sentence of your doom,
As, in letters of the lightning, traced upon a scroll of gloom !

" Go ! the western tribes shall meet you, ye will be an handful then,
And shall perish in your weakness — perish from the minds of men !
Like yon rushing highland river, in its mountains wild and free,
In the ocean lost forever.   Thus shall be your destiny ."

The Highlands of the Hudson were not called Matteawan
mountains, as stated by Moulton.   The Indians had no names
for mountain ranges, but designated different parts or peaks by
different names.   In the patent known as the Little Nine
Partners, one of the more eastern peaks of the Highland range
is called *Weputing*, from *Weepitung*, literally tooth mountain,
probably from its resemblance to a molar tooth.   The nearest
approach to a name for the range was that which the Indians
sometimes applied to themselves —*Wequehachke*, or " the people
of the hill country." [1]   The Dutch used Hoogland or Hogeland in speaking of the range, and, like the Indians, gave names
to particular peaks, as Anthony's Nose, Dunderberg, Buttaberg,
etc.

[1] Hogeland, or Hoogland, Dutch for
Highlands, a name applied to the Highlands of New York.   The Indians called
them *Wequehachke*, the hill country.—
*Memorials Moravian Church*, 146.

*Matteawan* was the Indian name for what is now called Fishkill creek, but which the early settlers denominated the " Fresh
kil or creek." The meaning of the word has been defined
as " good furs," and Moulton has endeavored to associate
it with the incantations of Indian priests, but on no positive
authority. *Matta*, in the Massachusetts dialect, is the elementary form of negative words, and generally used for *no ; wa* is
inanimate motion. This interpretation applied to the creek,
would be " no water " or " little water or motion." Another
classification would be *ma*, large water ; *tea*, valley or landscape ; *wan*, inanimate motion — literally "the large water in the
valley," *wan* perhaps referring to that portion of the creek near
its confluence with the Hudson.

What is now known as Wappinger's creek, while appropri-
ately preserving the name of its aboriginal owners, was not so
called by them, but by the very beautiful name, *Mawenawasigh*.
The precise meaning of the phrase cannot be given. *Ma* is
the Algonquin for large water ; *we* is also water ; *na* is excellence, fairness, abundance, something surpassing; *wasigh* is
apparently a corrupt rendering of *wassa*, light or foamy water.
A large stream of excellent water, or a large waterfall, would
seem to cover the original definition. Such names are beautiful without interpretation, and far more appropriate than many
English geographical terms. Wappinger's Falls, the name of the
village near the locality from which it takes its name, might well
be changed to *Mawenawasigh*.

*Apoquague* was the Indian name of what is now called Silver
lake, in Fishkill. The name signifies " round pond." *Wic-
copee* was the Indian name of the highest peak in the Fishkill
mountains on the south border of East Fishkill, and also of the
pass or gorge in the mountains through which the Indian trail
formerly ran. An Indian castle is traditionally located here,
and another at *Shenandoah*. It is said that at Fishkill hook
remains of an Indian burial ground have been found, and also
that apple trees planted by them were still bearing within the
memory of the earlier inhabitants.

An explanation of *Wappingers* may be proper in this connection. Although passed irrevocably into history, the term is a

corruption of *wabun*, east, and *acki*, land which, as applied by
the Indians to themselves, may be rendered Eastlanders, or Men
of the East. The French preserved the original very nearly in
*Abenaqué*, and Heckewelder in *Wapanachki* (note, *ante* p. 45).
The Dutch historians are responsible for *Wappingers*, perhaps
from their rendering of the sound of the original word, and perhaps as expressing the fact that they were, in the Dutch language, *wapen* or half-armed Indians.

Fourteen miles west of the Hudson and a few miles north of
Poughkeepsie was *Querapoquett*, from whence the boundary of
the Sackett tract ran north-east to a tree on the east side of
the *Wesiack* subsequently known as Ten Mile river. Of the
Indian name, O'Callaghan says: " *Wissayck*, rocky country,"
from *qussuk*, a rock, and *ick*, a locality." A more correct explanation is probably derived from *wassa*, light, and *ick*, locality —
the light or bright waters. It was in this district that the
Moravians found their fields of labor in the villages of *Shecomeco*,
*Wechquadnach* and *Pachgatgoch*. The former name is preserved
in that of the stream upon which the village stood, while the
second is applied to the lake now called Indian pond.

A tract of meadow land "lying slanting to the Dancing
Chamber," north of Wappinger's creek, had for its eastern
boundary a creek called *Wynogkee*. Schoolcraft defines Poughkeepsie as signifying safe harbor, from *apokeepsing ;* but the
interpretation is open to question. In early documents the
name is variously spelled. In a deed to Arnot Veil, 1680,
covering the tract, the boundaries are described as " beginning
at a creek called *Pacaksing*, by the river side ;" in a petition from
Wm. Caldwell the orthography is *Pogkeepke ;* in an affidavit by
Myndert Harmense, it is *Pokeepsinck ;* in other papers the prevailing orthography is *Poghkeepke*, and finally it is found applied
to a pond of water, lying in the vicinity of the city, and its signification given ; or muddy pond, an explanation which accords
with the accepted interpretation of *Ramepogh* — a simple generic
term for pond, or ponds, modified by locality or character.
West of Poughkeepsie, and constituting the boundary of the
Veil tract was *Matapan* fall or creek. In the geographical
terms of this district *ma*, *mata* and *matea*, frequently occur.

Crum Elbow creek was called *Equorsink*, and the lands ad-joining, on the Hudson, *Eaquaquanessink;* so given in a patent to Henry Beekman, the bounds of which ran from the Hudson " east by side of a fresh meadow called *Mansakin* and a small creek called *Mancapawimick*." In a patent to Peter Fal-conier and others the lands are called *Eaquaquannessinck,* the meadow *Mansakin,* the small creek *Nancapaconick,* and the Crum Elbow *Eaquarysink.* The boundary line of the " Great Nine Partners patent" began " at the creek called by the Indians *Aquasing* and by the Christians Fish creek." The Christians spoken of made free use of the word Fish, no less than three streams emptying into the Hudson being given that name. The signification of the Indian name, however, is not involved in the Dutch designations. In this case *Aquasing* apparently indicates stony, from *qusuk.* Roeloff Jansen's kil was the dividing line between the *Mahicans* and the *Wappingers,* a fact which has not only been already stated but which the reader will recognize in the change in dialect shown in the geographical terms. The creek was called *Sankpenak.* In the Livingston patent, of which it formed the southern boundary, the names of a number of localities are given, and, in some cases, their signification. In his first purchase were " three planes" or tracts of " flat lands" called *Nekankook, Kickua,* and *Wicquaskaka,* lying on the Hudson between " a small creek or kil" lying over against Katskill, called *Wackan-hassack,* and a place called by the Indians *Swaskahamuka.* His second, or *Taghkanick* tract, began at a place called *Minis-sichtanock;* thence west along a small hill " to a creek" called *Quissicheook;* thence " to a high place" called *Skaanpook,* which, " a little lower down" is called *Twastawekah;* then south along the foot of the high mountains " to the path that goes to *Wawijchtanok,* " to a hill called by the Indians *Mananosick;*" then west to " a creek" called *Nachawawachkano,* " which creek empties into the *Twastawekah,*" the place " where the two creeks meet being called *Mawichnanck*." His third purchase began at a creek called *Wachankasigh;* thence to a place called *Wawanaquassick,* " where the heaps of stones lye," near the head of a creek called *Nanapenahekan,* " which comes out of a

marsh lying near unto the said hills of the said heaps of stones
upon which the Indians throw another as they pass by, from
an ancient custom among them ;" then to the " northernmost
end of the hills that are to the north of *Tacahkanick,* known
by the name of *Ahashewaghkick ;*" then " along the said hills to
the southernmost end of the same, called *Wichquapakkat.*" In
the line of the boundaries " a rock or great stone" is called
*Acawaisik,* and " a dry gully at Hudson's river," *Sackahampa.*
*Taghkanick,* the name now applied to the entire range of hills
forming the eastern boundary of the manor lands, was originally
local, as appears not only from the names given to the north
and south ends respectively, but from the fact that the Indians
had no titles for entire mountain ranges. The name is pronounced Toh-kon-ick, and is said to have been given to a spring
on the west side of the mountains in Copake. Copake lake
was called *Kookpake.* (*See Mahopac.*) *Scompamuck* was the
name of the locality now covered by the village of Ghent.

*Wawanaquassick,* " where the heaps of stones lye ;" has its
plural in *wa-wa ; na* signifies good ; *quas* is stone or stones, and
*ick* locality. The name is without commemorative character.
Of the custom referred to in the quotation, the Rev. Gideon
Hawley writes : " We came to a resting place, and breathed
our horses, and slaked our thirst at the stream, when we perceived our Indian looking for a stone, which having found, he
cast to a heap, which for ages had been accumulating by pas-
sengers like him, who was our guide. We inquired why he
observed that rite. He answered that his father practised it
and enjoined it on him. But he did not like to talk on the subject. I have observed in every part of the country, and among
every tribe of Indians, and among those where I now am in
a particular manner, such heaps of stones or sticks collected on the like occasion as the above. The largest heap
I ever observed, is that large collection of *small* stones
on the mountain between Stockbridge and Great Barring-
ton. We have a Sacrifice rock, as it is termed, between
Plymouth and Sandwich, to which stones and sticks are always
cast by Indians who pass it. This custom or rite is an acknowledgment of an invisible being. We may style him the unknown

God, whom this people worship. This heap is his altar. The stone that is collected is the oblation of the traveler, which, if offered with a good mind, may be as acceptable as a consecrated animal. But perhaps these heaps of stones may be erected to a *local* deity, which most probably is the case."

There has always been manifested a disposition to invest the unexplained customs of the Indians with suppositions and super- stitions. Mr. Hawley's description is marred in this respect. The custom referred to had nothing of worship in it, nor was it in recognition of an " unknown God," or of a " local deity." The stone heaps were always by the side of a trail or regularly traveled path, and usually at or near a stream of water. The Indians paused to refresh themselves, and, by throwing a stone or a stick to a certain place, indicated to other travellers that a friend had passed.

*Twastawekak,* was the name of what is now known as Klaverack creek. *Machackoesk* was the name of a tract lying on both sides of Kinderhook creek ; *Pomponick* that of another tract in the same vicinity, and *Kenaghtequak* that of a small creek. The New England path, one of the routes of travel between the Indians of the Hudson and those of the east, ran along a portion of the boundary line of the Kinderhook patent. Kinderhook is Dutch of course, but is said to have had its origin in the fact that the point was a favorite place for the children of the Indians to practice their games, and perhaps the only point at which they could be observed from vessels passing on the river, as the Dans-Kammer was the only point at which devil worship was similarly observed. There is a fragrance in the fact that makes the name more palatable than most of the Dutch geographical terms.

*Schodac,* to which tradition assigns the important position of the capital of the *Mahicans* at the time of the discovery, is now covered by the village of Castleton. The name is from *skootag,* fire, and *ack,* place.

*Sannahagog* is the name given for the tract of land extending on the east side of the river from Beeren island to Smack's island. Beeren island was called *Passapenock* and subsequently, Mahican island. It was occupied by the *Mahicans* until the war of 1689, when they were "persuaded to goe and live at Katskill," where they would be in greater readiness for the public service. *Cachtanaquick* is described as an island· over against Beeren island. The island opposite Albany known as Smack's, was called "*Schotack* or Aepjen's island." *Poetanock* was the name for Mill creek, opposite Albany, and *Semesseeck* that for a tract through which it passed. Another tract adjoining took its name from its owner, *Paep-Sikenekomtas*, abbreviated to *Papsickenekas*. *Petuquapoen* and *Tuscumcatick* are names applied to what is now Greenbush. *Keeseywego* was the name of a kil opposite Albany, described as being " 1200 rods from Major Abram Staets's kil." *Paanpaack* was the name of the tract now covered by the city of Troy. *Taescameasick* and *Sheepshack* are now covered by Lansingburgh, and *Popquassick*, which is described as " a piece of woodland on the east side of the river near a small island commonly known as whale fishing island," is also supposed to be a part of the town of Lansingburgh. *Panhoosick* was the name of a tract north of Troy, and is still preserved in that of one of the towns of Rensselaer county and in Hoosick river. A small stream flowing into the Hoosick from the south was called *Tomhenack* creek, and one from the north bore the name of *Poquampacak*. Further east the *Wallomschock*, after taking in several tributary mountain streams from Vermont, adds its waters in considerable volume. The Indian village of *Schaticook* which stood at the confluence of the Hoosick and Hudson, has already been referred to. *Dionondahowa* is given as the Indian name for the falls on the Batten kil below Galesville, Washington county, and *Tioneendogahe* to the kil itself. (*Patent to Schuyler.*) The same name was also applied to the outlet of Lake George, now called *Ticonderoga*, by which it is known in its many historic associations. It is a generic term and appears under different orthographies and interpretations. " *Tionderoga*, meaning the place where two rivers meet. The French called it Carillon, on account of the noise of the waterfall at the outlet." (*Brodhead.*) " *Tsinondrosie*, or *Cheonderoga*, signifying brawling water, and the French name, Carillon, signifying a chime of bells, were both suggested by the noise of the rapids." (*Ga-*

*zetteer.*)   "*Dionderoga*, ' place of the inflowing waters ; ' *Ticon-deroga*, from *ti*, water.; *on*, hills ; *dar*, precipitous rocks, and *oga*, place." (*Schoolcraft.*)   *Quequicke* was the name of the falls on the Hoosick east of the bounds of Schaticook, now known as Hoosick Falls.   In answer to the claim that the Hoosick takes its name from Abraham Hoosac, one of the early settlers, is the positive assertion, in one of the first patents, that a tract, "twenty-five English miles north-east of the city of Albany," was "known by the Indian name of *Hoosack*."   The name is from *hussun*, stone, and *ack*, place — literally "stony country." A strata of round stones, such as are used for street pavements, apparently underlies the entire valley.

On the west side of the Hudson and the harbor of New York are the *Neversink* hills.   The name, according to School-craft, is from *onawa*, water, between the waters, and *sink*, a place ; but this interpretation appears to be forced.   The word probably signifies a place abounding in birds.   Hudson found the Indians there "clothed in mantles of feathers.   *Amboy*, according to Heckewelder, is from *emboli*, and signifies a place resembling a bowl or bottle.   *Epating*, in the rear of Jersey city, is from *ishpa*, high, and *ink*, a place — hence *Ishpatink*, or *Espating*, a high place, supposed to be Snake hill. (*O'Callaghan.*)   Schoolcraft applies the same term to "the high sandy bank now known as Brooklyn Heights."   *Arissheck* was the name of Paulus Hook, now Jersey City.   *Hoboken-hacking* was the name of the tract now embraced in the site of Hoboken, and is said to have meant tobacco pipe.   The term was frequently used to express crookedness, and in this instance was applied to the form of the river shore.   *Raritan*, a forked river ; *Passaic*, from *Pakhsajek*, a valley ; *Gamoenapa*, the aboriginal for Communipau ; the Raritan Great Meadows were called *Man-kack-ke-wachky* ; *Wiehacken* is still preserved in the name of Wehawken ; Hackinsack river perpetuates the name of the Hackinsacks and is the modern rendering of the original *Ack-kin-kas-hacky*.   The name is said to mean, "the stream that unites with another in low level ground."   *Haque-quenunck*, sometimes spelled *Aquackanonk*, was the name for the ract now covered by the city of Patterson, and *Totama* the name of the falls — a word signifying to sink, to be forced down under weight by water. *Watchtung* — literally mountain — was the name of a range of hills lying some twelve miles west of the Hudson; *Ramspook* or *Ramapo*, a river into which empties a number of round ponds; *Pompton*, "crooked mouth," referring to the manner in which the Ringwood and Ramapo rivers pass down and discharge themselves into the *Pompton*.

It is said that the *Tappans* derived their name from *Tuphanne*, a cold stream, signifying the people of the cold stream. *Kumochenack* was the name for Haverstraw bay. A small stream flowing into the Ramapo river was the *Chesekook*, a name also applied " to a tract of upland and meadow " embraced in and known as the " Chesekook patent," which covered a large portion of the original county of Orange, now Rockland. A small stream emptying into the Hudson just below Stony point, was called *Minnisconga*, from *minnis* an island, *co* or *con*, object, and *ga* a place, referring without doubt to Stony point itself which was then an island. The site of the present town of Orange-town was called the *Narrasunck* lands as late as 1769, a name which probably has its signification in *na* and *unk*, " good land." Verdrietig hook, or Tedious point, as the Dutch called it from the fact that it was generally so long in sight from their slow-sailing sloops, was called *Quaspeck*, from *qusuk*, a stone.

Opposite Anthony's Nose, was a " small rivulet called by ye Indians *Assinnapink*," or " the stream from the solid rocks." South of this rivulet was *Tongapogh* kil, and north of it *Pooploop's* kil, the latter apparently the name of an Indian owner. Buttermilk falls were called the Prince's falls, evidently from their ownership by a prince of " the people of the hill country." Plum point, north of the Highlands, was called *Cowonham's* hill, and the rocky island lying opposite, *Poleber's* island, which has been corrupted into Pallopel's island, and invested with a Dutch tradition which is not its own.

That which has been known as the Murderer's creek, from a period anterior to Van der Donck's *Map of New Netherland* (1656), enters the Hudson at Cornwall, and originally formed the starting point for the line which divided the counties of Orange and Ulster. That its name was derived from some unex-

plained event or hostile action on the part of the Waoran-
ecks appears to be conclusively established from the fact that
it was applied to it only until it reached the castle of that
chieftaincy on the north spur of *Schunemunk* mountain, about
seven miles from its mouth. Tradition affirms in explanation,
that at an early period a company of traders entered the
creek with their sloop and were enticed on shore, where they
were murdered on a hill still known as Sloop hill in commemoration of the event ; and this explanation is strengthened
by the fact that the name of the hill is coexistent with that of
the creek. It is here that Paulding locates his beautiful story
of *Naoman*, so generally accepted as history :

" Little more than a century ago, the beautiful region watered
by this stream was possessed by a small tribe of Indians, which
has long since become extinct, or incorporated with some other
savage nation of the west. Three or four hundred yards from
where the stream discharges itself in the Hudson, a white family,
of the name of Stacy, had established itself in a log house, by
tacit permission of the tribe, to whom Stacy had made himself
useful by a variety of little arts, highly estimated by the savages.
In particular, a friendship existed between him and an old Indian,
called Naoman, who had often came to his house and partook
of his hospitality. The Indians never forgive injuries nor forget
benefits. The family consisted of Stacy, his wife, and two
children, a boy and a girl, the former five, and the latter three,
years old.

"One day Naoman came to Stacy's hut in his absence, lighted
a pipe, and sat down. He looked very serious, sometimes
sighed very deeply, but said not a word. Stacy's wife asked
him what was the matter — if he was sick. He shook his head,
sighed, but said nothing, and soon went away. The next day
he came again and behaved in the same manner. Stacy's wife
began to think strange of this, and related it to her husband,
who advised her to urge the old man to an explanation, the next
time he came. Accordingly, when he repeated his visit, the day
after, she was more importunate than usual. At last the old
Indian said : ' I am a red man, and the pale faces are our enemies ; why should I speak ?' ' But my husband and I are

your friends; you have eaten salt with us a hundred times, and my children have sat on your knees as often. If you have anything on your mind, tell it me." " It will cost me my life if it is known, and the white-faced women are not good at keeping secrets," replied Naoman. " Try me and see." " Will you swear, by your Great Spirit, that you will tell none but your husband ? " " I have none else to tell." " But will you swear ? " " I do swear, by our Great Spirit, I will tell none but my husband." " But if my tribe should kill you for not telling ? " " Not if your tribe should kill me for not telling."

" Naoman then proceeded to tell her, that, owing to some encroachments of the white people below the mountains, his tribe had become irritated, and were resolved, that night, to massacre all the white settlers in their reach ; that she must send for her husband, inform him of the danger, and as speedily and as secretly as possible, take their canoe and paddle with all haste over the river for safety. " Be quick, and do nothing that may excite suspicion," said Naoman, as he departed. The good wife sought her husband, who was on the river fishing, told him the story, and, as no time was to be lost, they proceeded to their boat, which was unluckily filled with water. It took some time to clean it out, and meanwhile, Stacy recollected his gun which had been left behind. He proceeded to the house and returned with it. All this took up considerable time, and precious time it proved to this poor family. The daily visits of old Naoman, and his more than ordinary gravity, had excited suspicion in some of the tribe, who had, accordingly paid particular attention to the movements of Stacy. One of the young Indians, who had been kept on the watch, seeing the whole family about to take to the boat, ran to the little Indian village about a mile off, and gave the alarm. Five Indians collected, ran down to the river where their canoes were moored, jumped in and paddled after Stacy, who, by this time, had got some distance out in the stream. They gained on him so fast that twice he dropped his paddle and took up his gun. But his wife prevented his shooting, by telling him that, if he fired, and they were afterwards overtaken, they would meet with no mercy from the Indians. He accordingly refrained, and applied his paddle till the sweat rolled in big drops from his forehead. All would not do ; they were overtaken within a hundred yards from the shore, and carried back, with shouts of yelling and triumph.

" When they got ashore, the Indians set fire to Stacy's house, and dragged himself, his wife and children to their village. Here the principal old men, and Naoman among them, assembled to deliberate on the affair. The chief men of the council stated, that some one of the tribe had, undoubtedly, been guilty of treason, in apprizing Stacy, the white man, of the designs of the tribe, whereby they took the alarm, and well nigh escaped. He proposed to examine the prisoners, to learn who gave the information. The old men assented to this, and Naoman among the rest. Stacy was first interrogated by one of the old men, who spoke English and interpreted it to the others. Stacy refused to betray his informant. His wife was then questioned, while at the same moment, two Indians stood threatening the two children with tomahawks, in case she did not confess. She attempted to evade the truth, by declaring that she had a dream the night before, which alarmed her, and that she had persuaded her husband to fly. ' The Great Spirit never deigns to talk in dreams to a white woman,' said the old Indian. ' Woman, thou hast two tongues and two faces. Speak the truth or thy children shall surely die. The little boy and girl were then brought close to her, and the two savages stood over them ready to execute his bloody orders.

" ' Wilt thou name,' said the old Indian, ' the red man who betrayed his tribe ? I will ask three times.' The mother answered not. ' Wilt thou name the traitor ? This is the second time.' The poor woman looked at her husband, and then at her children, and stole a glance at Naoman, who sat smoking his pipe with invincible gravity. She wrung her hands, and wept, but remained silent. ' Wilt thou name the traitor ? 'Tis the third and last time.' The agony of the mother waxed more bitter ; again she sought the eye of Naoman, but it was cold and motionless. The pause of a moment awaited her reply, and the tomahawks were raised over the heads of the children, who besought their mother not to let them be murdered.

"'Stop!' cried Naoman. All eyes were turned upon him. 'Stop!' repeated he, in a tone of authority. 'White woman thou hast kept thy word with me to the last moment. I am the traitor. I have eaten of the salt, warmed myself at the fire, shared the kindness of these Christian white people, and it was I that told them of their danger. I am a withered, leafless, branchless trunk; cut me down if you will; I am ready.' A yell of indignation sounded on all sides. Naoman descended from the little bank where he sat, shrouded his face with his mantle of skins and submitted to his fate. He fell dead at the feet of the white woman by a blow of the tomahawk.

"But the sacrifice of Naoman, and the firmness of the Christian white woman, did not suffice to save the lives of the other victims. They perished — how, it is needless to say; and the memory of their fate has been preserved in the name of the pleasant stream, on whose banks they lived and died, which, to this day, is called the Murderer's creek."

Six miles west of the scene of this tradition is the mountain range called *Schunemunk*, or, as in the early deeds, *Skonnemoghky*, on the northern spur of which, and near its base was the castle or village of the' clan to whom it refers, and where they continued to reside until after considerable settlements had been made around them. The name is also spelled *Skonanoky*, and is apparently derived from *Shunna*, sour, and *na* excellent, *nuk*, local — probably referring to the abundance of wild grapes found there. On the east side of the mountain, in the town of Cornwall, and near the centre of the Wilson patent, was an Indian burial grond, so designated in a survey by General James Clinton. In its vicinity on the north is a hill which was called *Winegtekonk*, now known as Woodcock mountain. Further west, in the town of Goshen, what is called Run-bolt's-run, preserves in its name and source, the name and place of residence of *Rombout*, one of the chiefs who signed the deed for the Wawayanda tract, whose wigwam stood beside the spring from which the stream flows. A modern tradition associates the name of *Wawastawa*, another of the grantors of the tract, with the stream, through his daughter, to whom a Frenchman named Boltez made love. The maiden rejected his suit and fled towards her father's cabin. Just then her father's shrill whistle was heard, and she paused in her flight and exclaimed, " Run, Bolt, Run ! " an exclamation which, when the story came out, was applied to the streamlet. On Sugar Loaf mountain, in Chester, was an Indian village and burial ground some time after the advent of the whites. It is said that the chieftaincy located here paid tribute to the Senecas as late as 1756. *Mistucky*, a locality in Warwick, is probably an abbreviation of *Miskotucky*, a compound word implying red hills or red plains. *Pochuck*, a name applied to one of the streams of that town as well as to the district known as Florida, seems to retain the root term for bog or muddy land.

*Jogee Hill*, in the town of Minisink, takes its name from and preserves the place of residence of *Keghgekapowell* alias *Joghem*, one of the grantors of lands to Governor Dongan in 1684. A considerable canton is said to have resided in the vicinity at an early period, and that *Joghem* remained an occupant of this hill long after his brethren had departed for the west. Arrowheads and small images of various kinds have been found here, and among other articles an Indian tomahawk the whole of which is a pipe, the pole being the bowl, and the handle the stem. *Minnisink* is from *Minnis*, an island, and *ink*, locality, and not from *Minsis*, the name of the wolf tribe of the Lenapes. The name has a very general application to lands, in Pennsylvania as well as New York, known as the Minnisink country. It had its origin in the tradition that the land was covered with water before the Delaware broke through the mountain at the water gap, or Pohoqualin, and is said to mean the land from which the water is gone.

Entering the Hudson south of Newburgh is *Quassaick* creek. The name is from *qussuk*, a stone, and the signification stony brook. Partly in Newburgh and partly in New Windsor is what is called *Muchattoes Hill*, a name apparently derived from *Muhk*, red ; *at*, near or by, and *os*, small — a small red hill near the river.

North of Newburgh the rocky peninsula known as *Dans-Kammer* point is a feature in the landscape as well as in the history of the river. It was at this place that the Indians held their worship of the devil, on one occasion four or five hundred being seen here engaged in that service. There were two grassy plots on which the dances and other orgies were held, the one called the large Dans-Kammer, and the other the little Dans-Kammer. The first is now occupied by the Armstrong house ; the second was on the rocky point which retains the name. The place has its story as well as its history. " Hans Hansen," the story says, " was the son of Jacobus Hansen, one of the first settlers in the vinicity of Albany, and, except an occasional skirmish with the Indians, had enjoyed undisturbed peace and honor in the small circle that constituted his settlement. He had now arrived at such an age that the affairs of his farm were too fatiguing for his declining years ; and Hans being the eldest son, the superintendency necessarily devolved on him ; but so important a station could not be properly filled without the assistance of a *vrouw*. Hans accordingly looked among the fair of his acquaintances, and, with the consent of his parents, paid his addresses to Miss Katrina Van Vrooman, whose residence was but a mile from his own habitation. Those were " matter of fact " days, and the girl consented, without any flirtations, to become his wife. The wedding day was appointed, and the neighbors invited ; but before the ceremony could be performed, it was necessary to obtain a license from the governor, whose residence was in New York.

" Hans accordingly prepared to go thither for his license, and a party of his young friends, as well as his prospective bride, determined to accompany him. Katrina invited to the excursion an old squaw named Leshee, to whom she was much attached, but who was regarded by some as having intercourse with the Evil One, and was often consulted even in matters of importance by the superstitious Dutchmen. The day of the departure was marked by a severe storm, from which Leshee boded illluck ; but the party were impatient of delay, and proceeded on their journey.

" The affianced pair, after three days' journey, reached the house of the governor, obtained the necessary license, and then proceeded without delay homeward. On the evening of the sixth day they reached the Dans-Kammer. The place was known to them, and the company resolved to stop there and partake of some refreshments. Leshee remonstrated against visiting the scene of the rites and sacrifices of her tribe, and repeated the old prophetic lines —

> For none that visit the Indian's den
> Return again to the haunts of men ;
> The knife is their doom, oh, sad is their lot ;
> Beware! beware of the blood-stained spot.

But the evening was beautiful, the place attractive, the Indians at peace, their war-whoop hushed and their sacrificial fires extinguished ; hence they resolved to land. Drawing up their boats on the sandy beach, they seated themselves on the site of the Indians' place of worship — partook of their refreshments, joined in the dance, smoked the pipe and told the story.

"In company with one of his friends, Hans wandered over the plain, and on turning espied the sparkling of an eye in a thick cluster of bushes. Knowing that it was no one of his party, he proceeded cautiously, without appearing to observe it, until he came near enough to see it was an Indian, when, raising his rifle and taking deliberate aim, he directed his companion to make close search. Finding but one, they bound him and took him to the company, who were preparing to leave, and some of whom were already in their boats. Hans soon recognized the Indian as one with whom he had recently had trouble. He questioned him closely, but he refused to explain his presence or his purposes. Finding his efforts fruitless, Hans prepared to embark, when the Indian broke the silence by a shrill yell.

"The result was soon manifest. A company of warriors, who had concealed themselves and their canoes above the point, were seen darting forward with appalling velocity. Hans' only hope of escape was his boats. The Indians drew nearer and nearer — they were within an arrow's flight, and yet Katrina and two others were on shore. Hans faltered a moment when he saw the danger to which Katrina was exposed ; but it was momentary. Placing his knife at the breast of his captive, he shouted to the Indians, that if they approached a step, their chief should die ; but if they permitted the company to embark, their chief was free.   The Indians knew the determination of Hans, and stopped ; the females were got on board, and Hans had stepped to shove off the boat.   Just then the quick voice of the chief was heard, commanding his warriors to proceed. They hesitated until a reproach from their chief, when they again came forward with the rapidity of thought.

"Death now seemed the immediate doom of the party ; but Hans, always ready in emergency, was prompt in this.   He placed the chief before him and proceeded in this manner on board his boat.   As he expected, the Indians dared not risk their chieftain's life, for they well knew the quick arm of Hans would place him between the arrow and its intended victim. Just at the point of safety, the Indians separated so that they could kill their enemy without endangering the life of their chief. Hans again raised his knife, and proclaimed that the first arrow that flew the chief should die.   But the enmity of the chief was stronger than his love of life.   He gave the war-whoop — a cloud of arrows darkened the air — the glittering knife descended and the chief was no more.   Wounded, Hans stepped on board his boat and shoved off.   The Indians flew to their canoes ; the pursuit was speedy and the arm of Hans weak from loss of blood.   He was soon overtaken and carried back in company with Katrina and her friends.   Speedily the bridal pair were tied to trees and tortured in all the ways savage barbarity could devise.   Then gathering the materials for the fire, they kindled the flame and celebrated the dance of death around their victims in fiendish glee, until the forms of Hans and his fair bride were mingled with the ashes of the pyre — their embrace of love was at the stake of death.

"The remaining captives were treated more humanely, and were subsequently ransomed by their friends."   Such is the tradition.

There is no more familiar name, in Orange county, than that of *Wawayanda*, nor one the significance of which is less clearly known.   It first appears in 1703, in a petition from Dr. Staats in which he states that a tract which he had purchased, called

*Wawayanda*, or *Woerawin*, was "altogether a swamp." Its next use is in the deed and patent of Wawayanda, granted in 1703, while yet Staats's petition was under consideration. Staats's purchase was never definitely located, but that it covered a portion of the Drowned lands is known from the fact that the Wawayanda patent included the lands which he claimed. In the deed from the Indians, and in the patent, the description implies that the name embraced more than one tract, the language being "called by the name or names of *Wawayanda*;" while the deed to Staats is apparently located by the name of *Woerawin*, a term which may be derived from *woreco*, handsome, or *wooreecan*, good, or from *wewocan*, from *wewau*, waters, and *wocan*, barking or roaring, a term descriptive of the roaring of waters at a high fall, or in a rushing rapid stream in a flood. The distinction between the terms more clearly appears when considered in connection with the use of local and general terms in other patents. In the deed to Governor Dongan for the Evans patent the language is, "comprehending all those lands, meadows and woods called " by specific names, "together with the hills, valleys, woods," etc., surrounding and adjoining or within a district defined by certain natural boundaries, while *Minnisink* embraced an undefined territory. The explanation would seem to be that *Woerawin* was the name of a particular part of the tract, while *Wawayanda* was a *district* embracing several well known and occupied lands, or a *village* and its dependencies. This explanation accords with the name itself. *Wa*, according to Schoolcraft, is a reflective plural and may mean *he* or *they*, or, by repetition, *we;*[1] it has no descriptive significance whatever. *Aindau-yaun* is my home ; *Aindau-yun*, thy home ; *Aindau-aud*, his or her home ; *da*, town or village. From these terms we have *Wa-wa-yaun-da*, signifying "our homes or places of dwelling," or "our village and lands." Accepting the last, we find on the tract a Long house, situated on what is still called Long house creek, which was undoubtedly the seat or castle of the canton.

[1] Substantives are generally combined with inseparable possessive pronouns prefixed. The duplication *nana, wawa, wawall*, distinguishes the double plural, or combination of both the noun and possessive pronoun in the plural ('our fathers').—*Zeisberger's Grammar.*

The stream of water now known as the Tinbrook,—from the German Tinn Brock, or thin brook,—was called by the Indians *Arackhook*, or *Akhgook*, the Delaware term for snake, the reference no doubt being to the extremely sinuous course of its flow, which resembles the contortions of a snake when thrown upon a fire. In 1701, Robert Sanders[1] filed a petition for a patent to a tract of land described as " beginning at a fall (*i. e.*, a stream of water) called *Arackhook* and running thence *northerly* on the *east* side of the Paltz creek until it comes to a place called *Kackawawook*, and from thence due east four miles into the woods, and from thence parallel to Paltz creek until a due west line shall touch the aforesaid fall." He stated that he had held the land since June 4th, 1689 ; that all the Indians formerly owners were dead, and asked that a patent be issued to himself, his son Thomas, and Johannes Bush, William, Sharpas, and Joseph Cleator. He renewed the petition, April 18th, 1702, calling the tract *Oghgotacton*, and stated that his title was derived from a loan which he had made to the Indian proprietor, who, as well as all his relations, were then dead. In confirmation of his claim he presented the following paper :

" Whereas, *Pungnanis* is indebted to Robert Sanders the value of seventy pounds, and being ten years gone to the *Ottowawas*, and his brother *Corpowin*, now going to the war, desires that ye said Robert Sanders may keep the land of his brother, called *Oghotacton*, till his brother pays him the said sum of seventy pounds,[2] Robert Sanders comes to me to ask for leave to take this land from the said *Corpowin*, and I do give him authority to take," etc., etc. Signed by Gov. Dongan, June 4, 1689.

A patent was issued to Sanders under this petition, but, for some reason which does not appear, was not taken up by him.

---

[1] Robert Sanders, of Albany, was a distinguished and intelligent Indian trader. He became well versed in the languages, both of the Mohawks and the River Indians, and acted as interpreter between them and the English on several occasions. He enjoyed the confidence of the Indians to a high degree, and was made governor of Schenectady, occupying that post at the time of the massacre. He was particularly designated, by Mr. Miller, as a proper person to furnish the government information in regard to the condition of Canada. He rendered himself so obnoxious to the French governor there, in consequence of his opposition to the Jesuit missionaries among the Five Nations, that he was the subject of special complaint to Governor Dongan in 1687.— *Munsell's Annals of Albany.*

[2] Less then seventy dollars of United States currency.

On the 30th of June, 1712, a patent was issued to Henry Wileman covering the same tract but extending its boundaries west to the falls in the Walkill at Walden, the inference doubtless being that the word " fall " in Sanders' boundary had reference thereto. The Tinbrook enters the Walkill on the east about half a mile from the falls at Walden.

Much has been written in explanation of the word *Shawangunk*, and yet the solution of the term is far from satisfactory. The Rev. CHARLES SCOTT, in a paper read before the Ulster Historical Society,[1] remarks very properly that the interpretation by Schoolcraft, so extensively copied, that the word means white rocks, from *shawan*, white, and *gunk*, rock — alluding to the white cliffs which face the mountains west of Tuthiltown, is not sustained by any known vocabulary of Indian dialects. The word comes down to us in two principal forms, *Shawangunk* and *Chawangong*, the first in the Dutch records of the Esopus wars, and the second in some of the early English patents. In the deed to Governor Dongan, in 1684, it is specified as a certain tract of land, the language being, " all those lands, meadows and woods called Nescotack, Chawangon," etc. The patent to Thomas Lloyd, Feb. 22, 1686, is described as at the place called by the Indians *Chawangong*. Says Mr. SCOTT of the latter : " This tract of land was situated on the west side of Shawangunk kil, and north of what is now known as McKinstry's tannery. The next locality, to the north, was named by the Indians *Nescotonck*. On the south was *Schanwemisch*, or as the Dutch pronounced it, *Wishauwemis*, the beech woods, or place of beeches." In this manner he localizes the application of the name. He continues :

" This fixes with some accuracy the bounds of the original Indian Shawangunk. It was a section of fine low land, situated mainly on the west side of Shawangunk kil, for about five miles, from near the mouth of the Mary kil, to the mouth of the Dwars kil. Two miles to the west, and near the foot of the mountain, was a flat called *Weighquatenheuk*, the place of willows ; and about two miles east, on the Wallkill, another fine region of meadow and maize fields, which they designated

[1] Vol. I, part III, 229, etc., of *Proceedings*.

*Wanoksink*, or the place of sassafras. It was the seat of the main settlement of the Esopus tribe, on the east side of the mountains, and had, on its southern border, the village, or castle, which was destroyed by the Dutch in September and October, 1663. This, and nothing else, was the Shawangunk of the red man. From thence the name began to spread, when the country was opened to European settlement, until it became widely used. First, the kil was made to assume it, instead of its appropriate *Achsinink;* then the settlers along the kil for miles were said to have it for their home ; then the mountains or high hills running from Rosendale to Minnisink, were thus designated; and finally the precinct and afterwards the township. And here let it be remarked that the name belongs in no sense whatever to the mountains now bearing it. The Evans patent calls them the high hills of *Pitkiskaker* and *Aioskawosting.* In local records, they are for years termed simply the high hills or the steep rocks.

After a careful analysis of the word, he concludes :

" I venture to interpret : *Shawangum* — south water. Shawangunk, etc., the place on or at the south water, water being referred to generically, and not specifically, as the proper name of the kil. But to what kil and to what locality is Shawangunk relatively south ? Take the map of Ulster county, and notice the position, in respect to each other of the Rondout and of the Shawangunk kils ; and remember that the Indian paths from one valley to the other, ran almost due north and south, and one good reason is manifest. The warrior and the hunter passed either from the north part of Shawangunk proper through the traps, to Marbletown, or from the south part of the same, by Awosting lake — the Long pond — to the Kerhonkson. Stand upon the mountain top and glance down either path, to the winding streams, and upon their corn fields, and the meaning of the north water or the south water, can be easily understood. Again, at either terminus of the Aioskawosting, or southern path, were Indian villages and settlements of cultivated fields. The one was on the north water and the other on the south, for in truth they thus stood towards those opposite points of compass. The above mentioned villages became afterwards the sites of the old fort and the new fort, mentioned in the second Esopus war."

While Mr. Scott's investigation has brought out many facts of interest, it is not clear that he is correct in locating the name, or in explaining its meaning. If the name relates to a particular tract of land, then in that tract must be found its explanation; if in any stream of water, as the south water, its explanation must be sought there. The solution may be in one of the paths or trails which he describes as crossing the mountain and extending into the southern country, one of which was taken by the Long Island Indians who accompanied Kregier's expedition, in 1663, being the shortest route to their homes. This trail continued across the present county of Orange, where it formed one of the boundary lines of the lands of Christopher Denn, and is described in one of his deeds as the Chauwungonk path. It connected with the main trail which ran from Hackinsack to the Minnisink country, partially described in the *Journal of Arent Schuyler* in 1694. Whether called the north or south trail it led to and took its name apparently from one particular locality. This locality would seem to be indicated in the word itself. The first part or noun of the word, *shawan* or *chawan*, would seem to be from *jewan*, swift current or strong stream; *onk* or *gonk*, a place, literally the country of the strong stream, or the rapid water settlement, or if interpreted in connection with some part of the Wallkill, as indicating a specific portion of the Chawangong trail, the reference may be to a place where the shallowness of the current gave to it rapidity and yet afforded a fording or crossing place. To precisely such a place the trail in question led and the ford there established was not only used by the Indians and the early settlers, but is still used as such. Another interpretation is derived from *shong'*, the Algonquin for mink, and *um* or *oma*, water, or *onk*, a place or country. This would give the mink river, or the mink country. Still another is derived from *cheegaugong*, the place of leeks, and has no little force in the abundance of wild onions which are still found in that section of country. Indeed, so universal is this pest of the farmer there, that they might well have given their name to the stream, the valley, and the mountains.

The name of the Indian castle destroyed by Kregier, and which is described "as being situated at the head of the Kerhonkson," has not been preserved, unless it has that preservation in the name of the creek itself. It is altogether probable that such is the fact as it would accord with Indian custom, as illustrated in the case of the *Pakadasank*, to which reference will be made hereafter. In regard to this fort, as well as that called the New fort, Mr. Scott, in another paper, says :

" From the Delaware to the Hudson there once existed two great pathways of Indian travel. The one started from the mouth of the Neversink or Mahakemack, at Port Jervis, and passing by the ancient Peenpack, and through Mamakating hollow, struck the Rondout at Napanoch. Thence following that stream through Wawarsing and Rochester, it passed over in Marbletown to the Esopus, and skirted the latter to its mouth at Saugerties. The other crossed the mountain range at Minnisink, to the eastern valleys, and followed the Shawangunk, the Wallkill and the Rondout to the Hudson. The first may be distinguished as the Mamakating, and the second as the Shawangunk trail. From trail to trail the cross paths may yet be traced, and in some places have been marked upon the mountain rocks by the passing footsteps of ages."

It was on the Mamakating trail, about twenty-three miles south-west of Kingston, that he locates the Old fort, or that destroyed by Kregier on the 31st of July, and designates its site as being " on the south side of the Kerhonkson, near the line between Rochester and Wawarsing, just north of what is called Shurker's hill, and about three miles from the mouth and at the head of the Kerhonkson." The New fort, or that destroyed on the 4th of October, he says, " was in the town of Shawangunk, on the east bank of the Shawangunk kil, and twenty-eight miles from Kingston." He adds : " Whatever doubts there may be as to the Kerhonkson village, or the Old fort, there can be none as to that situated on the Shawangunk. From the first settlement of the country the place has been called The New Fort. The village which was found abandoned on the 4th of October, was in the vicinity of Burlingham. An Indian burial ground marks the spot, and a path led from thence to the hunting house at Wurtsboro." The site of the New fort, and the trails are described as follows :

" The mouth of the Shawangunk kil is six miles away, and most of that distance is occupied by fine and fertile lowlands. From the water rises an abrupt declivity, of irregular formation, reaching, it may be, an elevation of 75 or 80 feet, and then spreading out into a beautiful sandy plateau of twenty or thirty acres. The hill side is covered with the original forest, and broken up into what seem to be artificial mounds. On the edge of the plain overlooking the creek, the fort was situated, and the wigwams a little distance below. To the north, along the kil, extends a flat of moderate dimensions ; but on the opposite side are some of the finest lowlands in Ulster county. Here the Indians planted their maize, and one spot is yet distinguished as Basha's cornfield. The plateau is covered with flints and arrow-heads, which every ploughing turns up to the hands of those who prize them. From this village a pathway, yet preserved, led across the mountains to Wawarsing and the Kerhonkson settlement, just twelve miles to the north. This was the Wawarsing trail, so well known to all the early inhabitants of Shawangunk and Rochester. Another trail bore off to the traps, and through the clove to Marbletown. And yet a third passed eastward to the Hudson, through Montgomery and New Windsor, and branching, near the Wallkill, to the south, gave access from the Esopus clans, to the wigwams of the Haverstraws and Hackinsacks."

That the valley of the Wallkill was thickly peopled at the time of the discovery, there is no question. Along its banks and tributary streams imperfect but conclusive evidence is found of occupation both by permanent and temporary villages, and in the old patents are many names of localities which investigation would clothe with interest. Skirting along the eastern base of the Shawangunk mountains is a stream called the *Pakadasank* which took its name from an Indian village or castle at its head. The location of this village entered into the discussion in defining the boundaries of the Evans patent, and is referred to, in a paper bearing date in 1756, as follows :

" But what proves that point past contradiction is the description given of the western bounds of Evans's first purchase, which expressly says it extended all along said hills, etc., and the river Pakadasank southerly to a pond called *Mallolausly* (Maretange), lying on the top of the said hills. Nothing could more plainly point out where that pond lies, and which is the right pond, than the river Pakadasank which takes its rise at the foot of the said hills, opposite the said pond and extends *northerly* along the foot of the said hills from a place called Pakadasank, where the Indians who sold the land had a large settlement, and from that place to the head of the said river, and nowhere else, the said river is called by that name. And the said Indian settlement called Pekadasank is said to be included in the first purchase, but the line run from Stony point excludes that land for it is southward of their pond."

The Pakadasank has its source or head in Maretange pond on what was formerly called the *Alaskayering mountains* or Minnisink hills, flows north through the western part of the town of Crawford, and empties into the Shawangunk kil. Another stream, called the Little Pakadasank has similar source and outlet. There is reason for supposing that the Indian village, from which both streams took their name, was in the present town of Crawford, Orange county.

One of the boundaries of the Paltz patent, now known as Paltz point, was called and known by the Indians, *Maggrnapogh.* In the Ulster records is this certificate : " These are to certify that the inhabitants of the towns of New Paltz, being desirous that the first station of their patent named Moggonck might be kept in remembrance, did desire us, Joseph Horsbrook, John Hardenburgh, Roeleft Eltinge, Esq., justices of the Peace for the county of Ulster, to accompany them, and there being Ancrop, the Indian, then brought us to the High Mountain which he named *Maggrnapogh*, at or near the foot of which hill is a small run of water and a swamp which he called Moggonck, and the said Indian Ancrop affirms it to be the right Indian names of the said places as witness our hands this nineteenth day of December, 1722." Ancrop was at that time sachem of the Esopus Indians.

Schoolcraft has preserved a pictographic inscription on the Esopus rocks, " which, from its antiquity and character appears to denote the era of the introduction of fire-arms and gunpowder among the tribes inhabiting that section of the valley of the Hudson." [1] He says :

" The location of the inscription is on the western bank of the Hudson, at Esopus landing. Other indications have been reported, at sundry times, of the skill of these ancient Indians in inscribing figures on rocks. Tracks of human feet are among these objects; but the progress of building in that. vicinity, and the existence of but little curiosity on that head, appears to have destroyed these interesting traces of a people who now live only in history. The traditions of Ulster county do not refer to a period when this inscription was not there. The inscription may be supposed, if the era is properly conjectured, to have been made with metallic tools. The lines are deeply and plainly impressed. It is in double lines. The plumes from the head denote a chief, or man, skilled in the Indian medico-magical art. The gun is held at rest in the right hand; the left appears to support a wand. It is in the rampant Indian style. Such an inscription, recording the introduction of the gun, would not be made when that era had long past and lost its interest. Indians never resort to historical pictography when there is nothing new to tell. Thus the Indian pictography throws a little light on the most rude and unpromising scene ; and if the sources of these gratifications are but small, we are indebted to them for this little. No attempt of rude nations to perpetuate an idea is ever wholly lost."

*Atkarkarton*, the Indian name for Kingston, was not the name of an Indian village, but for a tract called by the Dutch the Great Plot, or meadow on which the Indians raised corn and beans. *At* is equivalent to *at* or *by* the waters.

Nutten Hook, at Katskil, was called by the Indians *Kockhachchingh ;* a place known to the Dutch as the Flying corner, was called by the Indians, *Machawanick ;* a small stream which enters " the creek called the Kats kil" on the south, was called *Quatawichnaak ;* Silvester Salisbury, in 1678,

[1] *History of the Indian Tribes of the United States*, part iii, 73. *Ante*, p. 157.

obtained " five great flats or plains" called *Wachachkeek*, *Wich-quanachtekok*, *Pachquyak*, *Assiskowachkok*, and *Potick*; a tract sold to Jacob Lockerman was bounded on the south by a creek called *Canasenix*, " east on the river in the Great Imbocht where Loveridge leaves off, called by the Indians *Peoquanackqua*, and west by a place called by the Indians *Quachanock* ; " and Henry Beekman had a tract " under the great mountains called Blue hills, by a place called *Kiskatameck*." The *Mahican* village known as *Potick*, was apparently located west of Athens, where the name is preserved in Potick hill and Potick creek, the latter forming the west line of the town. It may be added that the term Katskil was applied by the Dutch as descriptive of the totemic emblem of the Indians, a wolf.

Wanton island, a short distance north of Katskill landing, is the site of a traditionary battle between the *Mahicans* and the *Mohawks*. Like other traditions which are woven into history, the issue involved in the conflict is a pure fiction. The tradition is related by Stone, in his *Life of Brant*, as follows :

" Brown, in his *History of Schoharie*, gives a singular tradition in regard to the kings of the *Mohawks*, of which I have found no other mention. The *Mohawks* and *River Indians* were once bitter enemies, the former becoming the terror and scourge of the latter. Brown states that the last battle between the *Mahicans* and *Mohawks* took place on Wanton island, in the Hudson river, not far from Katskil. The question between them was, which should have the honor of naming their king, or which should have the tribute of the river tribes. Both nations collected their utmost strength upon that island, for the purpose of a final decision, and fought a pitched battle, which continued during the whole day. Towards night, the *Mohawks*, finding that the *Mahicans* were likely to prove an overmatch for them, deemed it necessary to resort to stratagem, for which purpose they suddenly took to flight, and gained another island in the evening. They here kindled a great number of fires, and spread their blankets on some bushes, gathered and disposed around them for that purpose, as though they themselves had encamped by their fires as usual. The

*Mahicans* following on, landed upon the Island in the depth of night, and were completely taken in by the deception. Supposing that the *Mohawks* were sleeping soundly beneath their blankets, after their fatigue, the *Mahicans* crept up with the greatest silence, and pouring a heavy fire upon the blankets, rushed upon them with knives and tomahawks in hand, making the air to ring with their yells as they fell to cutting and slashing the blankets and bushes instead of Indians beneath them. Just at the moment of their greatest confusion and exultation, the *Mohawks*, who had been lying in ambush flat upon the ground at a little distance, poured a murderous fire upon their foes, whose figures were rendered distinctly visible by the light of their fires, and rushing impetuously upon them, killed the greater part and made prisoners of the residue. A treaty was then concluded, by which the *Mohawks*, were to have the king and the *Mahicans* were to hold them in reverence, and call them Uncle. Hendrik was the king first named such by the *Mohawks*, after this decisive victory; " who lived to a great age," says Brown, " and was killed at the battle of Lake George under Sir William Johnson."

The boundary line of the Coeymans tract began at a point on the west shore of the Hudson called *Sieskasin*, described as " opposite the middle of the island called by the Indians *Sapana-kock*." *Caniskeck* is also the name for a tract in the town of Coeymans about ten miles south of Albany. *Coxackie* or *Kuxa-kee* has had several interpretations. Schoolcraft defines it as "the place of the cut banks," where the current deflected against the western shore had gradually worn away the land. O'Callaghan says that the word is a corruption of the Algonquin Kaaks-*aki*, from *Kaak*, a goose, and *aki*, locality, "the country of the wild goose." Another interpretation is *Cook-sockuy*, signifying owl-hoot. The most satisfactory explanation will be found perhaps in *co*, object, and *aki*, land, the reference being to the clay banks which rise there to the height of 100 feet, and form a conspicuous object in the river scenery. *Neweskeke* or *Naveskeek*, about ten miles south of Albany, is described as being a corner or neck of land having a fresh water river running to the east of it.

Coeyman's Hollow was called *Achquetuck*, and the creek, *Oniskethau*. Another creek is still known by the Indian name, *Hahnakrois*.

Coeyman's Creek.

*Sunckhagag* is recorded as the name of the tract from Beeren island to Smack's island.[1] The boundaries extended two days' journey into the interior. *Tawalsontha* was the *Mahican* name of the creek now called Norman's kil, in the town of Bethlehem, and *Tawassgunshee* that of the mound on which Fort Orange was erected. Schoolcraft gives *Tawasentha* as the orthography of the former term and regards it as signifying "the place of the many dead," adding that the *Mohawks* once had a village there, and that in excavating the road to Bethlehem an Indian burial ground was opened. But the Mohawks never had a village there, and the interpretation is in apparent violation of the custom of the Indians in bestowing names. We have yet to find the name of an Indian burial ground, and especially a stream of water and a burial ground bearing the same name.

[1] The name appears on both sides of the river, *ante*, p. 374.

*Schenectady*[1] is said to signify "beyond the plains." School-craft gives *Con-no-harrie-go-harrie* as the original name of the site of that city, and says "the name is in allusion to the flood wood on the flats." Another authority gives *Oron-nygh-wurrie-gughre* as the name of the region immediately around the city, but it has been very wisely dropped notwithstanding its signification, maize lands. *Canastagione*, a tract in Albany county, is said to mean the great maize land, from *onuste* (Mohawk) maize, and *couane*, great. It is added that *Niskayunah*, the present name of this tract, is only a variation of *Canastagione*, and is derived from *onatschia* another Iroquois word for maize, the *o* and *t* being dropped. (*O'C.*)

*Saratoga* is said to be derived from *soragh*, salt, and *oga*, a place, the place of the salt springs. Schoolcraft says the word is from *assarat*, sparkling waters, and *oga*, a place, but evidently bases his interpretation on the hypothesis that Saratoga springs are referred to. The name was first applied, however, to the site of the present village of Schuylerville on the Hudson, and in that connection is said to signify swift water. On Sauthier's map the name is given to a lake west of Schuylerville. Gov. Dongan endeavored to reclaim the Mohawk converts from Canada and settle them here in 1687. He writes: "I have done my endeavors and have gone so far in it that I have prevailed with the Indians to consent to come back from Canada on condition that I procure for them a piece of land called *Serachtague* lying upon Hudson's river about forty miles above Albany, and there furnish them with priests." A fort was subsequently erected there and a settlement formed. In the war of 1745, the fort was destroyed by the French, together

[1] The Iroquois name for the spot where Albany now stands was *Skenectadea*. In regard to this and other Iroquois geographical names in that vicinity, Dr. Mitchill, in answer to an inquiry from the Rev. Dr. Miller, in 1810, on information from John Bleecker, for many years an interpreter of the Iroquois, as well as from the Oneida chief, Louis, and other Indians, writes that *Canneoganakalonitàde* was their name for the Mohawk river; *Skenectadèa*, the city of Albany; *Ohnowalagàntle*, the town of Schenectady; *Càhohàtatèa*, the north or Hudson river; *Tioghsáhronde*, the place or places where streams empty themselves. "What their etymologies are," he adds, "I have not been able to ascertain, except as to *Skenectadèa*, Albany, which signifies the place the natives of the Iroquois arrived at by travelling through the pine trees."—*Collections of the New York Historical Society*, I, 43.

with about twenty houses; thirty persons were killed and scalped, and about sixty taken prisoners.[1]  The Indians were not occupants of the place at the time of this occurrence.  Waterford, Saratoga county, was called *Nachtenack*, and the island, known as Long Island, near Waterford, *Quahemiscos*.  There is apparently a mixture of the *Mahican* and *Mohawk* dialects in some of the names in this section of the state.

*Cohoes*, a term still preserved in the falls of the Mohawk, was not the name of the falls but of the island below them, and, 'from its diminutive termal *oes*, is presumed to mean simply a small island.  Regarding *co* as expressing object, the first syllable may have reference to the falls, in which case the rendering would be, the island at the falls ; or applied to the falls, would class them as *small* compared with Niagara.  The term is *Mahican*, and is applied in another form to a district in New Hampshire, the *Coos* country.  Van der Donck says of the falls, as they appeared in 1656 : " The water glides over the falls as smooth as if it ran over an even wall and fell over the same.  The precipice is formed of firm blue rock ; near by and below the falls there stand several rocks, which appear splendid in the water rising above it like high turf-heaps, apparently from eight, sixteen, to thirty feet high ; very delightful to the eye.  The place is well calculated to exalt the fancy of the poets.  The ancient fabulous writers would, if they had been here, have exalted those works of nature, by the force of imagination, into the most artful and elegant descriptive illusions.  The waters descend rapidly downwards from the falls, over a stony bottom, skipping, foaming and whirling boisterously about the distance of a gun-shot or more."

[1] *Ante*, p. 205.

FINIS

# ERRATA.

Page 9, 9th line, for *then*, read than.
" 9, 19th line, for *hospitality, so*, read hospitality. So he.
" 18, 11th line, for *Agassis*, read Agassiz.
" 24, 9th line, for *make*, read also.
" 27, 21st line, for *sacrifice and fires*, read sacrificial fires.
" 27, 22d line, for *Kitzinaeka* read Kitzinacka.
" 27, 29th line, for *were*, read where.
" 29, 26th line, for *presents be*, read presents were.
" 29, 27th line, for *it*, read was.
" 32, 5th line, for *called*, read asked.
" 63, 3d line, for *at*, read above.
" 66, 14th line, for *causes,*, read cause.
" 87, 10th line, for 1680, read 1630.
" 154, 24th line, for *soon he*, read soon as he.
" 172, 27th line, for *concede*, read accede.
" 176, 13th line, for *permanent*, read their.
" 187, 11th line, for *others* read other.
" 197, 26th line, for *Totakik*, read Potatik.
" 253, 4th line, for *Mahicans*, read Mohegans.
" 261, 1st line for *predecessors*, read predecessor.
Errors in uniformity of orthography not noted.

# INDEX.

406      *INDEX.*

Wappingers, continued —
with the, 136 : encouraged by English to revolt, 155 ; solicit peace for Esopus Indians, 155; take part in war of 1689, 178 ; removal of clans to Otseningo, 231 ; claim lands in Dutchess county, 252 ; aid Americans in war of Revolution, 286 ; signification of name, 370

Wappinger's creek, aboriginal name of, 84, 370

Warrawakin, sachem of Seatalcats, 74

Warranawonkongs, location of, 71, 94; wars with the Dutch (see Esopus Indians),

Warren Bush, settlement at, destroyed, 285

War song of Lenapes, 32

Wars, Cresap's, 285 ; Esopus, first, 120, 133 ; Esopus, second, 146 ; French, and Indian, 1787, 171 ; 1702, 187; 1744, 203; 1785, 208 ; Iroquois and the French, 172 ; King Philip's, 62 ; Lenapes for independence, 216; Lenapes, etc., 1793, 291 ; Mahicans and Manhattan, 105; Mahicans and Mohawks, 58, 158 ; Minsis and Senecas, 67, 145 ; Mohawks and the French, 131, 174; Montauks and Narragansetts, 76 ; Pontiac's conspiracy, 243, 246; Queen Anne's war, 187 ; Revolutionary war, 258 ; Raritans and the Dutch, 101; Senecas and Minsis, 67, 145 ; Senecas and the French, 145, 169 ; Tuscaroras and North Carolina, 190 ; Weckquaesgeeks and the Dutch, 102, 108, 111, 119, 121

Wassenaar and De Laet's account of subtribal organizations, 71

Wasenssne, sachem of Tankitekes, 80

Washington, Major George, commands expedition against the French, 210 ; holds conference with Lenape and Seneca chiefs, 210 ; attacks the French in ambush, 210 ; retreats to the great meadows, 211 ; withdraws from Ohio valley, 211

Warwarsinks, location of, 95

Wawayanda, signification of, 385

Wawiachech, sachem of Pennacooks, 193

Wawyachtonocks, location of, 85

Wayne, Gen., defeats Western tribes, 292 ; makes treaty of Greenville, 292

Weapons of war, 25

Weckquaesgeeks, location of, 78 ; a warrior of, killed, 101 ; attacked by the Dutch, 103; murder Ann Hutchinson, 112 ; castles of, destroyed, 114 ; treaty with, 117

Weckquaesgeek territory, 366

Welsh colonization of America, 17, 45

Werekepes, a Haverstraw chief, 92, 94

Weskheun, sachem of Kitchawongs, 79

Weskora, sachem of Weckquaesgeeks, 79

Wessickenaiuw, sachem of Weckquaesgeeks, 79

Westenhucks, location of, 85

Westenhuck, Mahican national council at, 89

Western controversy, parties to, 258

Western tribes, alliance of 1793, 292

Whitneymen, sachem of Matinecocks, 74; negotiates peace, 117

Wiekajocks, location of, 85

Willehoosa, cavern on Shawangunk mountains, 96

Wiltmeet, Indian castle of, 95 ; destroyed by the Dutch, 137

Wiltwyck, the old village of Esopus, 147 ; houses burned at, 147; council of war at, 149

Winnequaheagh, sachem of Secatogues, 75

Wyandance, sachem of Montauks, 75 ; death of, by poison, 76

Wycombone, sachem of Montauks, 76

Wyoming, lands at, purchased by Susquehanna Company, 215

Wyoming lands, 250, 25, 264, 265 ; massacre at, 276, 277

Yonkers, aboriginal name of, 77, 365

# Hope Farm Press & Bookshop
www.hopefarm.com

## ___INDIAN TRIBES of Hudson's River Vol I to 1700

E.M. Ruttenber. Volume one of this invaluable resource begins the best history of Native Americans in New York State. It covers from Henry Hudson's exploration, through the Esopus Wars, and up to and including the formation of the Iroquois Confederacy. 200 pages 6x9 with index and map cover ISBN #0-910746-98-2 Paper **$12.95**

## ___DELAWARE INDIANS A BRIEF HISTORY

Adams, Richard. A turn-of-the-century comprehensive history by a descendant of Chief White Eyes. Includes customs, folklore, religion and first-person accounts of all their military involvement through the Civil War. The text makes liberal use of original source material, with footnotes and an appendix, for a true account of the "Original People". 80 pages 6x9 index Paper **$8.95**

## ___HISTORY OF GREENE COUNTY

Vedder, Jesse Van Vechten. Charles Dornbusch Memorial Edition. A Reprint of the original 1927 village by village OFFICIAL history of Greene County by the then County Historian. Covers from 1651-1800 with an update to 1926/7 and a NEW 25 page name index. 237 pages 6x9 b&w photos Paper **$14.95**

## ___HISTORY OF SCHENECTADY COUNTY

Van Santvoord. This reprint of the 1887 brief history of a pivotal Mohawk Valley county includes the 1690 French & Indian sacking of Schenectady. map 48 pages 8.5x5.5 Paper **$6.95**

## ___THE CONCISE HISTORY OF ORANGE COUNTY

Rev Corning. From the Colonial period to the 20th century, when Orange County grew from an Indian ravaged frontier to a densely populated economic power, this is an historical overview of one of New York's original counties. With 25 b&w photos. 136 pages 7x10 indexed Paper **$13.95**

## ___REVOLUTIONARY WAR CHRONOLOGY & Almanac

Hilowitz, Harv. When the author couldn't find a concise account of the Revolutionary War, he wrote one! History teacher Harv Hilowitz chronicles the war battle-by-battle, campaign-by-campaign, for an easy understanding of this complex subject. With 6 maps by the author. A must for every student of history. 50 pages 5.5x8.5 Stapled **$7.50**

## ___MILITIA: New York State's Provincial & Revolutionary Military

Organizations. Brink, Benjamin Myer. (from Olde Ulster Vol VII c1911) This little gem is packed with minutia. From the differences in color and style of the uniforms of various units, to the names of all the officers and an outline of the battles engaged - including 4 pages (w/map) of the taking of Forts Clinton and Montgomery by the British in 1777. 25 pages 5.5x8.5 Stapled **$5.00**

## ___Reminiscences of the Revolution LeLoop's Bloody Trail

Arthur Reid. Early Washington County, Burgoyne's defeat, and the death of Miss McCrea all come together in this bloody Rev War booklet c 1859. 32 pages 5.5x8.5 Stapled **$6.50**

**Order Online - OR Add $3.95 for the 1st and $1 each addt'l book**
**Mail to: Hope Farm Press 252 Main St Saugerties NY 12477**